UNIONISM AND RECONSTRUCTION
IN TENNESSEE

WILLIAM GANNAWAY BROWNLOW. FROM A PORTRAIT IN THE POSSESSION OF
THE TENNESSEE STATE LIBRARY AND REPRODUCED BY ITS PERMISSION.

UNIONISM AND RECONSTRUCTION IN TENNESSEE

1860–1869

BY

JAMES WELCH PATTON, Ph.D.

PROFESSOR OF HISTORY
CONVERSE COLLEGE

GLOUCESTER, MASS.

PETER SMITH

1966

To

<small>My Father and Mother</small>

JAMES WESLEY PATTON

<small>AND</small>

ELIZABETH WELCH PATTON

PREFACE

THE HISTORY of the Civil War and reconstruction periods in Tennessee presents a number of novel characteristics. Tennessee was the last state to secede from the Union and the first of the seceded states to be restored to its constitutional relations with the Union. It was specifically exempted from the provisions of the Emancipation Proclamation; it was the only Southern state to escape the terrors of military reconstruction; and, to a much greater degree than the other Southern states, it avoided the menace of the carpet baggers. In large measure the explanation of this singular record is to be found in the political and intellectual background of the state and the character of its economic and industrial resources, factors which alike made secession undesirable and the speedy readmission of the state an event to be eagerly anticipated; the early occupation of the state by the Federal forces, making possible the erection of a military government under Andrew Johnson, a native Tennessean, possessing the confidence of President Lincoln and ardently desiring the restoration of his commonwealth to the Union; and, to an even greater degree, the remarkable character and activity of the reconstruction governor, William G. Brownlow.

Intense in his prejudices, extreme in his actions, and at times inconsistent in his policies, William G. Brownlow was guided throughout his gubernatorial career by a determined and unremitting desire to restore the state as speedily as possible to its former position in the Union. In his estimation the most reasonable and plausible method of achieving this end was by identifying his policy with that of the congressional Radicals. To this policy everything was made to conform. Brownlow was

not an advocate either of emancipation or of Negro suffrage, but he adopted both when it became evident that
such a course would reconcile the state with the Federal
government. In his gubernatorial policy there is clearly
seen the reflection of events that were occurring at Washington. Although there is ample room for criticizing the
policy adopted by the Governor, it deserves much commendation, for rigid, extreme, and inconsistent as it was
with that of his earlier career, it still saved the state from
the disasters of congressional military reconstruction
that other Southern states experienced.

It is the purpose of this study to trace the history of
the commonwealth of Tennessee through that turbulent,
bewildered, and unhappy period from 1860 to 1869—to
show the forces and factors that kept the state from
seceding until the pressure of events proved that neutrality would be impossible; the factors and events that
contributed to its early restoration to the Union, the
policy of the reconstruction governor and the changes in
it that occurred in response to the demands of the Radical party at Washington; and to estimate the ultimate
effect of this policy upon the state. To these topics are
of necessity added the chapters dealing with the Freedmen's Bureau and the Ku Klux Klan, bridging a gap in
the story that would otherwise be caused by the omission
of an account of the activity of these picturesque and
important institutions.

I take this opportunity of expressing my gratitude to
the numerous persons who have aided me in the preparation of this work. Especial thanks are due to the late
Mr. Selden Nelson and the late Miss Mary Boyce Temple
of Knoxville for permission to use the papers of their
respective fathers, Thomas A. R. Nelson and Oliver P.
Temple; to Mrs. Mary Brownlow Akin of Knoxville for
the use of some scrap-books of her father, William G.
Brownlow; to Mrs. John Trotwood Moore, state librarian

of Tennessee, for many valuable suggestions and mate-
rials; to Dr. W. A. Provine, secretary of the Tennessee
Historical Society, for many helpful suggestions regarding the use of the papers of that organization; to Mr. and
Mrs. W. B. Romine of Pulaski for permission to repro-
duce two illustrations from their *Story of the Original
Ku Klux Klan;* to Miss Laura Luttrell of the Lawson
McGhee Library at Knoxville and Dr. Albert Ray New-
some, secretary of the North Carolina Historical Commission; and to August Cook for drawing the end sheets.

This study is the outgrowth of investigations begun
in the seminar conducted by Professor J. G. de Roulhac
Hamilton at the University of North Carolina. I wish to
make grateful acknowledgment to Professor Hamilton
for his inspiration and encouragement in the prosecution
of the work and to Professor William Whatley Pierson,
Jr., also of the University of North Carolina, for many
valuable criticisms and suggestions. I am indebted to
my wife, Carlotta Dorothea Patton, for many helpful
suggestions and for numerous aids in reading the proof
and making the index.

JAMES WELCH PATTON.

Converse College,
Spartanburg, South Carolina,
October 24, 1933.

TABLE OF CONTENTS

ILLUSTRATIONS

UNIONISM AND RECONSTRUCTION
IN TENNESSEE

CHAPTER I

THE SECESSION OF TENNESSEE

TENNESSEE was singularly free from secession propaganda prior to 1860. The geographic location of the state, the social and intellectual background of its people, and the economic situation alike made secession from the Union undesirable. Impractical scholars and theorists, it is true, wrote that the days of the Union were numbered, that the South would no longer submit to the tyranny and oppression of the North,[1] but the popular leaders of the state were those who supported the Union. Tennessee was the stronghold of the conservative Whig party, which was devoted from its inception to the theory that the preservation of the Union was the *summum bonum* of American endeavor. That the popular leaders of the state were nationalists is especially illustrated in the case of John Bell, doubtless the most popular man in the state and prior to 1860 a constant supporter of the Union cause. Entering Congress in 1826, he frequently referred with pride to the fact that his majority had been increased by the suffrages of several free Negroes.[2] He united with Chase and Sumner in their fight against the threatened "Crime against Kansas,"[3] and he was the only Southern senator to oppose the repeal of the Mis-

[1] J. G. M. Ramsey, the noted Tennessee historian, wrote to L. W. Spratt, of Charleston, South Carolina, in 1858, "I conceal from no one my deep conviction that the days of our present Union are numbered. . . . Our people will never again be a unit. . . . The high toned New England spirit has degenerated into a clannish feeling of profound Yankeeism. . . . The masses of the North are venal, corrupt, covetous, mean, and selfish. The proud Cavalier spirit of the South and of the slave-holder—the virtue and integrity of the Huguenot, the probity and honor of the Presbyterian not only remain but have become intensified. . . . We are essentially two people." Copy in the McClung Collection, Lawson McGhee Library, Knoxville, Tennessee.

[2] W. G. Shotwell, *The Civil War in America*, I, 10.

[3] Joshua W. Caldwell, "John Bell of Tennessee," *American Historical Review*, IV, 659.

souri Compromise.[4] Yet in spite of all these considerations he remained popular in Tennessee and was the choice of the people of that state for president in 1860.

The social and economic interests of Tennessee bound its inhabitants to the North equally as strongly as to the South. Speaking for the Breckenridge ticket at Knoxville in 1860, William L. Yancey made a fatal mistake and lost votes for his candidates when he scornfully asserted that "in the North women work and white men black boots and drive carriages, while we in the South are more elevated and have negroes to do this."[5] His audience was composed largely of non-slave-holders, themselves not averse to performing these menial functions. The economic interests of the state were such as to make its continued existence in the Union both profitable and desirable. Tennessee could by no means be classed as a typical cotton and plantation state. The ratio of slaves to white people in the state in 1860 was less than one to four, and was constantly decreasing.[6] Out of a population of 1,109,801 there were only 36,844 slave owners, and of these only one man owned more than three hundred slaves. Only forty-seven men owned over one hundred slaves each.[7] A large section of the state was better adapted to the production of live-stock and food-stuffs than to cotton raising, and although these commodities found a ready market in the large plantations of the South they were also finding other markets among the growing population of the North and West. The importance of this fact was stressed by Dr. Felix Robertson in an address to the people of Tennessee in 1861,[8] and the Knoxville *Whig* asserted in 1860 that the state was in no position to secede because of the dependence

[4] A. C. Cole, *The Whig Party in the South*, p. 294.
[5] Knoxville *Whig*, Sept. 22, 1860.
[6] *A Century of Population Growth*, p. 140.
[7] *Eighth Census of the United States, Agriculture*, p. 239.
[8] Nashville *Banner*, Jan. 31, 1861.

of its population upon the North for manufactured goods.[9]

In large measure the intellectual and religious leaders of the state championed the cause of the Union against the attacks of their more rabid associates in the lower South. A Tennessean, William H. Sneed, introduced a resolution at the Southern Commercial Convention at Knoxville in 1858, declaring it inexpedient and against public policy to reopen the African slave trade.[10] This indicates that the people of Tennessee were not inclining sympathetic ears to the proposals for the extension of the slave power that were continually coming from the South, and as the secession movement increased in violence they turned more and more to the Union in search of a remedy for their troubles. On Thanksgiving Day, 1860, the Rev. C. T. Quintard, afterwards Bishop of the Protestant Episcopal Diocese of Tennessee, delivered a sermon on "Obedience to Rulers," which contained a strong plea for the Union,[11] and in the same year Bishop James Hervey Otey lamented the condition into which the Southern agitators had plunged the country. His words were almost prophetic:

The cry, like a death-knell rings through our borders. "The Union is dissolved! and the sun of our glory has gone down." Ruin with its weird shriek of despair spreads its dark wings over all the land, and foreshadows the "desolation that comes like a whirlwind." Every face gathers blackness, every bosom heaves a sigh, and every eye drops a tear. Well may we then, if not now, take up the lament of Christ over Jerusalem, and say, "O my country! if thou hadst known, even thou, at least in this day, the things which belong to thy peace! but they are hid from thine eyes."[12]

[9] Knoxville *Whig*, Nov. 10, 1860.
[10] *DeBow's Review*, XXIII, 309.
[11] A. H. Noll, *Doctor Quintard, Chaplain C. S. A. and Second Bishop of Tennessee*, p. 10.
[12] W. M. Green, *Memoir of Bishop Otey*, p. 348.

In 1860 the Nashville *Banner,* one of the leading Whig organs of the state printed a vigorous editorial against secession,

Let every true and honest citizen of the South beware. The vilest, most damnable, deep laid, and treacherous conspiracy that was ever concocted in the busy brains of the most designing knave is being hatched to destroy his liberties by breaking up this government. If the people do not rise in their strength and put back these meddling politicians the latter will chloroform them with sectional prejudice, and then ride over them rough-shod before they can recover from the narcotic.[13]

To the list of the names of the enemies of secession should be added by all mèans that of the editor of the Knoxville *Whig,* the virile and caustic William G. Brownlow. In an editorial in 1860 he poured a stream of withering scorn upon the secessionists,

We are for the cónstitutional Union party, and we shall fight to the bitter end the thieving, lying, all pervading corruption and wasteful extravagance of the Buchanan wing of Democracy; the fire-eating, union dissolving, political charlatanism of the Southern extremists; the squatter-sovereignty and disguised abolitionism of the Douglass wing, and the treacherous adherents who have traded alone upon the political capital of a petty demagogue, and last, but not least, we shall fight the sectionalism of the Northern Republicans as a band of outlaws, menacing the integrity of the Union.[14]

So strong were the influences against secession and so thoroughly were they supported by the people that there seems to be much truth in the statement of one writer to the effect that "the secession or rebellion of Tennessee was a rebellion of office-holders and politicians" in which "the people arrayed themselves on the side of the government; the office-holders and politicians arrayed themselves on the side of the rebellion."[15]

Notwithstanding, however, the strength of the forces

[13] Nashville *Banner,* Jan. 20, 1860.
[14] Knoxville *Whig,* June 9, 1860.
[15] J. S. Hurlburt, *History of the Rebellion in Bradley County,* p. 37.

that were arrayed against secession in the state, they
were all broken down between November, 1860, and June,
of the following year; and by the middle of the summer
of 1861 Tennessee was a loyal member of the organization later known as the Confederate States of America.
A number of reasons may be advanced in explanation
of this somewhat sudden reversal of state policy. The
more potent of these reasons are the persistent action
of Governor Harris, who was determined to carry the
state out of the Union at all costs; the failure of the
Washington Peace Conference to arrive at any satisfactory means of compromise between the sections; and
the gradual deflection from the Union cause of the old
Whig leaders, particularly John Bell. It will be observed that the election of Abraham Lincoln as president is not given as a cause of the secession of the state.
There was no Lincoln ticket in Tennessee in the election of 1860, and the electoral vote of the state was cast
for a native son, the popular John Bell.[16] In voting
for a man who represented a compromise element, as
Bell certainly did, Tennesseans gave evidence of their
intention to remain neutral as long as possible. The
presidential campaign of 1860 was attended by no undue
violence or demonstrations in the state, and neither before nor after the election was there any disposition to
withdraw from the Union because the returns gave the
coveted place to the Republican candidate.[17] William
G. Brownlow, although a strong supporter of the Bell
and Everett ticket, declared on September 18 that "when
the secessionists go to Washington to dethrone Lincoln,
I am for seizing a bayonet and forming an army to resist such an attack, and they shall walk over my dead

---

[16] Edward McPherson, *Political History of the . . . Rebellion*, p. 1.
See also Marguerite B. Hamer, "The Presidential Campaign of 1860 in
Tennessee," *East Tennessee Historical Society Publications* III, 3-22.

[17] *American Annual Cyclopedia, 1861*, p. 677.

body.''[18]   A similar sentiment was expressed by Nathaniel G. Taylor, one of the Bell electors, in a debate in Knoxville.[19]

After the election was over and the result was known, there was still no disposition to regard the situation as alarming. "Let every man put his foot on secession," said the Memphis *Enquirer*, "it is no remedy for Southern wrong, or it is only a madman's remedy."[20]   Similar expressions of feeling were manifested in the editorials of the Memphis *Bulletin*,[21] and the Nashville *Banner*.[22]   The precipitate action of South Carolina was regarded with both contempt and ridicule. E. G. Sevier, writing from Kingston on December 25, was especially critical of the action of the legislature of that state:

Oh, this South Carolina frenzy surpasses in folly and madness, in absurdity and wickedness, anything which fancy in her wildest mood has heretofore been able to conceive. But I am glad to say that Tennessee yet stands firm, and will, I trust, to the end. There is no safety for the border states, except in the Union. It is a fearful debt which the authors of our present and prospective disaster will have to pay.[23]

Dr. William R. Sevier, writing from Jonesboro in the same month, expressed similar opinions:

The wicked disregard which South Carolina has paid to the views, interests, and perils of the border states, should preclude her from any great share of our sympathies, especially when we remember that a portion of her men are now advocating, in the legislature, a monarchical government and boldly expressing an utter want of confidence in the people or in a democratic government.[24]

[18] Knoxville *Register*, Sept. 20, 1860.
[19] Thomas W. Humes, *The Loyal Mountaineers of Tennessee*, p. 80.
[20] Memphis *Enquirer*, Nov. 13, 1860.
[21] Memphis *Bulletin*, Nov. 12, 1860.
[22] Nashville *Banner*, Nov. 13, 1860.
[23] Letter of E. G. Sevier to Thomas A. R. Nelson, December 25, 1860, in Nelson Papers, Lawson McGhee Library, Knoxville, Tennessee.
[24] Letter of William R. Sevier to Thomas A. R. Nelson, December 11, 1860, in Nelson Papers, Lawson McGhee Library.

In one of the most sensible and temperate editorials of his entire career, Brownlow, in his Knoxville *Whig,* called attention to the fact that although Lincoln might be the most aggressive and violent of all abolitionists he would be restrained by the Constitution, the Senate, the House of Representatives, the Supreme Court, and the various other checks and balances of the United States government from any action detrimental to the South.[25] To a correspondent in South Carolina the same editor wrote in deprecation of the action of the Methodists of that state who were reported to favor secession, "You may leave the vessel,—you may go out in the rickety boats of your little state, and hoist your miserable *cabbage-leaf* of a Palmetto flag; but depend upon it, men and brethren, you will be dashed to pieces on the rocks."[26]

While these strong sentiments against secession were being expressed and while the majority of the people of the state were apparently regarding the election of Lincoln with lackadaisical apathy, a small but active and belligerent minority of pro-slavery men and politicians was bestirring itself. Immediate action was demanded by the leader of this group, the governor, Isham G. Harris. He was in constant communication with the secession leaders in the other states and was intent upon following their example.[27] Nicolay and Hay, in their monumental work on Lincoln, aver that he was "no doubt under secret promise" to these leaders,[28] but this statement cannot be definitely substantiated. He was, however, an active and aggressive defender of the doctrine of state rights, secession, and slavery, and he regarded the election of Lincoln as an auspicious pretext upon which to perfect his designs to lead the state out of the Union. Largely because of the strong sentiment against this end, however, his first efforts were premature.

[25] Knoxville *Whig,* Nov. 17, 1860.　[26] *Ibid.,* Dec. 8, 1860.
[27] C. R. Hall, *Andrew Johnson, Military Governor of Tennessee,* p. 2.
[28] Nicolay and Hay, *Abraham Lincoln, A History,* IX, 250.

On December 7, 1860, Harris issued a call for the legislature to meet in extra session on January 7, 1861, "to consider the present condition of the country."[29]   In this procedure he was supported by a considerable element of the population of West Tennessee, where feeling had become so intense that Andrew Johnson was burned in effigy because he had denounced secession in the United States Senate.[30]   In his opening message to the members of the legislature upon the occasion of their assembling in January the governor was far from conciliatory. He recited a long list of "outrages" which had been perpetrated upon the South by the North and advocated that these should be terminated by a series of amendments to the Federal Constitution which should permanently tie the hands of the Northern majority. Apparently, however, he had no hopes for the success of such pacific proposals, for he confessed that it was his belief that "the work of alienation and disruption has gone so far that it would be extremely difficult, if not impossible, to arrest."[31]   He therefore suggested that the legislature call a convention which should consider the matter of Federal relations.[32]   As the members of the existing legislature had been elected without any reference to Federal affairs it was deemed wisest to submit the question of calling a convention to the people of the state in the form of a referendum, and an act was accordingly passed on January 19, calling for an election to be held on February 9 at which the people should vote for or against a convention "to consider the existing relations between the Government of the United States and the people of the State of Tennessee, and to adopt such measures for vindicat-

---

[29] *Senate Journal, 33rd Tennessee General Assembly, Extra Session, 1861,* p. 3.

[30] Knoxville *Whig,* Jan. 5, 1861. Johnson was burned in effigy at Memphis on December 22, 1860.

[31] *Senate Journal, 33rd Tennessee General Assembly, Extra Session, 1861,* pp. 12-13.

[32] *Ibid.,* p. 15.

ing the sovereignty of the state, and the protection of its institutions, as shall appear to them to be demanded."[33] The act further provided that when voting on the question of the calling of the convention the people should vote for delegates to the convention in case it should be held. It also provided that no ordinance or resolution of secession which might be adopted should "be of any binding force or effect until it is submitted to and ratified and adopted by a majority of the qualified voters in the state."

In East Tennessee, the citadel of opposition to Harris, the people were intensely loyal to the Union, and they immediately organized for the approaching contest. The ablest and most influential men were selected in every county as Unionist candidates for the convention. Nathaniel G. Taylor was nominated in Carter County, James W. Deaderick in Washington, R. A. Crawford in Greene, John Netherland and W. C. Kyle in Hawkins, R. M. Barton in Jefferson, John F. Henry in Blount, John Baxter, Connally F. Trigg, and Oliver P. Temple in Knox, and men of like character in the other counties. William G. Brownlow, through his *Whig*, wrote editorials in his bravest words and bent all of the energies of his powerful pen to the support of the Union. On January 26 he declared,

We have no parties but Union men and Disunionists. Let the good people of East Tennessee see to it that not a single Disunionist shall go to the Convention. There is no dodging the issue. Hold them to it and require every candidate to speak out. We must face the real issue.[34]

The several candidates at once entered the canvass. In their speeches a decided intention to defeat secession was manifested, and this sentiment was shared by their audiences. Oliver P. Temple described the scene at Fair Garden in Sevier County where he spoke in the late part of January,

[33] *Acts, 33rd Tennessee General Assembly, Extra Session, 1861*, pp. 16-17.
[34] Knoxville *Whig*, Jan. 26, 1861.

A number of the mountain men had their guns with them, significant of the use that they were to make of them in the near
future. I spoke outdoors, with all the earnestness of my nature,
for between two and three hours. As I unfolded to the people
the secession plot to break up the government of their fathers,
indignation and determination settled on their brows. A grave
and terrible calamity presented itself, which could only be
averted by a united people at the ballot-box. And never was
there a more determined crowd than this one. There was not a
disloyal man in it. A few, very few, of those who were present
may have become Confederates afterwards; but they were all
true on that day, and true at the election five days later.[35]

In all of the recorded speeches made in this canvass
there was an absolute absence of all timidity, ambiguity,
or apology for the advocacy of the supremacy of the national government. They were aggressive in the extreme
against secession, and the speakers were sustained and
encouraged by a public sentiment that was almost unani-
mous. The campaign ended on the night before the election in a speaking and torch-light procession in East
Knoxville, but by this time it was already a foregone
conclusion that the Union party would be victorious at
the polls. This victory proved to be even more overwhelming than its enthusiasts had anticipated. The proposition to call a convention was negatived by a vote of
68,282 to 59,449,[36] and the simple question of secession,
which was in effect voted on in the choice of delegates,
was defeated by a majority of 91,803 to 24,749.[37]

For a brief period following the election there was a

---

[35] O. P. Temple, *East Tennessee and the Civil War*, p. 173.

[36] *War of the Rebellion, Official Records of the Union and Confederate
Armies*, series IV, vol. I, p. 901. Statement of J. E. R. Ray, secretary of
state of Tennessee, under seal, January 31, 1862. (This publication will
hereafter be referred to as *O.R.*)

[37] J. W. Fertig, *The Secession and Reconstruction of Tennessee*, p. 20.
East Tennessee voted against secession by five to one, Middle Tennessee by a
majority of 1,382, and West Tennessee gave a majority of 15,118 for it.
It is to be observed that the interests of the last named section were more
similar to those of the lower South than were the predominant interests of
the other sections of the state.

cessation of the secession activity on the part of the majority of the people of the state. The electorate, acting in its sovereign capacity, had spoken clearly, and there was little disposition to question the decision. Robert Hatton, a member of Congress, writing from Lebanon to his colleague, Thomas A. R. Nelson, on March 27 stated that "all is quiet here. Secession is making no headway. Can't for the present. Trust it never may."[38] The governor, however, did not cease his agitation even in the face of this overwhelming vote against secession. Absolutely self-confident and thoroughly undaunted, he refused to acquiesce in the will of the people as expressed at the polls and continued his aggressive attempts to effect the secession of the state. That this was his attitude is well illustrated in a letter written to him by a strong supporter, H. S. Bradford, on July 12,

Eternal vigilance is the price of liberty. All honor to the man who, chief among the rest, aroused her [Tennessee] to a sense of impending danger. Long and laboriously, but with willing hands, have you labored in the cause of the South.[39]

Harris's enemies as well as his friends were alive to the extent of his activities, and in a speech in Wilson County Ex-Governor William B. Campbell charged that it was the governor's intention to use troops in order to intimidate the people into secession.[40]

With all of his activity, however, the governor could not have succeeded in carrying the state out of the Union had not other events occurred which moved the leaders of the state in the same direction. One of the most important of these events was the failure of the Washington Peace Conference to arrive at any satisfactory agreement. Much significance was attached to the outcome of

[38] Letter of Robert Hatton to Thomas A. R. Nelson, March 27, 1861, in Nelson Papers.
[39] Letter of H. S. Bradford to Isham G. Harris, July 12, 1861, in Governors' Papers, Harris Administration, State Library, Nashville.
[40] Letter of B. W. Harris to Isham G. Harris, Jan. 21, 1861, in Harris Papers.

this convention in Tennessee. The state was ably represented by a distinguished delegation, including such men
as Samuel Milligan, Robert L. Caruthers, A. W. O. Totten, F. K. Zollicoffer, and others. Hiram P. Bell, an
agent sent to Tennessee by the Georgia Secession Convention, who conferred with Governor Harris and other
prominent leaders, reported that the prevailing sentiment in the state seemed to be that the action of Tennessee would depend largely on the issue of the Washington conference.[41] The failure of this conference, followed closely by the attack upon Fort Sumter and the
President's call for troops, deflected from their conservative and neutral position the most valiant defenders of
the Union in Tennessee.

The change that came over the state pursuant to the
call for troops on the part of President Lincoln was almost complete. Harris, seeing in the demand a suitable
weapon for the further extension of his secession propaganda, indignantly declared that "in such an unholy
crusade no gallant son of Tennessee will ever draw his
sword,"[42] and at the same time called a second extra
session of the legislature to meet on April 25.[43] Meanwhile the state was transformed into a hot bed of radical
secession feeling. An examination of the correspondence
of several prominent men of the period reveals the most
bitter and violent hatred of the North. That the time for
debate was over and the time for action had come, in the
minds of these leaders, is shown in a telegram from R. G.
Payne, refusing to speak at Trenton against Emerson
Etheridge on April 16. "If Etheridge speaks for the
South," said he, "we have no reply. If against it *our
only answer to him and his backers must be cold steel
and bullets.*"[44]

[41] *O.R.*, series IV, vol. I, pp. 177-81.
[42] Letter of Harris, in the collection of the Tennessee Historical Society,
Nashville.
[43] *Senate Journal, 33rd Tennessee General Assembly, 2nd Extra Session,
1861*, p. 3.
[44] Horace Greeley, *The American Conflict*, I, 483.

For a short time the old Whig leaders, whose political creed was love and service of the Union, attempted to stay this rising tide of secession feeling. On the same day that the governor sent his reply to the President's demand for troops, an "Address to the People of Tennessee" was issued by Neill S. Brown, Russell Houston, John Bell, Baillie Peyton, and several other prominent Whig politicians. These men assumed a neutral position and condemned both secession and coercion. They disapproved of the policy of the President and applauded Governor Harris's stand against it, but they did not think it the duty of the state "to take sides against the Government" as in so doing Tennessee would "terminate her grand mission of peacemaker between the states of the South and the general government."[45] The present duty of the state, they continued, was to maintain a strict position of independence and to "hold a conference with her sister slaveholding states yet in the Union, for the purpose of devising plans for the preservation of the peace of the land." William B. Bate thought that he could "see a dagger behind that smile in the shape of a central republic," but added that the secessionists "will grind out the idea."[46]

This neutral position, however, could not be maintained, and the irresistible tide of secession swept these leaders before it. About April 30 Neill S. Brown declared in a public letter that "the first duty is to arm at once; and to talk of keeping out of such a conflict, if it comes, is simply idle."[47] A letter from Felix K. Zollicoffer, who had served as a member of the Washington Peace Conference, announced similar sentiments, "Let us emulate the glorious example of our fathers in arms. We must not, cannot stand neutral and see our Southern

[45] Frank Moore, *Rebellion Record*, I, 71.
[46] Letter of William B. Bate to Leroy P. Walker, April 28, 1861, in *O.R.* series I, vol. LII, part II, p. 73.
[47] *American Annual Cyclopedia, 1861*, p. 679.

brothers butchered.''[48]   The Protestant Episcopal Bishop
of Tennessee, James H. Otey, who had looked upon the
course of South Carolina as ''infamous'' and had wished
''to see Buchanan impeached and tried for neglecting to
enforce the laws'' in November, 1860,[49] likewise changed
his sentiments.   On July 17, 1861, he wrote to a friend
in Virginia,

Your views, like mine, I doubt not, have undergone a great
change in regard to the moral aspect of the contest. Since Mr.
Lincoln's proclamation, and the attitude assumed, and the purposes proclaimed by the North, I have no sympathy with the
U. S. Government—no respect for its rulers—very little regard
for the Northern people. Our duty is clearly and unequivocally
to repel force by force, and to make every sacrifice rather than to
submit to an administration that tramples down every barrier
raised by our Forefathers for the protection of personal, social,
and public rights.[50]

Perhaps in no case was this change in sentiment so
clearly illustrated or so significant as in that of John
Bell. Slow and indecisive, he proved himself lacking in
leadership in this crisis, which was doubtless the supreme
event in his career. Physically he was a man of courage,
but at this time he seemed powerless to resist the counter
current of public opinion.   When a crowd waited upon
him, after the firing upon Fort Sumter, with music, shout-
ing, and hurrahs, he yielded to the overpowering Southern sentiment and went over to the cause of the Confederacy. As the leader of the Union party in Tennessee
he was, in all probability, the one man who could have
kept the state in the Union. and for his so-called ''treason'' he was bitterly assailed by writers and politicians in
the North. ''Of the many who weakly, culpably allowed
themselves to be beguiled or lured into complicity in the

[48] *Ibid.*, p. 679.

[49] Letter of James H. Otey to Edward C. Burks, Nov. 23, 1860, *American Historical Review*, XXXI, 98.

[50] *Ibid.*, p. 100. Letter of James H. Otey to Edward C. Burks, July 17, 1861.

crime of dividing and destroying their country," said
Horace Greeley, "there is no name wheron will rest a
darker stigma than that of John Bell."[51]   James G.
Blaine wrote,

If Mr. Bell had taken firm ground for the Union, the Secession
movement would have been to a very great extent paralyzed in
the South. . . . A large share of the responsibility for the dangerous development of the Rebellion must therefore be attributed
to John Bell and his half million Southern supporters who were
of the old Whig party.   At the critical moment they signally
failed to vindicate the principles upon which they had appealed
in the preceding canvass for popular government.[52]

These criticisms were harsh and obviously unsympathet-
ic, but it can scarcely be doubted that if John Bell, with
his wide influence, his commanding personality, and his
immense popularity, had dared to make the fight for the
Union that was made by Andrew Johnson or even William G. Brownlow, the result of the secession agitation
in Tennessee might have been very different.[53]

The second extra session of the legislature met on
April 25.   Governor Harris, in a spirited message, informed the members that a state of war existed already
by the act of the President of the United States, and urged
the passing of ordinances of secession and of union with
the Confederacy.   In order to decrease the expense and
delay, he suggested that the legislature, instead of calling a convention for the purpose, should frame an ordinance of secession and submit it directly to the people of
the state for their ratification or rejection, "since it is
the voice of the people that is to be heard."[54]   Acting

[51] Horace Greeley, *op. cit.*, p. 482.
[52] James G. Blaine, *Twenty Years of Congress*, I, 310-11.
[53] See Joshua W. Caldwell, "John Bell of Tennessee," *American Historical Review*, IV, 662-64, for a defense of Bell's action.   When the state
was invaded by United States troops Bell left for the lower South.   When
the war ended he returned to Tennessee, broken in health and spirit, and died
in Stewart County, near Bear Spring furnace, in 1869.
[54] *Senate Journal, 33rd Tennessee General Assembly, 2nd Extra Session,
1861*, p. 11.

upon this suggestion the legislature passed on May 6 "A Declaration of Independence and Ordinance Dissolving the Federal Relation between the State of Tennessee and the United States," and provided that this act should be submitted to the people for ratification on June 8.[55]

This act of the legislature was greeted with both approval and reprehension over the state. The Memphis *Avalanche* hailed it as "the fruition of years of struggle and toil, and anxious and often despairing effort, in the cause of Southern rights," and exclaimed with great warmth of sentiment "Welcome, thrice welcome, glorious Tennessee, to the thriving family of Southern Confederate States."[56] At the other end of the state, however, the procedure was met with opposition and denounced by Brownlow, in the Knoxville *Whig*, as "the most outrageous, high-handed and infamous legislation ever known to the civilized world."[57] Nor were the border-state papers more charitable. "The spirit of secession appears to have reached its culminating point in Tennessee," said the Louisville *Journal*. "Certainly, the fell spirit has, as yet, reached no higher point of outrageous tyranny. The whole of the late proceeding in Tennessee has been as gross an outrage as ever was perpetrated by the worst tyrant of all the earth."[58]

Without waiting for the ratification of the secession ordinance, the legislature, now completely under the domination of the governor, continued with its high-handed procedure, and took steps to unite the state with the Confederacy. On April 30 the members were addressed by Henry W. Hilliard, of Alabama,[59] who had been appointed by Jefferson Davis as special commissioner to Ten-

---

[55] *Acts, 33rd Tennessee General Assembly, 2nd Extra Session, 1861,* pp. 13-18.

[56] Memphis *Avalanche*, May 6, 1861.

[57] Knoxville *Whig*, May 18, 1861.

[58] Louisville *Journal*, May 13, 1861.

[59] *Senate Journal, 33rd Tennessee General Assembly, 2nd Extra Session, 1861,* p. 30.

nessee.[60] As a result of his address, which was aggressive and spirited, a joint resolution of both houses was passed on May 1, authorizing the governor to appoint three commissioners to negotiate with Hilliard.[61] Harris, thereupon, selected Gustavus A. Henry, A. W. O. Totten, and Washington Barrow, with whom Hilliard drew up an agreement known as "A Convention, Agreement, and Military League." By the terms of this agreement the military forces of the state were placed "under the chief control and direction of the President of the Confederate States, upon the same basis, principles, and footing, as if the said state were now . . . a member of the Confederacy." The legislature ratified this convention immediately and invited the Confederacy to make Nashville its permanent capital.[62]

Meanwhile preparations were made for the approaching election. Speeches were made throughout the state and a great change took place in public sentiment within a few days.[63] "Feeling in favor of our Government rises to enthusiasm," wrote Hilliard to Robert Toombs.[64] J. A. Minnis, of Memphis, writing to Thomas A. R. Nelson, reported that "West Tennessee is now almost one military camp; the people are in earnest, not so much excited as they were, excitement giving away to cool determination and a preparation for the contest."[65] Men were not lacking who were willing to make sacrifices for the Confederacy. S. U. Collins wrote to Governor Harris that he had accumulated "some of the goods of this world," and that he would spend his resources and "be stripped naked and turned out into the world" rather

---

[60] O.R., series I, vol. LII, part II, p. 82.

[61] Senate Journal, 33rd Tennessee General Assembly, 2nd Extra Session, 1861, pp. 67-68.

[62] Acts, 33rd Tennessee General Assembly, 2nd Extra Session, 1861, p. 19.

[63] Letter of Henry W. Hilliard to Robert Toombs, O.R., series I, vol. LII, part II, p. 76.

[64] Ibid.

[65] Letter of J. A. Minnis to Thomas A. R. Nelson, in Nelson Papers.

than see his "neighbors and their children in bondage, and subjects of the Lincoln Vandal Government."[66]   A similar attitude was expressed by James T. Shields in an eloquent speech at Bean's Station on May 18, in which he bitterly denounced the "Mercenary Yankees" and called upon every man to fight for the South and for slavery.[67]   Andrew Johnson, returning to East Tennessee from Nashville, "had his nose pulled on the way; and was hissed and hooted at all along on his route" because of his defense of the Union.[68]   Few men in the state dared to raise their voices against this overwhelming tide of pro-slavery and pro-Southern sentiment; but as usual William G. Brownlow and the Knoxville *Whig* were on the side of the Union.   "Let every man, old and young, halt and blind, contrive to be at the polls on that day," he urged.   "If we lose then, our liberties are gone and we are swallowed up by a military despotism more odious than any now existing in any monarchy of Europe."[69]

It is difficult to ascertain with any degree of accuracy the amount of pressure that was brought to bear upon the voters of the state during the campaign by Harris and his agents; certainly it was considerable.   It is generally conceded that in many of the counties of Middle and West Tennessee it was dangerous for one to vote against secession, and there were reports, fairly well substantiated, to the effect that large numbers of soldiers were brought in from the other Southern states, passed off as Tennesseans, and allowed to cast their votes against the Union.   There is some direct evidence showing that pressure was exerted by the disunionists. When Emerson Etheridge attempted to make a Union speech at Paris, the meeting was broken up by secessionists, and in the disorder that followed one Union man was

[66] Letter of S. U. Collins to Isham G. Harris, in Harris Papers.
[67] Pamphlet in Nelson Papers gives the speech in full.
[68] Letter of Gideon J. Pillow to Leroy P. Walker, *O.R.*, series I, vol. LII, part II, p. 69.
[69] Knoxville *Whig*, May 11, 1861.

killed.[70] Although it was in the nature of Unionist propaganda, the Greeneville Convention, meeting a short time later, issued a declaration of grievances definitely asserting that the election had been attended with violence. Conceding the fact that this is a partizan statement, it must still be admitted that the character of its framers entitles their words to some credence:

So far as we can learn the election held in this state on the eighth day of the present month was free, with few exceptions, in no part of the state other than East Tennessee. In large parts of Middle and West Tennessee no speeches or discussions in favor of the Union were permitted. Union papers were not allowed to circulate. Measures were taken in some parts of West Tennessee, in defiance of the Constitution and the laws, which allow folded tickets to have the ballot numbered in such a manner as to mark and expose the Union votes. . . . Disunionists in many places had charge of the polls, and Union men, when voting, were denounced as Lincolnites and abolitionists.[71]

However this may be, the returns showed that, at the polls, the Declaration of Independence and Ordinance of Secession was approved by a vote of 108,399 to 47,233.[72] Secession thus became an accomplished fact in Tennessee.

This account would be incomplete, however, if some notice were not taken of the valiant attempt on the part of the inhabitants of East Tennessee to remain in the Union. This opposition to the secession movement is known in the Confederate military records as "The Revolt of the Unionists in East Tennessee," and it brought down upon the people of that section the full force of the vengence of the Confederate Government, causing terrible suffering and innumerable hardships. This period will be described later, but the account of the inception of the movement belongs to the present discussion.

In the election of June 8, seventy per cent of the votes

[70] O.R., series I, vol. LII, part II, p. 69.
[71] Ibid., part I, p. 148.
[72] Ibid., series IV, vol. I, p. 901.

against secession were cast in East Tennessee, a section
where only forty per cent of the entire vote of the state
was cast.[73] The inhabitants of this region had little
sympathy or interest in common with the slave-holding
people of Middle and West Tennessee, where the large
majorities for secession had been piled up. This section,
frequently called the Switzerland of Tennessee, was
separated from the other sections by geographic, social,
and economic barriers. For the most part its people were
small farmers, and there were relatively few slaveholders
among them. The ratio of whites to slaves in the whole
section was about twelve to one in 1860.[74] These people.
loved the Union as heartily as they despised the philosophy of the slaveholder and the secessionist; and they
could not be induced to renounce their allegiance, even
by fire-eaters like William L. Yancey or "eagle-orators"
like Gustavus A. Henry who were sent among them.[75]
In addition to these small farmers the Unionist element
could count upon the support of a small but powerful and
aggressive group of conservative Whig politicians in the
urban districts, including such men as Horace Maynard
and Thomas A. R. Nelson. These men were determined
to carry on the program of the Whig Party, to which they
considered John Bell, Baillie Peyton, Neill S. Brown,
and others had proved unfaithful.[76]

From the time of its origin these uncompromising
Whigs had regarded the secession movement with horror
and disgust. They viewed with apprehension and dismay
the course of events at Nashville, and after the ordinance
of secession was passed they prepared for decisive action.

[73] O. P. Temple, *op. cit.*, p. 199.

[74] *Eighth Census of the United States, Agriculture*, pp. 238-39.

[75] Gustavus A. Henry, a native of Clarksville, was sent into East
Tennessee in 1861 to organize the secessionist sentiment. He was a fluent
speaker, and was usually referred to as "the Eagle Orator." William
L. Yancey also made a number of fiery speeches in East Tennessee during
the presidential campaign of 1860. He was a supporter of the Breckenridge ticket.

[76] O. P. Temple, *op. cit.*, p. 221.

To this end a number of prominent leaders, in May, 1861, united in issuing a call for a convention to meet in Knoxville on May 30.[77] This call met with an enthusiastic response, and on the day appointed the leading Union men of East Tennessee assembled at Knoxville. The convention met in a beautiful grove in what is now East Knoxville, and Thomas A. R. Nelson was chosen as permanent chairman. Speeches were made by Nelson, Thomas D. Arnold, and Andrew Johnson. The military league was strongly denounced and vigorous and emphatic resolutions in favor of the Union were adopted. Since the people were to vote on the question of separation on June 8, it was deemed most advisable to adjourn and await their decision. In order, however, to meet any exigencies that might arise by reason of the election, it appeared expedient to the leaders that the convention should meet again at a later date. Resolutions were therefore adopted "that when the convention adjourns, it adjourns to meet again at such time and place as the president, or vice-president in his absence, may determine and publish."[78]

After the adjournment of the convention many of its members went before the people urging the defeat of the ordinance of secession at the polls. Thomas A. R. Nelson issued an address "To the People of Tennessee" calling upon them to "arrest the despotism of 'King Harris' and retrieve the blunders of a misguided legislature."[79] James P. Swann addressed a long letter "to the Freemen of Jefferson County," imploring them to support the Union in the June election,[80] and William G. Brownlow, with his usual bitter sarcasm, exposed the inconsistencies in the arguments of Gustavus A. Henry who was making disunion speeches in East Tennessee.[81]

As soon as the result of the election was ascertained,

[77] *O.R.*, series I, vol. LII, part I, p. 148.
[78] Knoxville *Whig*, June 8, 1861.   [80] *Ibid.*, June 1, 1861.
[79] *Ibid.*   [81] *Ibid.*

the president of the convention issued a call for its reas-
sembling on June 17, this time at Greeneville. That place
was more suitably located for a meeting of this kind,
for threats had been made against some of the more
prominent Unionists in Knoxville.[82] On the appointed
day the convention met, but under circumstances far
different from those under which the first meeting was
held. Then it was a mere assembling of the people who
wished to keep the state in the Union; now it was a revolutionary body composed of Unionists in a state that had
withdrawn from the Union. Because of this situation it
was necessary that they should proceed with caution. The
first three days were consumed in offering speeches and
resolutions, some of them wild and visionary, and all of
them revolutionary. On the first day Thomas A. R.
Nelson submitted a long paper entitled a "Declaration of
Grievances" which was an able, bitter, and daring ar-
raignment of the secession party in Tennessee. This
paper was referred to the business committee for consideration, and after considerable toning down it was
adopted on the fourth day without division.[83] The document was a work of remarkable ability and expressed in
a very clear but eloquent manner the attitude of the
people of East Tennessee. It contained a charge that
the election of June 8 had been attended with violence and
duress on the part of the disunionists and expressed a
desire to disregard the results of the election. The language was eloquent and impressive:

We prefer to remain attached to the government of our fathers.
The constitution of the United States has done us no wrong. The
Congress of the United States has passed no law to oppress us.
The President of the United States has made no threat against
the law-abiding people of Tennessee. Under the government of
the United States we have enjoyed as a nation more of civil
and religious freedom than any other people under the whole

[82] *Ibid.*, June 22, 1861.
[83] *Proceedings of the East Tennessee Convention Held at Knoxville,
May 30-31, 1861, and at Greenville, June 17, 1861*, p. 19.

heaven. . . . The cause of secession or rebellion has no charm
for us, and its progress has been marked by the most alarming
and dangerous attacks upon the public liberty. . . . Its whole
course threatens to annihilate the last vestige of freedom.[84]

A long list of disorders that were "the fruits of secession" was then recited, and a committee of three, John
Netherland, Oliver P. Temple, and James P. McDowell,
was appointed "to prepare a memorial and cause the
same to be presented to the general assembly of Tennessee, now in session, asking that the counties composing
East Tennessee and such counties in Middle Tennessee
as desire to co-operate with them, may form and erect
a separate state."[85]

A petition embodying these resolutions was presented
to the legislature on June 20. It was referred to a joint
committee, but no action was ever taken upon it.[86] Thus
ended the last attempt to defeat the secession movement
in Tennessee. That this movement was not fully concurred in by a large element of the people of the state
is well illustrated in the words of one of their number:

The rebellion itself was a strange thing, and everything about it
was strange in the extreme. It had strange statesmen, strange
politics, a strange religion, and strange Gods. Strange Gods indeed the rebels must have had that could so deceive and mislead
them, and false prophets that the Lord did not send.[87]

[84] *Ibid.*, pp. 20-21.   [85] *Ibid.*
[86] *Senate Journal, 33rd Tennessee General Assembly, 2nd Extra Session,
1861*, pp. 176-77.
[87] J. S. Hurlburt, *op. cit.*, p. 24.

Chapter II

CIVIL AFFAIRS IN TENNESSEE, 1861-1865

On July 22, 1861, Tennessee became a member of the Confederate States of America.[1] The duration of the administration of the Confederate government in the state, however, was not lengthy; it ended with the surrender of Fort Donelson on February 16, 1862. Up until the occurrence of this event the government was fairly prosperous and stable. The executive, the legislative, and the various other branches of the administration functioned as well as could be expected under the existing conditions. There was much excitement and confusion attendant upon the outbreak of hostilities, and the chief interest of the legislature was in plans and preparations for the conflict; but nothing occurred to detract seriously from the supremacy of the civil authority of the state. The popularity of the governor, already quite extensive, was enhanced by the success of the secession movement in which he had played a conspicuous part. This fact was amply illustrated in the result of the gubernatorial campaign of 1861, in which the Unionist party was confounded and completely defeated. Actuated by a desire to rebuke his "numerous Southern calumniators" and "for the sake of the three thousand dollars per annum," William G. Brownlow announced his candidacy for governor on a platform endorsing the Lincoln Inaugural Address and strongly critical of secession. Avowing that his eyes had not been blinded by gazing "through telescopes made of cotton stalks" he proceeded with an eloquent denunciation of the perpetrators of disunion:

The leaders in this movement to dissolve this Union, the great citadel of our liberties, and the depository of the hopes of the

[1] *Journal of the Confederate Congress*, I, 272.

human race, will go down to their graves without any halo of glory surrounding their brows, while on their heads will be gathered the hissing curses of all generations, horrible as the forked-tongued snakes of Medusa. Their ghosts will stand on the highest and blackest eminence of infamy, the detestation of mankind. Having met a traitor's death, they will each and all fill a traitor's grave, over which there will be no requiem but the groans of the oppressed and the execrations of the good. Their monuments will be the human bones upon foundations slippery with human blood. However high may have been their elevation in office, their fall will be like that of Lucifer. And whilst from their bad eminence they shall turn from beholding the glories of that Constitution and Union against which they rebelled in the year of grace 1861, to survey the barren waste, the boundless and bottomless pits, of Secession, they will exclaim, like Lucifer, their "illustrious predecessor":

> "Farewell, happy fields! where joy forever dwells!
> Hail, horrors! hail, infernal world! and thou,
> Profoundest hell! receive thy new possessor!"[2]

Impassioned as this announcement was it failed to evoke any great enthusiasm. Moreover, Brownlow was suffering from bronchitis, rendering it impossible for him to canvass the state or speak to the people other than through the columns of his newspaper; and he withdrew from the contest in favor of William H. Polk, a Middle Tennessee man who, it was supposed would have more strength in the western part of the state and be more likely to defeat secession. Polk, however, became a secessionist after June 8, and consequently was repudiated by East Tennessee where he had made a strong appeal.[3] After this event the election was a mere formality. There was some talk of putting forth Connally F. Trigg in East Tennessee,[4] but this plan did not materialize, and Harris was elected virtually without opposition.

[2] Knoxville *Whig*, Mar. 23, 1861.

[3] Letter of William H. Polk to Thomas A. R. Nelson, July 10, 1861, in Nelson Papers.

[4] Knoxville *Whig*, July 13, 1861. O. P. Temple, *op. cit.*, pp. 227-28.

One of the most outstanding events of the Confederate period in Tennessee was the congressional election of 1861. This election occurred on the first Thursday in August, the same day upon which the election for governor and other state officers was held. The ordinance of secession had provided that the state should have as many delegates in the Congress of the Confederate States as it had been entitled to in that of the United States, and that these delegates should be elected from the congressional districts then established by law and in the mode and manner prescribed for the election of members of the United States Congress.[5] The loyalist element in the First, Second, Third, and Fourth Districts was of considerable importance, and loyal candidates were nominated for Congress in these districts. Secessionist candidates were likewise nominated. In the First and Second Districts, the loyalist candidates, Thomas A. R. Nelson and Horace Maynard were respectively elected over their Confederate opponents.[6] Claiming that their election by loyal men entitled them to seats in the United States Congress, they both departed for Washington after the election. Maynard alone was successful, and he was given a seat in the Thirty-seventh Congress.[7] While passing through Virginia Nelson was arrested and carried to Richmond by the Confederate authorities. After a short imprisonment he took the oath of allegiance to the Confederate Government and returned home.[8] The secessionist candidates in these two districts acknowledged their defeat and declined seats in the Confederate Congress.[9]

In the Third District the election was claimed by both parties. The secessionist candidate accepted a seat in

[5] *House Journal, 33rd Tennessee General Assembly, 2nd Extra Session, 1861*, p. 56.
[6] *House Reports*, 37 Cong., 2 Sess., No. 32.
[7] *Congressional Globe*, 37 Cong., 2 Sess., p. 2.
[8] Knoxville *Whig*, Aug. 10, 1861.
[9] *Journal of the Confederate Congress*, I, 337, 340, 357.

the Confederate Congress,[10] and George W. Bridges, the Union candidate, succeeded in escaping through the lines with the intention of demanding a seat in the United States Congress. He was decoyed back, however, by a false report that his wife was dying, and was for a time kept a prisoner in his own house. Later he escaped, made his way to the North by means of the Underground Railway, and arrived in Washington on February 23, 1863, just nine days before the adjournment of Congress. He was allowed to take his seat and served for the few remaining days of the term.[11] A similar situation prevailed in the Fourth District where both Andrew J. Clements, the Unionist candidate, and William H. DeWitt, the secessionist candidate, claimed the victory. DeWitt accepted a seat in the Congress of the Confederate States,[12] and Clements made his way to Washington where he was accorded a seat in the United States Congress.[13]

Early in 1862 the Confederate government in Tennessee was overthrown. After the fall of Fort Donelson a panic seized the governor and the legislature, and Nashville was evacuated on February 23. The legislature adjourned to Memphis where it met on February 20. After passing acts authorizing the state banks to remove their locations in case of invasion and other acts, enabling the governor to provide for emergencies, it adjourned *sine die* on March 20.[14] The governor sought refuge with the Confederate Army of Tennessee, where he remained until the end of the war. Organized civil government in the state thus came to an end. Martial law was declared in West Tennessee by General Grant;[15] East Tennessee had

[10] *Ibid.*, p. 337.

[11] *Congressional Globe*, 37 Cong., 3 Sess., pp. 1295-96.

[12] *Journal of the Confederate Congress*, I, 357.

[13] *House Reports*, 37 Cong., 2 Sess., No. 9.

[14] Joshua W. Caldwell, *Constitutional History of Tennessee*, p. 277. See also, *The Great Panic, By an Eye Witness*, a graphic account of the evacuation of Nashville.

[15] *O.R.*, series I, vol. VII, p. 655.

already been occupied by the Confederates and was virtually under martial law;[16] and Middle Tennessee became the theater of the struggle between the opposing forces of the North and the South.

On March 3 President Lincoln, looking toward the restoration of Federal authority in the state, appointed Andrew Johnson military governor of Tennessee.[17] The difficulties devolving upon the holder of this office were numerous and almost insuperable. For various reasons Johnson was unpopular with the inhabitants of Tennessee. His violent opposition to slavery and secession, together with the fact that he had retained his seat in the Senate of the United States in the face of the secession of his state, rendered him obnoxious to the Southern Democratic Party. At the same time his support of the Breckenridge and Lane ticket in 1860[18] had made him unpopular with the Unionists of East Tennessee, an unpopularity which was made all the more complicated by the long-standing personal antagonism between himself and William G. Brownlow, who was now the leader of this group. Likewise his devotion to the Democratic party, in spite of the fact that he possessed the unqualified confidence of the President, was destined to win opposition for him among certain radical elements in the North and in the national administration.

Johnson's unpopularity was further increased by the nature of the position to which he had been appointed. This position was an anomalous one. Had he come as an alien conqueror, or as the temporary occupant of a territory shortly to be annexed to the United States, the principles of international law and the history of his country would have furnished him with rules and precedents upon which to base his actions. In the one case he would have

[16] Knoxville *Whig*, Aug. 10, 1861. Address of General Zollicoffer to the citizens of East Tennessee.

[17] *O.R.*, series I, vol. IX, p. 396.

[18] O. P. Temple, *Notable Men of Tennessee*, p. 392.

been bound only by the rules and regulations of martial law; in the other he would have had the benefit of the constitutional rules and precedents applicable to the government of territories for his guidance. As it was, however, no path had been blazed for him; he must wait for the difficulties to appear and then settle them as best he might.

These difficulties were of two kinds, administrative and constitutional. No specific instructions were given him to determine his relation to the inhabitants of the state. "You are hereby appointed," ran his commission, "military governor of the State of Tennessee, with authority to exercise and perform, within the limits of that State, all and singular the powers, duties, and functions pertaining to the office of military governor (including the power to establish all necessary offices and tribunals and suspend the writ of habeas corpus) during the pleasure of the President, or until the loyal inhabitants of that state shall organize a civil government in conformity with the Constitution of the United States."[19] There was no explanation or specification as to what these "powers, duties, and functions" were. Moreover, there was no uniform political status that might be applied to the people of the state of Tennessee. They might be divided into at least three classes. There were in the first place those who had remained firm in their loyalty to the Union, and it was the duty of the military governor, as the agent of the Federal executive, to secure for them the constitutional guarantee of a republican form of government, protect their persons and property, and restore to them the rights of loyal citizenship. Secondly, there were the active secessionists, who were to be disarmed and brought into subjection to the Federal government. And lastly, there was a class consisting of those persons who had remained, or attempted to remain, hon-

[19] O.R., series I, vol. IX, p. 396.

estly and sincerely neutral. These must be impressed
with the ability and determination of the Federal government to maintain itself against its enemies and to re-
assert its authority in the state. At the same time it was
necessary that care be taken not to excite their hostility
or apprehension by harsh or illegal acts, or threatened
interference with the rights or institutions to which they
were devoted. To adjust all of these unique complica-
tions, the utmost firmness, tact, and courage were requisite.

Another administrative difficulty grew out of the fact
that, in the territory to be administered by Johnson, the
armies of Halleck and Buell were operating in the face
of the enemy. To provide for this contingency Johnson
had been created a brigadier general, but these commanders, accustomed by training and precedent to make
everything subordinate to the success of their military
plans, were certain to view with impatience and intoler-
ance the projects of a civil officer of whose very presence
they disapproved.[20]

The constitutional difficulties of the military governor
were perhaps less acute, but they were still unpleasantly
annoying. The validity of Johnson's position under the
Constitution was seriously questioned. Its chief spon-
sors rested upon the guarantee clause of the Constitution and contended that the Confederacy had attempted
to subvert the true republican form of government. The
loyal citizens of the state, they claimed, had the right to
call upon the United States Government to make good this
guarantee, and to that call the government was obligated
to respond.[21] Thaddeus Stevens dissented from this
view. He contended that the seceding states were out of
the Union; that the rights and guarantees of the Constitution did not extend to their citizens; that they were
enemies to be conquered; and that the authority of the

[20] O.R., series I, vol. X, part II, p. 11.
[21] House Miscellaneous Documents, 39 Cong., 1 Sess., No. 55.

military governor existed by virtue of no clause of the Constitution, but only by the fiat of the commander-in-chief of the army.[22] Still a third view was developed by Representative Olin of New York. He repudiated Stevens' thesis that the states were out of the Union, but declared that the appointment of the military governor was justified, not by the guarantee clause of the Constitution but by military necessity.[23] It is not the purpose of this writer to debate the old question as to the status of the seceding states; but the contemporaneous dissenting views are analyzed in order to illustrate the fact that even in the national administration there was not a harmonious attitude with reference to conditions and policies in Tennessee.

It was only to be expected that the appointment of Johnson would lead to the outburst of a storm of fierce and vindictive disapproval. Plots were formed against his life; guerilla bands attempted to intercept his train and take him to the lower South to answer for his "crimes"; and his mail was filled with warnings and threats. An anonymous correspondent wrote,

Go it, Andy, this is your day. But while you are going so high you must not for get that evry dog has his day and the day is not far advance when you will have your just day, and that day cannot come until you are tared and fethered and burnt. We are preparing a knise coat of feathers for that orcation, so when we have the chanse we will turn your black skin red, and then andy your black friends will not know you.[24]

A Confederate soldier wrote to his wife that men in the army had vowed to take Johnson's life and would do so if they were allowed to leave their commands;[25] and at least one plot, sanctioned by General Braxton Bragg, to kidnap him by an organized force, is reported.[26]

[22] *Congressional Globe*, 37 Cong., 3 Sess., pp. 239-44.
[23] C. R. Hall, *op. cit.*, p. 35.
[24] Johnson Papers (Library of Congress), vol. li, p. 1023.
[25] *Ibid.*, vol. xvii, p. 3810.
[26] E. L. Drake, *Annals of the Army of Tennessee*, I, 312.

Johnson inaugurated his administration with a proclamation or "Address to the People," explaining his position and indicating the policy that he proposed to follow. This proclamation was especially conciliatory in its tone and general content. After referring to the happiness and prosperity of the people of Tennessee while the state was yet in the Federal Union, he reviewed the existing situation in the state:

The executive has abdicated, the legislative has dissolved, the judiciary is in abeyance. . . . The archives have been desecrated; the public property has been stolen and destroyed; the vaults of the state bank violated and its treasures robbed, including the funds carefully gathered and consecrated for all time to the instruction of our children. In such a lamentable crisis, the government of the United States could not be unmindful of its high constitutional obligations to guarantee to every state in this union a republican form of government.[27]

The only purpose of the military government, he said, was to aid in the prompt restoration of the state to its former place in the Union. If the people would consent to further that purpose, no unnecessary obstacles would be placed in their way. There should be no humiliating requirements of probation or atonement. The sole condition prescribed was submission to the Constitution and the laws of the United States, and a complete amnesty was specifically offered to all private citizens who would renounce their disloyalty and return to their allegiance to the United States Government.[28]

Upon the completion of his inaugural address Johnson's first task was to select his cabinet or corps of lieutenants. Edward H. East was appointed secretary of state; Joseph S. Fowler, comptroller; Horace Maynard, attorney-general; and Edmund Cooper, private secretary and confidential agent.[29]

[27] John Savage, *The Life and Public Services of Andrew Johnson*, pp. 250-51.
[28] *Ibid.*, pp. 251-53.   [29] Nashville *Union*, Apr. 27, 1862.

It was the firm belief of Johnson that the great masses of the people of the state were loyal at heart and that they had been forced into the rebellion under duress or else duped by the falsehoods of their leaders. In this belief he was supported by General Don Carlos Buell and other Union commanders in the state at this time.[30] In order that this obstruction might be removed and that the masses might be facilitated in returning to their allegiance, two policies were determined upon. In the first place, prominent secession leaders were to be silenced or removed from the state. Active measures were taken to this end, and seven prominent citizens of Nashville, including six clergymen, were arrested. Upon their refusal to take the oath of allegiance to the United States they were imprisoned and later exiled from the state.[31] Military supervision was extended to the press of the city. The *Daily Times* and the *Banner* were suppressed in April, and S. C. Mercer, a violent Kentucky Unionist, was imported to begin an administration paper, the *Daily Union*. The plants of the *Gazette* and the *Patriot,* as well as the Methodist and Baptist publishing houses, were seized and closed for propagating disloyalty.[32]

The second policy determined upon was that of encouraging and promoting the inarticulate Union sentiment in the state through a series of mass meetings, a policy that was especially facilitated by the success of the United States forces in the region. On April 17 Grant pushed Beauregard's army across the Tennessee River and thus freed the entire state, with the exception of East Tennessee, from any considerable Confederate opposition. As a result of this victory good times returned. Cotton rose in value, and business, which had been suffering from a severe depression since the evacuation of Nashville, was resumed. There was a temporary return to nor-

---

[30] *O.R.*, series I, vol. XVI, part I, p. 633.
[31] Nashville *Union*, July 5, 1862.
[32] *American Annual Cyclopedia, 1862,* p. 766.

mal conditions of life.[33] Several mass meetings were then arranged by Union men throughout Middle Tennessee with the support of the military governor. The most important one was held at Nashville on May 12 in pursuance to a call issued by several prominent men who favored "the restoration of the former relations of this state to the Federal Union."[34] A former governor of the state, William B. Campbell, presided and made an earnest and conciliatory appeal to all citizens to return to their old allegiance. As Johnson was the instigator of the meeting, Campbell's speech may be regarded as the official statement of the military governor's policy at that time.[35]

When these meetings had been held it was decided to test public opinion at the polls. On May 22 an election for circuit judge was held in the Nashville district. The result of this election, however, demonstrated that the administration had miscalculated the temper of the people, for the anti-administration candidate, Turner S. Foster, a man with a record of open disloyalty, was elected by a large majority.[36] Thus Johnson's first attempt to restore the state came to a somewhat inglorious end. This debâcle was quickly followed by the return of the Confederate armies to the state. Middle Tennessee was invaded by the cavalry detachments of Morgan and Forrest, disconcerting the plans of the Union generals. As a result of this, Johnson, who believed that these generals were not acting to the best advantage for the defense of the state, became involved in a series of violent controversies with Buell, Halleck, and Rosecrans, and their subordinates. These controversies, largely concerned with military questions, have no place in this account, but they virtually prevented, for a time, any further attempt at the civil reorganization of the state.

[33] Nashville *Union*, May 1, May 10, 1862.
[34] Frank Moore, *Rebellion Record*, vol. V. doc. 335.
[35] C. R. Hall, *op. cit.*, p. 48.
[36] Nashville *Union*, Sept. 20, 1862.

There were two elections, however, held in 1862 and 1863, respectively, which deserve some comment. The first was inspired largely by President Lincoln's sincere desire to effect the political regeneration of the border states. His proclamation of September 22, 1862, asserting his intention of recommending compensation for the slaves of all states not in rebellion that should voluntarily free their bondmen, and announcing emancipation by the executive on January 1, 1863, had not had the desired effect in Tennessee.[37] By taking prompt steps to reinstate their commonwealth as a member of the Union, Tennesseans might thereby share in any financial relief afforded by Congress to loyal slave states, and their Congressmen would have a hand in the measures adopted. Instead of availing themselves of this advantage, however, the Tennessee slaveholders disregarded it and sent large numbers of their slaves to the lower South as expeditiously as possible.[38]

In October, notwithstanding the precarious situation of the army, the President sent commissioners to Tennessee to stimulate popular sentiment favorable to the holding of congressional and state elections. The governor was requested to co-operate "in all available ways ... to give the people a chance to express their wishes at these elections,"[39] and although somewhat discouraged by the results of his previous experiments with popular sentiment he resolved upon one more attempt to gratify the President. Large areas in West Tennessee had been reclaimed by the Union forces, and the inhabitants were petitioning the governor to hold the regular elections for congressmen in the Ninth and Tenth Districts.[40] He therefore issued, on December 8, a proclamation calling for elections on December 29 for members of Congress

[37] James D. Richardson, *Messages and Papers of the Presidents*, VI, 96.
[38] Nashville *Union*, Nov. 27, 1862.
[39] *O.R.*, series III, vol. II, p. 675.
[40] Johnson Papers, vol. XXVI.

in these two districts. The "Union sentiment" in these
regions proved to be more apparent than real, and when
the nominating conventions met there was much "copperhead" feeling displayed. Fortunate, doubtless, for the
prestige of the President and the Governor, a well directed
raid by General Forrest and his cavalry interfered with
the opening of the polls. A battle was fought in sight of
one of the polling places, and the sheriff of another was
compelled to surrender his writs of election and give
bond that no election would be held. Alvin Hawkins, of
Huntington, the Union candidate for congressman in
the Ninth District, was compelled to leave the state to
avoid assassination. He later presented himself in Washington and demanded his seat in Congress, but as he
could only show that he had received 1,900 votes out of a
voting population of 18,000, and this by no very authentic proof, the election committee, to which his case was
referred, declined to allow him a seat.[41] Thus ended
Johnson's second attempt to restore the state government.

In August, 1863, on the date appointed by the state
constitution for holding gubernatorial and congressional
elections, there occurred, in the form of another election,
the last despairing episode in the political history of the
Confederacy in Tennessee. Regardless of their slight
hold upon the state, except in East Tennessee where they
had no political influence, the Confederates attempted to
hold an election. On May 23, Governor Harris, from his
position behind the lines of the Army of Tennessee, issued a proclamation calling for a convention to be held at
Winchester on June 17 for the purpose of nominating a
candidate for governor and a general congressional
ticket. "It is more important," declared the call, "that
this duty should be performed now than at any other
previous period in our history. We must exhibit to the

enemy an unalterable firmness of purpose and determination to preserve and perpetuate our free institutions.''[42] As the Union armies were in possession of the state, no regular method of naming the delegates was possible, and the convention which assembled was in no legal sense representative. Many of the delegates were refugees from counties which were then under the control of the Union forces. Harris himself addressed the meeting, and William Brimmage Bate of Castallian Springs was selected as a candidate for governor. Bate was at this time serving in the Confederate army, however, and he declined to accept the nomination. Judge Robert L. Caruthers of Lebanon was then named, and a full congressional ticket was drawn up.[43]

The Union leaders were also alert to the advantage of holding an election under the sanction of the state constitution and the control of the army. Horace Maynard, William G. Brownlow, and others issued a call,[44] and a Union convention, fully as irregular as the Confederate meeting at Winchester, assembled at Nashville on July 1. Instead of complete harmony of sentiment in the convention, however, there developed much dissension. The most significant disagreement occurred with reference to the purpose of the convention itself. The radicals declared that it should nominate a civil governor as well as candidates for the legislature and Congress. Another group suggested that the convention should constitute Johnson himself as provisional governor of the state, thus fortifying his position with the sanction of the people, and request him to issue writs of election to enable the people of the state to elect all of the state officers provided for in the constitution on the day fixed in that instrument. Still another group favored the election, by the convention, of a governor's council of

[42] Nashville *Union*, May 30, 1863.
[43] Nashville *Dispatch*, June 27, 1863.
[44] Nashville *Union*, June 23, 1863.

three members which should consult with and advise Johnson in the interest of the people until the full civil government should be restored.[45]

On the other hand it was pointed out that the convention was not a representative body and that it could not make Johnson a provisional governor. No civil functions, it was argued, could be exercised in Tennessee except under the constitution of the state, and this document was temporarily in abeyance. The only solution of the difficulty, then, was to attempt to restore the civil government under the constitution, an attempt which could not be consummated until the state was clear of the Confederate forces. As the first step in this direction had already been taken by the President in his appointment of the military governor, it was argued that the convention should do nothing except endorse the administration of Johnson. This position was strongly maintained by the East Tennessee delegates, who, being unable to hold an election in their region, had no desire to see the civil power re-established by the "less loyal" elements in Middle and West Tennessee. In the end this latter view prevailed, and resolutions were passed, declaring null and void all laws, resolutions, and ordinances passed by the legislature of Tennessee since April 12, 1861, and endorsing the administration of Governor Johnson. The importance of electing a state legislature was emphasized, and the military governor was requested to issue writs and appoint agents for holding such an election on the first Tuesday in August. The convention also named a Union state executive committee, as a permanent body, to keep an eye on the political situation and call another convention whenever such action was deemed to be necessary.[46]

The election day passed without any further demonstration from the administration party. They made no attempt to hold an election, Johnson maintaining that no

[45] *Ibid.*, July 2-8, July 18, 1863; Nashville *Dispatch*, July 3, 1863.
[46] Nashville *Union*, July 2-8, 1863.

Union strength could be developed in the state as long as the region was infested with the guerrilla bands.[47]   The Confederates went through the form of holding an election in August 4.[48]   Judge Caruthers was chosen as governor, and representatives to the Confederate Congress were named.   The vote, however, was exceedingly small and was confined largely to the army camps.[49] The whole proceeding was an empty formality and created no problem for the Johnson administration.   The representatives took their seats in the Confederate Congress at Richmond, but Judge Caruthers, an elderly and peaceful gentleman, made no attempt to take his office—nor could he have done so had he desired.

Another election was conducted on the same day, however, which created a very embarrassing problem for the Johnson administration to deal with.   There was in the state a considerable Union party, the leader of which was Emerson Etheridge of Dresden.   An outstanding Union leader during the secession period, he was now accused of being a copperhead, but his bold and fearless speeches, his imposing presence, and his fascinating manner had won for him a considerable following.   Relying upon the neglect of the Johnson party to name a candidate, Etheridge and his friends devised a scheme whereby an election for governor should be held on August 4.   The anti-administration candidate would thus secure the entire vote of the state and would, under the constitution, be the legal governor by action of the people.   This project was partly carried out.   An election was held in Bedford and Shelby counties, and William B. Campbell, the Etheridge candidate, received about 2,500 votes.[50]   It was perfectly apparent that this election had been held with-

[47] C. R. Hall, *op. cit.*, p. 99.

[48] E. H. Rennalds, Civil War Diary (typewritten copy in the Lawson McGhee Library).

[49] Charles A. Miller, *The Official and Political Manual of Tennessee,* p. 46.

[50] C. R. Hall, *op. cit.*, pp. 99-101.

out the necessary preliminaries, but the Etheridge party claimed that their candidate had received all of the votes legally cast and was thereby chosen governor. Etheridge even went to Washington and urged the President to recognize and install Campbell. He met with no success, but the affair embarrassed the administration by furnishing unfortunate evidence of the division in the ranks of the Unionists.[51]

Meanwhile the Federal armies were achieving success in the state, and Lincoln thought that his opportunity for restoring the Federal authority had arrived. After Bragg's evacuation of Chattanooga in September he suggested that Johnson take steps for the reorganization of the loyal state government and gave him specific authority, under the guarantee clause of the Constitution, to exercise all powers necessary for the restoration. The President was very explicit as to the character of the new government that was to be organized. "Let the reconstruction be the work of such men only as can be trusted for the Union," he wrote to Johnson. "Exclude all others and trust that your government so organized will be recognized here as being the one republican form to be guaranteed to the state, and to be protected against invasion and domestic violence."[52] These instructions should be borne in mind in studying Johnson's later policy of excluding the ex-Confederates from the polls. Mass meetings were held; Johnson outlined his policy; and high hopes were entertained for the speedy restoration of the state to the Union. Again the action was premature, for these hopes were shattered by the disaster of Rosecrans at Chattanooga.

Lincoln and Johnson were both deeply chagrined by the failure of the new scheme for reorganization, but circumstances proved that the reverses were only temporary. The Federal government planned a fall and winter

---

[51] Nashville *Union*, Oct. 1, 4, 1863.

[52] *O.R.*, series III, vol. III, p. 789; Nicolay and Hay, *op. cit.*, IX, 116.

campaign on a grander scale than ever before, and the
new generals who had come to the front in 1863, Grant,
Sherman, and Thomas, were able to retrieve the losses of
Chickamauga. With the exception of Hood's raid in
1864, Tennessee was permanently freed from the presence of Confederate troops, and the process of reconstruction could now be carried on without interruption.[53]

Inspired by these successes Lincoln issued, on December 8, 1863, his proclamation of amnesty and reconstruction. By the terms of this proclamation, amnesty and
pardon with certain exceptions were to be extended to all
Confederates upon their taking the oath of allegiance to
the power of the United States, and when loyal voters to
the extent of one-tenth of the voting population of 1860
should establish a state government this government
would be recognized as the true republican form, entitled
to all the guarantees and protection promised in the
Constitution.[54] In January, 1864, an agent was dispatched to Tennessee with the necessary blanks and
instructions to enroll all citizens who would take the oath
of allegiance. Johnson however, entertained little sympathy for the President's proclamation. Its terms were
not severe enough to satisfy him. Taking the amnesty
oath, he contended might set a former Confederate
right with the lawful authority, secure for him a pardon,
and absolve him from punishment for his treason, but
a more stringent oath should be required for admission
to the elective franchise. On January 21, 1863, at a mass
meeting in Nashville, arranged presumably at his insti-
gation, Johnson delivered an address setting forth this
view, and resolutions were adopted in full accord with
his desires.[55] Encouraged by the success of this meeting and by messages that came in from various parts of
the state, he issued a proclamation on January 26, call-

[53] James F. Rhodes, *History of the Civil War,* p. 299.
[54] Richardson, *op. cit.,* VI, 213.
[55] Frank Moore, *Rebellion Record,* vol. VIII, doc. 358.

ing for an election of county officers to be held on
March 5.[56]

At this election those presenting themselves to vote
should be required to take, in addition to the amnesty
oath, the following "test oath":

"I do solemnly swear that I will henceforth support the Constitution of the United States and defend it against the assaults of
all its enemies; that I will henceforth be and conduct myself as
a true and faithful citizen of the United States, freely and
voluntarily claiming to be subject to all the rights and privileges of such citizenship; that I ardently desire the suppression
of the present insurrection and rebellion against the government of the United States, the success of its armies, and the
defeat of all those who oppose them, and that the Constitution
of the United States, and all laws and proclamations made in
pursuance thereof may be speedily and permanently established
over all of the people, states, and territories thereof; and, further,
that I will hereafter aid and assist all loyal people in the accomplishment of all these results. So help me God."[57]

It will be observed that only by false swearing or a delib-
erate change of heart could a former secessionist obtain
a voice in the government of the state.

There were many judicious Union men in the state who
thought that Johnson was going too far in this procedure, and that by unnecessary severity he would defeat
his own plan. In the hope of checking him they appealed
to the President, but they received no encouragement.
"I have seen and examined Governor Johnson's proclamation", said Lincoln, "and I am satisfied with his plan,
which is to restore the state government and place it
under the control of citizens truly loyal to the government
of the United States."[58] But if the President was not
disposed to place obstacles in the way of the Governor,
the people of the state were. There was so much disorder
and confusion that the election of March 5 was little more

[56] *Ibid.*, doc. 340.
[57] *Ibid.*, vol. VIII, doc. 340.
[58] *O.R.*, series III, vol. IV, p. 141.

than a farce, and its results contributed to a severe decline in Johnson's prestige.[59]

The Governor was firmly determined, however, upon carrying out his plan, even in the face of the storm of abuse to which he was subjected. He proposed, therefore, to appeal to the citizens of East Tennessee with the hope of enlisting a solid loyal party in support of his policy. On account of the severe economic distress and serious social dislocations which the war had caused in that region the East Tennessee people were bitter and vindictive in their demands for "no concessions to traitors." It will be recalled that the Greeneville Convention of 1861 had adjourned to meet again upon the call of its president, Thomas A. R. Nelson. Upon Johnson's suggestion Nelson now reassembled the convention at Knoxville on April 12. This body proved to be unsuitable, however, as a weapon for the Governor's purpose. The old leaders were still conservative, and the majority still favored a settlement along the lines of the Crittenden Compromise. A minority supported Johnson, but neither party was able to carry the convention.[60] A movement to detach East Tennessee and form the region into a separate state showed some vitality for a time, but finally collapsed before the determined opposition of the Governor himself.[61]

Despite these repeated rebuffs Johnson saw one more illusive hope in the approach of the presidential campaign of 1864. Much prestige might be gained for the state if delegates from Tennessee should be admitted to the National Union Convention at Baltimore. With this end in view the permanent executive committee which had been appointed in 1863 issued a call on May 3 proposing that all unconditional Union men meet in their respective divisions of the state on May 30 for the pur-

[59] Nashville *Union*, Mar. 8, 1864.
[60] O. P. Temple, *Notable Men of Tennessee*, p. 407.
[61] Nashville *Union*, Apr. 17, 19, 30, 1864.

pose of electing delegates to this convention. The newspaper accounts of these meetings are so badly confused
that it is impossible to determine exactly what happened,
but it is certain that they supported Johnson's policy and
that they declared for him and Lincoln as party nomi-
nees.[62] Delegates to the national convention were
selected, and fortunately for the Unionists they were admitted at Baltimore.

A more important and more difficult task now remained—that of taking positive action in the approaching presidential campaign and pushing the Union party
to success in the state. Opposing the Union party were
two groups, the secessionists and the Union Peace party.
The former group could create no difficulty as its members could be readily excluded from the polls by the test
oath, but the latter was more formidable. Its members
stood upon their loyalty to the Union and their rights
under the Constitution, but they denounced the Emancipation Proclamation and attacked Lincoln and Johnson
for prolonging the war. Their candidate for the presidency was General George B. McClellan, who had been
nominated at Chicago by the Democrats on a platform
declaring that "justice, humanity, liberty, and the public
welfare demand that immediate efforts be made for a
cessation of hostilities."[63] In order to devise and dis-
cuss plans for dealing with this group, a Union convention was held at Nashville on September 5. At this convention the Radicals were strongly in the ascendency and
the Conservatives were completely overwhelmed. A
Lincoln and Johnson electoral ticket was nominated and
an executive committee of fifteen—five from each grand
division of the state—was appointed. Extremely difficult suffrage requirements were prescribed. Voters
should be required to take both the amnesty and test
oaths, but the taking of these oaths should be only pre-

[62] Nashville *Union*, June 11, 1864.
[63] N. W. Stephenson, *Lincoln*, p. 385.

sumptive evidences of loyalty. Moreover, the test oath
was amended so as to disfranchise the supporters of
McClellan, who had announced a desire for a cessation
of hostilities and a restoration of peace on the simple
basis of the Union, by the addition of a clause pledging
the voters to "oppose all armistices or negotiations for
peace with rebels now in arms."[64] Both the adherents
of the secessionist and the Union Peace parties were thus
excluded from the polls.

The McClellan supporters were so outraged by this
highhanded procedure that they sent a delegation to
Washington to deliver a protest to the President. When
John Lellyet presented the protest to Lincoln, however,
the latter merely inquired "how long it took you and the
New York politicians to concoct that paper"[65] and declined to interfere. "I expect to let the friends of George
B. McClellan manage their side of the contest in their
own way, and I will manage my side of it in my own
way," he added, and closed the interview. The delegation composed of several distinguished Conservative
Union men was outraged by this, and they forthwith withdrew the McClellan ticket in the state. "There will be
no election for President in Tennessee in 1864," they announced. "You and Governor Johnson may 'manage your
side of it your own way' but it will be no election."[66]

There was much excitement and confusion in the state
on the eve of the election. Lincoln and Johnson mass
meetings were held frequently and sometimes under
rather hectic conditions. A Negro torch light procession
was held in Nashville on October 24, and "shots were
freely fired." On this occasion Johnson made a violent
and ill-timed speech, resorting to the devices of a demagogue to sway the feelings of the ignorant and excited
blacks. The estates of the aristocracy, he said, should be

[64] *American Annual Cyclopedia, 1864*, p. 765.
[65] Edward McPherson, *Political History of the . . . Rebellion*, p. 439.
[66] *Ibid.*, p. 440.

confiscated and divided among the free farmers. "The great planters sneer at Negro equality," he declared, "while about their dwellings one may see mulatto children bearing unmistakable resemblance to their masters, the product of a concubinage compared to which polygamy is a virtue." Tennessee's destiny must be controlled by loyal men and "rebels must be dumb. Let them gather their treasonable conclaves elsewhere— among their friends in the Confederacy." Then looking upon the persecuted and despised crowd of Negroes before him, he expressed a wish that, as of old, a Moses might arise and lead them out of the land of bondage to the promised land of freedom. "You are our Moses," shouted the crowd. "Well then," said Johnson "humble and unworthy as I am, if no better shall be found, I will indeed be your Moses, and lead you through the Red Sea of war and bondage to a fairer future of liberty and peace."[67] McClellan meetings were broken up by soldiers,[68] and the election on November 8 was a mere farce with its outcome already predetermined. Only a few scattered votes were cast for McClellan and Pendleton. However, the electoral vote of Tennessee was not counted. Congress, by joint resolution rejected it on the ground that the state was in rebellion and that no valid election had been held.[69]

When the presidential election was over the occasion seemed propitious for the permanent restoration of the state to the Union. The initiative in this attempted procedure came from the East Tennessee Union Executive committee, which on November 12 issued a call for a state convention to meet at Nashville on December 19, "to form a ticket to run for a constitutional convention."[70] The entrance of the Confederate army into the state

[67] C. R. Hall, *op. cit.*, pp. 154-55, quoting the Cincinnati *Gazette*.
[68] Edward McPherson, *op. cit.*, p. 440.
[69] *Congressional Globe*, 38 Cong., 2 Sess., pp. 522, 533, 534, 574, 590.
[70] Nashville *Union*, Nov. 18, 1864.

under General John B. Hood, however, caused the proposed convention to be postponed until January 8, the anniversary of the Battle of New Orleans. As this date fell upon Sunday, the convention met on Monday, January 9.

Instead of serving as a preliminary convention, however, as the call had contemplated, the convention of January 9, after a series of debates, arrogated to itself constituent powers and framed two new amendments to the state constitution. The first of these abolished slavery, and the second prohibited the general assembly from passing any law recognizing the right of property in man. A schedule, appended to these amendments, repealed Section 31 of the state constitution, repudiated the ordinance of secession and the military league with the Confederate States, and declared null and void all acts of the Harris administration effected after May 6, 1861. It ratified an act of Johnson calling for an election on February 22 at which the people of the state should vote on the proposed amendments and the schedule. Provision was also made, in the event that the ratification of the amendments was successful, for an election of a governor and members of the general assembly, the latter to be voted for on a general ticket on March 4, and to assemble on April 2, following.[71]

The election was held on the appointed day, February 22, and the amendments were ratified by a vote of 25,293 to 48.[72] As this was more than ten per cent of the vote of the state in 1860 it was considered and held as a compliance with the President's proclamation of December 8, 1863, whereby he came under a special promise to guarantee to Tennessee a republican form of government and protect the state against invasion and domestic violence. When this had been accomplished, the election

[71] Nashville *Dispatch*, Jan. 10-16, 1865.
[72] Charles A. Miller, *The Official and Political Manual of Tennessee*, p. 48.

for governor and members of the legislature was held, and William G. Brownlow, who had been nominated by the convention, was elected. He was inaugurated on April 5, and Tennessee again came under a civil government.

CHAPTER III

THE CIVIL WAR IN EAST TENNESSEE

IN THE preceding chapters the progress and success of
the secession movement were described. It will be recalled that, although secession became an accomplished
fact in June, 1861, this was accomplished only as a result
of the victory of a numerical majority over the forces
of a vigorous, influential, and well organized minority.
In Middle and West Tennessee the members of this
minority group, who had been drawn largely from the
old Whig party, almost without exception acquiesced in
the result of the June election, found their way into the
Confederate forces, and became valiant defenders of the
Southern cause. There was no significant body of organized and articulate Union sentiment in these sections
subsequent to June, 1861. In East Tennessee, however,
the situation was entirely different. There the Unionists,
alleging that the decision at the polls on June 8 was fraud-
ulently obtained, refused to abide by its results. They
allied themselves with the new Republican party and continued, with fierce and unrelenting hostility, their opposition to the forces that had disrupted the Union. As a
consequence civil war with all of its horrors broke out in
East Tennessee, and the animosities and hardships which
were then created were long remembered. They bore a
very significant and important influence upon several of
the leaders of the subsequent period of reconstruction in
Tennessee.

As the supporters of the Confederacy in East Tennessee were largely of the wealthy and aristocratic classes
in the cities, while the Unionists came from the non-slave-
holding classes in the rural and mountainous region, the
war in that region assumed the character of a class strug-

gle as well as a political and military contest.[1] The contempt of the Unionists for the members of the aristocracy was very accurately expressed by William G. Brownlow when he described the latter as "descendants in direct line from some old foreigners who had been sold out upon shares to pay their passage to this country . . . who had taken their start in life by peddling upon pins and needles, by spading up gardens for other people, or by entering other people's lands, and, by hook or crook, securing their titles."[2] These two classes were innately and fundamentally incapable of understanding each other, chiefly because of their divergent social and economic interests. Inhabiting a region unsuited for the production of cotton, the Unionists of East Tennessee owned few slaves, and they followed William G. Brownlow in refusing to aid in inaugurating "a new reading of the Ten Commandments, so as to teach that the *chief end of Man is Nigger*."[3] On the other hand there was a disposition on the part of the slaveholders of the region to regard the Unionists as levellers, dangerous to the security of the institutions of the country.

To these fundamental social and economic differences must be added, as circumstances engendering animosity and distrust, the political and religious dissensions which were inflamed among the people by a group of clergymen, orators, and journalists. "No class of churchmembers," declared the Knoxville *Whig*, "have been so intemperate and as proscriptive as those preachers who have entered into this contest. The result is, that in all of the congregations of the country, there is a division in sentiment, and a portion of the congregations are unwilling to hear these men preach."[4] Among these agitators no one ex-

[1] Thomas W. Humes, *The Loyal Mountaineers of Tennessee*, p. 61.

[2] Knoxville *Whig*, Feb. 20, 1864.

[3] William G. Brownlow, *Sketches of the Rise, Progress, and Decline of Secession*, p. 29.

[4] Knoxville *Whig*, Aug. 31, 1861.

ceeded in force and vituperation the man who was here denouncing them, William G. Brownlow, and in force and acrimony he was followed closely by his sometime associate, Andrew Johnson.

Both of these men were active in the campaign against secession in 1861. A fair specimen of this activity is given in the account of an eye witness of Johnson's speech at Jonesboro, on May 6, 1861,

Such a time has never been since I have lived in the place. J[ohnson] rose to speak. The crowd at once commenced *booing, booing,* until it finally deafened you. He gave back for a little while, and then came forward and commenced. Such groans and cursing you never heard. They cursed him for a *God Damed Traitor*—told him he was hired by Lincoln to make speeches, asked how much he got—he again sat down. The crowd said Nelson might speak, but he should not. Nelson came forward and commenced. Some groaned for him a while, but he went on and did not speak long until a shower came up and he quit. A few went down into the basement story of the courthouse (which has been used as a *necessary* for a year or so), and Johnson spoke to a few old sore back union shriekers. The boys would occasionally thrust through the window a secession flag, and ball for him. When he went to start out to Nelson's they raised the shout, groaned and *booed* him out of town. . . . You never saw such a time. Men on horses ripping up and down the streets, screaming upon the top of their voices, "you damed traitor, you damed traitor."[5]

The character of the oratory and procedure indulged in by Johnson during this campaign was calculated to arouse rather than to allay animosity. On June 7 he spoke at Kingston, and the scene was vividly described by John Bell Brownlow, the son of William G. Brownlow, who had gone to warn Johnson that an attempt would be made upon his life if he boarded the train for Knoxville that night. "When I reached Kingston," said Brownlow, "Nelson, Johnson, and Trigg were speaking. Nelson was sitting on the stand asleep, and there was a large bucket

[5] Letter of W. H. Crouch to L. C. Haynes, May 6, 1861, in Nelson Papers.

of whiskey punch on the floor. Johnson had all he could hold and still speak. He swore that he 'was not afraid,' and said that he 'owned $12,000 in the stock of that railroad' and he 'would be damned if he would be driven from it by the traitors of the cotton states'."[6] Fortunately, however, he yielded to the advice of young Brownlow and returned with him to Knoxville in a buggy.

Much more important than Johnson as an agitator was William G. Brownlow. As the able editor of the Knoxville *Whig,* a journal having a wide circulation among the mountainous counties, and as an ex-circuit rider, honored and respected by the Methodists of East Tennessee, with all the devices and methods of a demagogue at his command, he was in a position to sway and excite the masses with great effect. He refused to eat in a lunch room at Athens because the proprietor was a secessionist,[7] and when asked by General Pillow to serve as chaplain of his brigade, he replied, "when I shall have made up my mind to go to Hell, I will cut my throat and go direct, and not travel around by way of the Southern Confederacy."[8] When prayers were requested for the Buchanan administration in certain quarters he declared that he would prefer to send his children to a dancing school than to see them gathered around the family altar offering supplications for the perfidious Democracy, and at the same time composed a prayer to "be used this winter by all *local* preachers in their public ministrations",

Almighty God, our heavenly Father, in whose hands are the hearts of men, and the issues of events, not mixed up with Locofocoism, nor rendered offensive in Thy sight by being identified with men of corrupt minds, evil designs, and damnable purposes, such as are seeking to up-turn the best form of government on earth, Thou hast graciously promised to hear the

[6] Letter of John Bell Brownlow to O. P. Temple, Aug. 14, 1860, in the Temple Papers, University of Tennessee Library, Knoxville.

[7] Knoxville *Whig,* Apr. 30, 1864.

[8] Frank Moore, *Rebellion Record,* I, 60.

prayers of those in an humble spirit, and with true faith,—
such as no *Secessionist* can bring into exercise,—call upon Thee.
Be pleased, we beseech Thee, favorably to look upon and bless
the Union men of this Commonwealth, and sustain them in
their praiseworthy efforts to perpetuate the Government, and,
under it, the institutions of our holy religion. Possess their
minds with the spirit of true patriotism, enlightened wisdom,
and of persevering hostility towards those traitors, political
gamblers, and selfish demagogues who are seeking to build up
a miserable Southern Confederacy, and under it to inaugurate
a new reading of the Ten Commandments, so as to teach that
the *chief end of Man is Nigger!* In these days of trouble and
perplexity, give the common people grace to perceive the right
path, which, Thou knowest, leads from the camps of Southern
mad-caps and Northern fanatics, and enable them steadfastly
to walk therein!

So strengthen the common masses, O Lord, and so direct
them, that being hindered neither by the fear of fire-eaters, nor
by the love of corrupt men in power, nor by bribery, nor by an
over-charge of mean whiskey, nor by any other *Democratic* pas-
sion, but being mindful of Thy constant superintendence, of
the awful majesty of Thy righteousness, of Thy hatred of a
corrupt Democracy and its profligate leaders, and of the strict
account they must hereafter give to Thee, they may, in counsel,
word, and deed, aim supremely at the fulfilment of their duty,
which is to talk, vote, and pray against the wicked leaders of
Abolitionism, and the equally ungodly advocates of Secessionism.
Grant that those of Thy professed ministers who are mixed
up with *modern Democracy,* and have become so hardened in
sin as openly to advocate the vile delusion, may speedily abandon
their unministerial habits, or go over to the cause of the devil,
that their positions may at least be unequivocal, and that they
may thereby advance the welfare of their country! . . .[9]

To one Jordan Clark, of Camden, Arkansas, who
wrote, probably in a facetious vein, that a report had
come to him that Brownlow was preparing to join the
Democratic party, the latter replied,

When the sun shines at midnight and the moon at mid-day;
when man forgets to be selfish, or Democrats lose their inclina-
tion to steal; when nature stops her onward march to rest, or

⁹ William G. Brownlow, *op. cit.,* pp. 28-30.

all the water-courses in America flow up stream; when flowers lose their odor, and trees shed no leaves; when birds talk, and beasts of burden laugh; when damned spirits swap hell for heaven with the angels of light, and pay them the boot in mean whiskey; when impossibilities are in fashion, and no proposition is too absurd to be believed,—you may credit the report that I have joined the Democrats!

I join the Democrats! Never, so long as there are sects in churches, weeds in gardens, fleas in hog-pens, dirt in victuals, disputes in families, wars with nations, water in the ocean, bad men in America, or base women in France! No, Jordan Clark, you may hope, you may congratulate, you may reason, you may sneer, but that cannot be. The thrones of the Old World, the courts of the universe, the governments of the world, may all fall and crumble into ruin,—the New World may commit the national suicide of dissolving this Union,—but all this, and more, must occur before I join the Democracy!

I join the Democracy! Jordan Clark, you know not what you say. When I join Democracy, the Pope of Rome will join the Methodist Church. When Jordan Clark, of Arkansas, is President of the Republic of Great Britain by the universal suffrage of a contented people; when Queen Victoria consents to be divorced from Prince Albert by a county court in Kansas; when Congress obliges, by law, James Buchanan to marry a European princess; when the Pope leases the Capitol at Washington for his city residence; when Alexander of Russia and Napoleon of France are elected Senators in Congress from New Mexico; when good men cease to go to heaven, or bad men to hell; when this world is turned upside down; when proof is afforded, both clear and unquestionable that there is no God; when men turn to ants, and ants to elephants,—I will change my political faith and come out on the side of Democracy.[10]

Brownlow's editorials in the Knoxville *Whig* displayed his intense hatred of the Confederacy. The following is characteristic of the general tenor of these editorials,

If we had the power, we would arm and uniform in Federal habiliments all the fowls of the air and the fishes of the sea— every wolf, panther, catamount, and bear in the mountains of America—every tiger, elephant, and lion in Europe—every

[10] *Ibid.*, pp. 62-64.

rattlesnake and crocodile in the swamps of Florida and South Carolina—every negro in the Southern Confederacy, and every devil in Hell, and turn them loose upon the Confederacy. Nay, we would poison the very air they breathe, the water they drink, and the food they eat. We would convert Hell itself into one great torpedo, and have it exploded under the very center of the Confederacy. Aye, we say put down the rebellion, and force rebels to lay down their arms, if, in so doing, we have to exterminate from God's green earth every living human being South of the Mason and Dixon's Line.[11]

Concerning Forest and Hardee, two prominent Confederate officers, he wrote on one occasion,

Had we our wish, we would throw Hell wide open, and place all such beastlike men and officers upon an inclined plane, at an angle of forty-five degrees, grease the plane with hog's lard six inches thick, with a wicket at the bottom, and send them, as one stream of traitors, robbers, and assassins, into the hottest part of the infernal regions.[12]

Likewise he was adept in appealing to the freedom-loving and democratic instincts of the Anglo-Saxons of the East Tennessee highlands. He constantly urged upon them the fact that,

We can never live in a Southern Confederacy and be made hewers of wood and drawers of water for a set of aristocrats and overbearing tyrants. . . . We have no interest in common with the Cotton States. We are a grain growing and stock raising people, and we can conduct a cheap government, inhabiting the Switzerland of America.[13]

His pen was extremely active in calling upon the Unionists of the region to speak out "in these times that try men's souls."[14]

Another cause for discontent in East Tennessee was the physical and material devastation wrought by the contending armies and by the depredations of camp followers and guerrillas on both sides. These "bush-

[11] Knoxville *Whig*, Aug. 10, 1865.
[12] *Ibid.*, Jan. 30, 1864.
[13] *Ibid.*, Jan. 26, 1861.   [14] *Ibid.*, Dec. 15, 1860.

whackers" and "partisan rangers" especially deserve
the most severe condemnation. Of them, Daniel Sullins,
an East Tennessee clergyman, wrote,

There were many good men who were Union men in the country, but they were powerless to prevent the state of things.
They might have done a little better than they did, maybe, if
they had tried hard. But let it be written as history that it
was not the men who wore the blue and the gray and stood on
the firing line in the day of battle who did these cowardly things.
No, it was whelps from another kennel, who cowardly came out
after the killing was over, with the instincts of a hyena to get
what they could out of the offal. I will not particularise the
fiendish acts that characterized and disgraced the time. Let
them go unnamed and be forgotten.[15]

At first the people of East Tennessee were disposed
to occupy a neutral position, but experience soon demonstrated that this was impossible. Because of the strate-
gic value of the region, it was inevitable that both the
North and the South would attempt to occupy it. The
Richmond *Enquirer* called it the "Keystone of the Southern arch." Not only did its passes afford avenues for
the armies to pass between the upper and the lower
South, but it was also a great storehouse of salt and
bacon, scarce and precious necessities of the soldier's life.
Its tremendous value, thus, justified almost any measure
calculated to secure it.

The attention of statesmen and military men in the
North was early directed to East Tennessee. This fact,
together with the urgent requests for aid which came from
the region, should have brought the Union forces into
East Tennessee during the first few weeks of the struggle. The government, however, moved with disastrous
slowness. As early as May, 1861, Andrew Johnson and
Horace Maynard besieged the President for prompt aid,
and in October William Blount Carter wrote to General

[15] Daniel Sullins, *Recollections of an Old Man; Seventy Years in Dixie,*
pp. 195-96.

Thomas that "whoever is the leader of a successful expedition into East Tennessee will receive from these grateful people a crown of glory of which anyone might be well proud."[16] A Southern sympathizer wrote to Jefferson Davis in November that these people "look for the establishment of the Federal authority with as much confidence as the Jews look for the coming of the Messiah, and I feel quite sure when I assert that no event or circumstance can change or modify their hope."[17] Moreover, the President was, from the beginning, impressed with the importance of occupying the region, and in this view he was supported by General Thomas, then operating in Kentucky. Some supplies and arms were sent in June,[18] and in October Lincoln pressed upon the war department the necessity of occupying Cumberland Gap, the outlet from East Tennessee to Virginia and Kentucky. When McClellan became commander-in-chief in November he assigned this task to his personal friend, General Buell, who was unfortunately bent upon striking at the center of the Confederate authority at Nashville. Johnson and Maynard telegraphed him that "our people are oppressed and pursued as beasts of the forest; the government must come to their relief,"[19] but Buell remained inactive, maturing his own plans, and meeting the importunities of Lincoln and McClellan with evasive replies until the Confederate occupation of East Tennessee was complete.[20] As a result the Union objective failed, and these faithful people were forced to undergo two years of extreme privation before deliverance came.

[16] O.R., series I, vol. IV, p. 230.

[17] Letter of A. C. Graham to Jefferson Davis, Goodspeed, *History of Tennessee*, p. 485.

[18] O.R., series I, vol. LII, part II, p. 115.

[19] *Ibid.*, series I, vol. VII, p. 480.

[20] C. R. Hall, *op. cit.*, p. 18. This is the administration view of Buell's conduct. Historians have differed as to the advisability of his plans; some claim that his plan to strike at the enemy's main force was better calculated than that of Lincoln and McClellan. It is certain, however, that the lack of candor in Buell's dispatches put him in bad odor with the administration.

Meanwhile the Confederates had been much more keenly aware of the advantage of possessing the region. Many of the accounts of their brutality and outrages are doubtless exaggerated, but it is certain that they were determined, by fair means or foul, to control the eastern part of the state. In August General Felix K. Zollicoffer was designated to reclaim it for the Confederacy. In an address to the people of East Tennessee he promised moderation and conciliation. "The military authorities," he said, "are not here to offend or injure the people, but to insure peace to their homes, by repelling invasion and preventing the horrors of civil war. Treason to the state government cannot, will not, be tolerated. But perfect freedom of the ballot-box has and will be accorded and no man's rights, property, or privileges shall be disturbed."[21] This policy failed, however, to effect the desired results, and more stringest measures were adopted. Crops were confiscated and sent South, and the Confederate conscription act was put into operation, tearing many Unionists from their homes for unwilling service in the ranks of the enemy.

One of the most important aspects of these stringent measures was the harsh treatment accorded to those persons suspected of bridge-burning. In many respects the burning of the East Tennessee bridges was one of the most hazardous events of the whole war. The execution of this attempt was arranged by the Rev. William Blount Carter,[22] after consultation with Lincoln, Seward, and

[21] Knoxville *Whig*, Aug. 10, 1861.

[22] Carter was a Presbyterian minister living at Elizabethton. He received from the Federal Government the sum of $20,000 for his activity in arranging the scheme for burning the bridges. The plans were carried into upper East Tennessee by his wife disguised as a mother going to visit a wounded son. William Blount Carter was the brother of General Samuel P. Carter. The latter was a graduate of the United States Naval Academy and was serving in the navy when the war broke out. Upon the urgent request of President Lincoln he resigned from the naval service and took command of the Federal forces in East Tennessee, with the rank of brigadier-general. After the war he reëntered the navy and rose to the rank of rear-admiral.

Top: CONFEDERATE SYMPATHIZERS REVILING THE CORPSES OF FRY AND HENSIE WHO HAD BEEN HANGED FOR BRIDGE BURNING. FROM AN ENGRAVING IN PARSON BROWNLOW'S BOOK.

Bottom: EAST TENNESSEE UNIONISTS ESCAPING ACROSS THE MOUNTAINS TO JOIN THE UNION ARMY. FROM AN ENGRAVING IN HARPER'S WEEKLY.

McClellan, and the plan was to burn, on the same night, nine bridges between Stevenson, Alabama, and Bristol, thus rendering useless 265 miles of railway and impeding the transportation of troops and supplies to the battle-fields of Northern Virginia. On the appointed night five of the bridges were burned, and, although Carter escaped, five of his associates were hanged under instruction from Judah P. Benjamin, the Confederate secretary of war.[23] The execution of two of these men, Fry and Hensie, was particularly fiendish and brutal. According to the current report they were hanged upon the same limb of an oak tree close by the track of the East Tennessee Railroad, and the trains were ordered to pass by them slowly, so that the passengers could see, kick and strike with canes their dead bodies, from the front and rear platforms of the cars, as they passed. After two days, however, such natural processes developed that the bodies had to be taken down in order that the passengers might pass the spot without offense. The military authorities also directed that many prominent Union men, suspected of various acts, ranging from uttering "Union talk" to bridge-burning, should be imprisoned at Knoxville or sent to Tuscaloosa, Alabama, where they suffered greatly.[24] Brownlow's *Whig* was suppressed, and the editor was committed to jail.[25]

Becoming restive under this condition of things and hoping for relief from the North, the Unionists began to organize military forces. As early as July Brownlow stated that there were 10,000 of them under arms,[26] and

He is said to have been the only man in the history of the United States to rise to such eminence in both branches of the service.

[23] *O.R.*, series I, vol. IV, p. 231.

[24] These events are recounted in some detail in Brownlow's *Sketches of the Rise, Progress, and Decline of Secession*. See especially pp. 311-12. Other good accounts will be found in Humes, *The Loyal Mountaineers of Tennessee*, and Temple, *East Tennessee and the Civil War*.

[25] Knoxville *Whig*, Oct. 24, 1861. Brownlow might have avoided this inconvenience merely by taking the oath of allegiance to the Confederacy but this he refused to do.

[26] *O.R.*, series I, vol. IV, pp. 365-66.

by November they had grown bold enough to avow their
purpose to resist the authority of the Confederacy. "The
Union feeling in this county is intense," wrote T. J.
Cannon from Loudon, "and all they want, in my opinion,
to induce a general uprising is encouragement from the
Lincoln armies. They have a great many arms, and they
are actually manufacturing Union flags to receive the
refugee Tennesseans when they return."[27] "A worse
state of feeling never prevailed in East Tennessee than
at the present moment," wrote R. G. Fain to Judah P.
Benjamin. "The belief that the enemy are about to enter
our borders has emboldened them to such an extent that
there is no telling what they may do."[28]. A Southern
sympathizer wrote to Jefferson Davis,

In my passage through East Tennessee I found a much more hostile and embittered feeling toward the Confederate Government
than I had supposed to exist. I found the emissaries of the Lincoln Government actively and constantly engaged in exciting
hatred and animosity towards our government. I believe the
people only await the occasion to revolt against the Confederate
Government.[29]

A similar view was expressed in the correspondence of
the Union Men. William Blount Carter wrote from
Kingston that,

This whole country is in a wretched condition; a perfect despotism reigns here. The Union men of East Tennessee are long-
ing and praying for the hour when they can break their fetters.
The loyalty of our people increases with the oppressions they
have to bear. Men and women weep for joy when I merely hint
to them that the day of our deliverance is at hand.[30]

In Morgan County the same writer found the Union
people "firm and unwavering in their devotion to our
government, and anxious to have an opportunity to assist
in saving it." The Confederates, he found, were continuing "to arrest and imprison our people."[31]

[27] Ibid., p. 233.
[28] Ibid., p. 231.
[31] Ibid., series II, vol. I, pp. 889-90.
[29] Ibid., pp. 369-70.
[30] Ibid., p. 329.

Top: REBELS WHIPPING A MAN FOR EXPRESSING UNION SENTIMENTS IN EAST TENNESSEE. FROM AN ENGRAVING IN PARSON BROWNLOW'S BOOK.

Bottom: BRUTAL TREATMENT OF THE REV. WM. H. H. DUGGAN BY THE REBELS. DUGGAN WAS A METHODIST MINISTER AND HAD PRAYED FOR THE UNION. FROM AN ENGRAVING IN PARSON BROWNLOW'S BOOK.

Many went North to join the Union armies. Camp
Dick Robinson in Kentucky offered them a convenient
rendezvous, and Dan Ellis, "the great Union guide,"
piloted hundreds of loyalists across the mountains to
this post.[32]

Determining to hold the region at all costs the Confederates inaugurated a reign of terror. Vigilance committees prowled over the country, armed to the teeth,
arresting men on suspicion of hostility to the new government, and shooting others down. The Unionists then,
despairing at length of relief from the North and regarding their houses and lives in danger, formed themselves
into secret "bushwhacking" societies, shot Confederates
from ambush and destroyed their property. This is turn
maddened the Confederates and provoked them to savage
retaliation. A civil and guerrilla war was thus begun, the
horrors of which almost defy description. The fact that
the Confederate armies were composed largely of Tennesseans, who were bitter political enemies of the Unionists and who keenly realized that, in the event of failure,
they had to expect the penalty of treason at the hands of
vindictive local enemies, tended to intensify their cruelty.
On the other hand, the Unionists, deprived of the stabiliz-
ing force and discipline of a regular military organization, were unrestrained in their acts. The Confederates,
operating from their center at Knoxville, terrorized the
country. In October Robertson Topp wrote that,

More than one hundred persons have been arrested in East Tennessee, without warrants in some cases, marched great distances,
and carried into court on no other charge than that they were
Union men. In one case an old man named Duggan, a Methodist
preacher, was arrested and carried 50 miles on foot—he a large
fleshy man—refused the privilege of riding his own horse, and
all they had against him was that in February last he prayed
for the Union. . . . Arrests are made by W. G. Swan, William

[32] These exploits were described, in a somewhat exaggerated manner,
by Ellis himself in, *Thrilling Adventures of Daniel Ellis, the Great Union
Guide of East Tennessee.*

Churchwell, John Crozier, John Crozier Ramsey, and others. . . . It is said that these men have private griefs and malice to gratify, and that they mean to bring down the avenging arm of the government to satisfy their passions.[33]

The Union leaders were silenced, and their papers were suppressed. The Confederate press waged an active propaganda, however. The Knoxville *Register* became the organ of the Confederate government, and a violent campaign was launched against the Unionists through its columns. In December, 1861, the *Register* stated that,

The time has come when their devotion to the memories of the past must yield to the exigencies of the present. The Union is now finally dissolved; the Federal Government is no longer administered according to the principles of the constitution, and each day's developments reveal more clearly the ultimate designs and fell purposes of the Northern people and government to crush out the most cherished institution and the most sacred rights of the South. The government at Washington has declared its purpose to abolish the institution of slavery and to subjugate the South to the military despotism which now rules supreme over all the states of the North; and the time has come for the people of East Tennessee to awake to a full consciousness of the part their interest and honor alike require them to take in the pending contest between the North and South, between liberty and despotism.[34]

In October of the following year the same paper stated that,

There breathes not a sane man in East Tennessee who will not acknowledge that the tastes of our people have been corrupted; that a radicalism in politics and religion has not been engendered; that feuds have not been created by the violence and acrimony with which politicians and parties have conducted their struggle for the ascendency in this portion of the state. We have been driven by the force of circumstances to give utterance to feelings embittered by the assaults of a press which once existed in this city, that did more to destroy the harmony of

[33] *O.R.*, series I, vol. IV, pp. 476-77.
[34] Knoxville *Register*, Dec. 20, 1861.

our people, to sow dissension in churches and among families and friends than any other publication ever issued in our country.[35] It never addressed itself to the reason of its readers but to the worst passions of men. It never argued any proposition, but was filled with fiercest denunciations, the most ribald jests, the vilest slanders. It spared neither the living nor the dead. The private character of no one escaped pollution; the very gravestones of departed statesmen and heroes were lifted up, and shafts of malice and hate were leveled at the reeking corpses of the entombed.[36]

Thomas W. Humes, who was living in East Tennessee at the time, wrote that,

Words of bitterness and wrath against the "yankees" and against Union men under several opprobrious names were freely used. Alienations of close kinsmen and ruptures of friendly relations were widened and deepened. Other swords there are besides those of steel wielded in civil wars, quite as sharp and effective as they in wounding feelings and cutting through social ties, as are metallic blades in severing limbs and piercing bodies.[37]

More serious and moderate men, however, lamented and regretted that such a state of affairs should have come to pass. David Deaderick wrote in his diary that,

God is doubtless punishing the whole people North and South for their sins. The nation had forgotten God, had magnified herself against Him. Had prospered as never nation had prospered before, and had never in thankfulness looked to the great source of all these blessings. Had deserted God's sabbaths, and in many ways repudiated his authority, and he has permitted the vile passions of men to rule them, and a cause of quarrel, which could have been, and should have been, adjusted peacefully, has brought on this terrible war.[38]

The following year, 1862, brought no relief. "Disloyalty increases here," wrote J. G. M. Ramsey to Gov-

[35] Clearly a reference to Brownlow's *Whig*.
[36] Knoxville *Register*, Oct. 10, 1862.
[37] Thomas W. Humes, *op. cit.*, p. 122.
[38] David Deaderick, Diary, p. 53. Deaderick was a Knoxville merchant, and his diary runs from 1825 to 1872. Typewritten copy in the Lawson McGhee Library.

ernor Harris. "Smith is in an enemy's country. You and the Richmond government never would believe how much of Lincolnism is spread over all East Tennessee."[39] Under such circumstances the Confederates met with little success in enforcing their conscription act. In April General E. Kirby Smith wrote to the Confederate adjutant-general that,

Every effort made by the state authorities to call out the militia of East Tennessee has proved unavailing. The county officers chosen in the recent state elections are generally open advocates of the Federal Government. The people only await the appearance of a Northern army to range themselves under their banner.[40]

At the same time Smith wrote to Major R. A. Washington, the assistant adjutant at Richmond, advocating the application of martial law in the region. He was firmly of the belief that this measure was an absolute necessity, since,

But six counties in East Tennessee are friendly to us; the others are disloyal; many in open revolt, in which there are organized armed bands that oppress men of Southern principles. In the recent state elections open and avowed supporters of the Federal Government have been elected to almost every office, and they will be installed on Monday next. Under their administration little justice will be meted to loyal citizens.[41]

With the introduction of martial law the Confederates were able to maintain a nominal ascendancy in East Tennessee for a time. In this they were facilitated by the heroic action of the Knoxville *Register* and by the resentment which the Emancipation Proclamation caused among the slaveholders of the region. When Thomas A. R. Nelson, formerly a strong and avowed Unionist, saw this document he issued an "Address to the People of East Tennessee" in which he affirmed that,

[39] Letter of J. G. M. Ramsey to Harris, Mar. 18, 1862, in Harris Papers.
[40] *O.R.*, series I, vol. X, part I, pp. 385-6.
[41] *Ibid.*, p. 390.

The last link is broken which bound me to the government for which my ancestors fought, and, whatever may be the course of others, I shall feel it my duty to encourage the most persevering and determined resistance against the tyrants and usurpers of the Federal administration who have blasted our hopes and are cruelly seeking to destroy the last vestige of freedom among us.[42]

In February, 1863, the *Register,* in a spirited editorial, issued a statement of "The Demands of the Crisis," declaring that,

It is time for every one who has the least spark of patriotism in his heart—every one who professes himself a citizen of Tennessee, and every one who would rather be a southern freeman than a bond slave of a yankee taskmaster, to be bestirring himself to see what he can contribute, either in personal services, money, or moral support, for the rescue of Tennessee from the grinding oppression of the foe that seeks her subjugation. Every city, every town, hamlet, and country cross-roads should be ablaze with the fire of indignant patriotism; the air should resound with the notes of the spirit-stirring drum, with the clang of arms, and the shouts of defiance to the invaders.[43]

What this enthusiasm would have resulted in can only be conjectured, for in September, 1863, the Union army under Burnside entered East Tennessee and occupied Knoxville. The situation was now reversed, the status of the Confederates changing from that of occupiers to that of invaders. On the whole, however, conditions were not improved, and in many cases they grew even worse. Daniel Sullins wrote that,

The worst elements of society were aroused, and bad men took occasion to vent their spite on such as they did not like. Old family feuds broke out afresh, and the land was full of murders and robbery. Bands of the worst men seized the opportunity, scoured the country by night, calling quiet old farmers to their doors and shooting them down in cold blood. This caused other bands to unite and retaliate. It was the reign of terror—war at every man's door, neighbor against neighbor. Neither property or life was safe by day or night.[44]

[42] *Ibid.,* series I, vol. XVI, part II, pp. 909-11.
[43] Knoxville *Register,* Feb. 13, 1862. [44] Daniel Sullins, *op. cit.,* p. 262.

Many lawless acts were committed by the Federals on
persons and property. There was a determination to
retaliate upon the Confederates for the treatment which
the Unionists had received at the hands of the former.
In his diary David Deaderick described the state of
affairs in and around Knoxville in December, 1863,

Citizens were arrested, in many cases Union men, so called, at
the instance of a personal enemy or on some frivolous charge
and put in prison. The county jail was used, and the house at
the northwest corner of Main and Prince Street near the Courthouse.. In many cases the prisoners were left ignorant of the
charges made against them. Some have lain in jail for weeks
or months, who were finally discharged, nothing having been established against them. No redress could be had by the sufferers
in such cases or outrages. The property of citizens, both union
and secession, has been taken from them by the military and
doubtless without authority often. Some of it has been paid
for at their own price, but in numerous instances no payment
has been made. The plea of military necessity must satisfy the
sufferer.[45]

Many refugee Tennesseans now returned, eager to
recoup their lost fortunes and to take vengeance upon
their former oppressors. Among these refugees was the
implacable Brownlow. In October, 1861, his newspaper
had been closed and he committed to prison. After remaining in the Knoxville jail until December, where, according to his journal, he was grossly ill-treated, he wrote
to Judah P. Benjamin the Confederate secretary of
war, "You are reported to have said to a gentleman in
Richmond that I am a bad man, dangerous to the Confederacy, and that you desire me out of it. Just give
me my passports, and I will do more for your Confederacy than the devil has ever done—I will quit the country."[46] Benjamin accepted this gratuitous proposal, and
Brownlow was shortly afterward sent through the lines

[45] David Deaderick, Diary, p. 69. Dec. 30, 1863.
[46] William G. Brownlow, *Sketches of the Rise, Progress, and Decline of
Secession*, p. 318.

to the North. His family was sent after him with little ceremony, and although he made considerable money by lecturing in the North, he was a heavy financial loser in the war.[47] Although he was accused of having a desire to profit materially by the success of the Union army and the confiscation of property, there seems to be little evidence to show that he was guilty of this. It is true, however, that, remembering his ill-treatment in the Knoxville jail, he desired revenge upon those who had been active in securing his imprisonment. His wrath was especially directed toward John Crozier Ramsey and the Confederate district attorney, John H. Crozier. Through his instrumentality the latter was committed to the chain gang where he died of ill treatment and humiliation.[48]

Brownlow re-established his newspaper under the title of the Knoxville *Whig and Rebel Ventillator* and began anew, and even more fiercely, his attacks upon the Confederate government. The following excerpt from one of his editorials is typical of his style:

Keep it before the people that it is proper and right for union men to shoot down upon sight, each and all of these murderers [those who had court martialled union men in 1861] and that it is the duty that East Tennessee union men owe to their country, to their God, and to their abused relatives to see that these men, each, anyone of them, or all, die violent deaths, if they shall

[47] John Bell Brownlow wrote in the margin of a file of his father's newspapers: ''The rebellion suspended and destroyed the editor's newspaper property, the most valuable in the whole southern confederacy, bringing him an income of about $10,000. Besides this he recovered in a lawsuit real estate to the value of many thousands by the verdict of the Rebel supreme court of Tennessee. This property was sold by order of the court just after he went north and the proceeds deposited by the rebel clerk of the chancery court with the rebel officers of the branch bank of Tennessee, who speculated with the money during the war; and the aforesaid clerk tendered to the editor confederate money after Burnside took East Tennessee, when said trash was worthless. The editor was a heavy loser by the war.'' Margin of the Library of Congress file of the Knoxville *Whig*, issue of June 11, 1864.

[48] Brownlow always wrote the names of these two men in his paper as John *Crow* Ramsey and John *Hoopee* Crozier.

dare to show themselves in East Tennessee during the present century.[49]

On another occasion he wrote in his paper,

We endorse all that Lincoln has done, and we find fault with him for not having done more of the same sort.   The Federal Government has been too slow and lenient to punish rebels, and to crush out this wicked, abominable, and uncalled for rebellion from its very commencement.   The mediation we shall advocate is that of the cannon and the sword, and our motto is—no armistice on land or sea until *all* the rebels, both front and rear, in arms and in ambush, are subjugated or exterminated.[50]

It is a well known fact that Brownlow was an extremist, and due allowance must be made for this fact; but it is also true that many prominent men, ordinarily of less extreme views and sentiments, shared these radical sentiments.   This fact is well illustrated in a speech delivered by Nathaniel G. Taylor in Faneuil Hall, Boston, on February 10, 1864.   In this speech Taylor said,

East Tennessee has drunk the fierce cup of suffering and nothing seems left to her now but to drain the bitterness to its very dregs. She has sacrificed everything but loyalty and honor; she has suffered everything but dishonor and death; and now destitution and famine, followed by despair and death, are tramping upon the thresholds of her sad homes, are entering their very doors, ready to consummate the sacrifice and to complete the offering.[51]

Then speaking of peace, he added,

Can we get peace by quibbling over questions of constitutional law and talking about violated rights, and the rights of traitors, if they will come back into the Union, while they are pointing their daggers at the very heart of our nationality itself?   No, sir, . . .   There is but one way I know of.   Let it gleam upon the bristling points of 1500,000 bayonets; let it blaze upon the glittering steel of 500,000 swords; let it leap from the mouths of

---

[49] Knoxville *Whig*, Apr. 9, 1864.
[50] *Ibid.*, Nov. 11, 1863.
[51] Edward Everett, *Account of the Fund for the Relief of East Tennessee*, p. 35.   The East Tennessee Relief Association was organized in Boston, and thousands of dollars were spent by it in alleviating the sufferings of the Unionists in East Tennessee.

10,000 cannon, and the echo of that thunder will bring peace to every home and house and heart throughout the length and breadth of our ruined country.[52]

The economic, social, and intellectual life of East Tennessee suffered greatly during the war. As the contest advanced, shops and mercantile houses were forced to diminish their stocks or close their doors entirely. Prices gradually increased until they became almost prohibitive. Many articles, in frequent or habitual use by the people, could not be had at any price. Coffee increased from fourteen cents to one dollar per pound; salt rose from two and one-half cents to thirty cents; brown sugar from twelve and one-half cents to seventy-five cents. Common calico increased eightfold, and wearing apparel of all kinds rose correspondingly. Gold and silver passed completely out of circulation. Then bank notes gradually disappeared. As the rate of interest and salaries continued on the same level, those who depended for maintenance upon incomes from loans or upon stipends for regular services suffered from this derangement of affairs. Debtors became increasingly anxious to pay their debts, as they could do so in the depreciated paper currency, which a citizen of loyalty to the Confederacy would not refuse or a citizen of loyalty to the Union dared not refuse.[53]

The intellectual life of the region was seriously restricted. The newspapers dwindled in size and sometimes did not appear at all. Even after the restoration of the Federal power in 1863 Brownlow was repeatedly forced to suspend publication of the *Whig* because of a lack of paper and ink. Moreover, any news from outside had to be shorn in its proportions and its color changed to suit the requirements of the political and military censors. The Richmond *Examiner* appears to have been the chief *foreign* paper in circulation, and its popu-

[52] *Ibid.*, p. 35.
[53] Thomas W. Humes, *op. cit.*, pp. 176-77.

larity was enhanced by its occasional criticisms of the
Davis administration. Even its dimensions were reduced
to one-half sheet of very inferior paper. If, by any
chance, a few newspapers were smuggled in from the
North and came into the hands of a Unionist citizen they
were regarded as worth their weight in gold. Their con-
tents were eagerly devoured, and they were then passed
covertly to other Unionists; and so they would continue
their rounds. Current literature, periodicals, and new
books found almost no access to the region. The only
books which had circulation were Bulwer's *A Strange
Story* and a translation of Victor Hugo's *Les Miserables*.
These had been reprinted at Richmond and were remark-
ably inferior in their mechanical execution. The paper
upon which they were printed vied in poverty and un-
happiness. The covering was of wall-paper with very
large figures, the mutilation of which, in adapting the
binding to its use, added to the grotesque appearance
of the book.[54]

In the great majority of cases friendly social intercourse between people of hostile opinions ceased. In
some instances, however, citizens of Unionist sympathies
who had influence with the military authorities performed
services for their Confederate friends and neighbors.
This, it seems, was not always a labor of love, however,
for instances are said to have occurred where a charge
of ten dollars was made for introductions to General
Carter.[55]

In Knoxville, especially, there was a great scarcity of
food, both for men and live stock. A number of horses
and mules left in an open field ate the manes and tails
of each other, and it was reported one night, facetiously
of course, that "the mules had eaten the fifth wheel of
a caisson." Fuel was exceedingly scarce, and fences and
buildings were frequently requisitioned to supply this
need.[56]

[54] *Ibid.*, pp. 198-99.   [55] *Ibid.*, pp. 230-31.   [56] *Ibid.*, pp. 272-73.

These conditions were somewhat relieved after the entrance of Burnside in 1863. In 1864 Brownlow spoke of the disappointment of the green flies "who are returning this year under the apprehension that the rebels are still holding the country."[57]

That the Unionists were keenly alive to the hardships which they had suffered, but which they had endured for the sake of the Union, is shown in a memorial which they sent to congress in 1864,

Their arms and ammunition were seized, before they could organize, by the rebel soldiers; and though the government, which owed them protection, did not protect them, yet their hearts clung to the government and they prayed for the union. Five thousand of their men have seen the inside walls of rebel prisons, and hundreds of them, covered with filth, devoured with vermin, famished with hunger, have died martyrs to their country there. Their property has been seized, confiscated; their houses pillaged; their stock driven off; their grain consumed; their substance wasted; their fences burned; their fields laid waste; their farms destroyed by friends as well as foes. The Rebels robbed them; the Federals devoured them; for they had short supplies, and our women broke their last biscuit, and gave them the biggest half, out of the mouths of hungry children. They gave up the last horse, mule, cow, sheep, hog, everything they had to the soldiers that neded them, because they were union soldiers, or were plundered out of them by the enemy. Their young men have been hunted like wild beasts, by soldiers, by Indians, sometimes by blood hounds, and when caught, tied two-and-two to long ropes, and driven before cavalry—thin-clad, barefooted, and bleeding—over frozen roads and icy creeks and rivers. Some have been beaten with ropes, with straps, and with clubs. Some have been butchered, others shot down in their own homes or yards—in the highroad, or the fields, or in the forests; others still have been hung up by the neck to the limbs of trees, without judge or jury. I have heard of no single neighborhood within the bounds of East Tennessee, whose green sod has not drunk the blood of citizens murdered.[58]

[57] Knoxville *Whig*, Apr. 30, 1864.
[58] Edward Everett, *op. cit.*, pp. 6-7. Memorial of N. G. Taylor to Congress.

These conditions, although they may have been slightly exaggerated by some of the writers who have been quoted, did exist, and they form the background of reconstruction in Tennessee.

CHAPTER IV

THE INAUGURATION OF THE BROWNLOW
ADMINISTRATION

ATTENTION has already been called to the intrepid and
eccentric character of the governor-elect. A more detailed description of this singular person will be instruc-
tive, for it was his character and personality that dominated the history of Tennessee during the entire reconstruction period. William Gannaway Brownlow was
born in Wythe County, Virginia, on August 29, 1805. Left
an orphan at an early age he was bound out to serve
an apprenticeship at the trade of house-carpenter. During the period of this apprenticeship the value of industry and the dignity of labor were so thoroughly impressed
upon him that he never forgot them. Years later he
wrote, "Though a Southern man in feeling and principles, I do not think it degrading to a man to labor, as do
most Southern disunionists. Whether East or West,
North or South, I recognize the dignity of labor and look
forward to a day, not very far distant, when educated
labor will be the salvation of this vast country."[1]

His education was somewhat imperfect and irregular,
even in the subjects taught in the common schools of the
country, but it was sufficient to admit him to the Methodist travelling ministry. Upon the completion of his
apprenticeship, having removed to Tennessee in the
meantime, he left the carpenter's trade and entered the
ministry.[2] Here he remained for about ten years, and
during the time availed himself of his position to study
and improve his limited education. This study, however,
was confined entirely to the English branches of knowl-

[1] William G. Brownlow, *Sketches of the Rise, Progress, and Decline of Secession*, p. 17.
[2] John B. McFerrin, *History of Methodism in Tennessee*, III, 325.

edge, and he developed into a master of invective and a coiner of coarse and crude phrases and metaphors. His style of writing and speaking, especially in his opposition to the institutions and proceedings of other denominations, was objected to, and in 1830 it became necessary for the Holston Conference to admonish him to alter his course in the future.[3] This admonition, however, proved to be of little effect, for his writings continued to abound in strong statements. His style was terse and bitter, but his writings contain scarcely any references or allusions to foreign or classical languages and literature.

Before the termination of his career as a circuit rider he entered upon that of an author and a political and theological pamphleteer. In 1832, while riding a circuit in South Carolina, he published a pamphlet violently attacking John C. Calhoun and the "Nullification Rebellion" as he termed the opposition of South Carolina to the protective tariff.[4] In 1834 there appeared from his pen *Helps to the Study of Presbyterianism*,[5] a violent denunciation of Calvinism in all of its aspects and modifications. This was followed, in 1844, by *A Political Register*, containing a critical attack upon Andrew Jackson and his attitude toward the second United States Bank, vigorous criticisms of James K. Polk, Martin Van Buren, and the Locofocos, and a vindication of the career of Henry Clay.[6] He was a firm adherent of the Know

[3] R. M. Price, *Holston Methodism from its Origin to the Present Time,* III, 257.

[4] Brownlow describes this pamphlet in his *Sketches of the Rise, Progress, and Decline of Secession,* pp. 22-24. I have not been able to find a copy of the original pamphlet.

[5] The titles of Brownlow's books are lengthy and descriptive. The full title of this one was *Helps to the Study of Presbyterianism or an Unsophisticated Exposition of Calvinism, with Hopkinsian Modifications and Policy with a View to a More Easy Interpretation of the Same, to Which is Added a Brief Account of the Life and Travels of the Author, Interspersed with Anecdotes.*

[6] *A Political Register Setting Forth the Principles of the Whig and Locofoco Parties in the United States, with the Life and Public Services of Henry Clay, also an Appendix Personal to the Author.*

Nothing party and published in 1856 a defense of its principles in *Americanism Contrasted with Foreignism, Romanism, and Bogus Democracy.*[7] In 1856 a religious controversy occurred, giving occasion for another of his works. One J. R. Graves, a Baptist clergyman and editor of the *Tennessee Baptist*, issued *The Great Iron Wheel*,[8] an attack upon the doctrines and polity of the Methodist Church. The book, which was really a series of letters, was addressed to Joshua Soule, the senior bishop of the Methodist Episcopal Church, South. Bishop Soule was at this time an aged and infirm man, quite unequal to the task of engaging in a religious debate, even had he the desire to do so, and Brownlow assumed the task of replying to Graves. This he did in *The Great Iron Wheel Examined, or its False Spokes Extracted*,[9] described by himself later as "a work of great severity, but written in reply to one of greater severity." The last of his books was the famous *Sketches of the Rise, Progress, and Decline of Secession*, commonly known as *Parson Brownlow's Book*.[10] This work was published in Philadelphia while the author was in exile from Tennessee in 1862. It contains accounts of his life and of his experiences and adventures while confined in the Knoxville jail. Throughout it is written in the most bitter language and is a terrible indictment of the secession movement and the Confederate government. It was very popular in the North, where it was used as Union propaganda, and he is said to have realized over sixty thousand dollars from its publication and sale.

[7] *Americanism Contrasted with Foreignism, Romanism, and Bogus Democracy, in the Light of Reason, History, and Scripture; in which certain demagogues in Tennessee and elsewhere are shown up in their true colors.*

[8] *The Great Iron Wheel, or Republicanism Backwards and Christianity Reversed in a Series of Letters Addressed to J. Soule, Senior Bishop of the M. E. Church, South.*

[9] *The Great Iron Wheel Examined or its False Spokes Extracted and an Exhibition of Elder Graves, its Builder.*

[10] The full title was *Sketches of the Rise, Progress, and Decline of Secession with a Narrative of Personal Adventures among the Rebels.*

Brownlow was a journalist as well as an author. His ventures in this field include the *Whig* and the Jonesboro *Review*. The former might be described as a peripatetic newspaper. It was first established at Elizabethton in 1839 as *Brownlow's Tennessee Whig*. During the following year the paper was removed to Jonesboro, where it remained until 1850 under the title of the Jonesboro *Whig and Independent*. In the latter year it was again removed, this time to Knoxville, where it was established under the name of *Brownlow's Knoxville Whig*. It was published at this place until 1862 when it was suppressed by the Confederate authorities because of its violent attacks upon the administration. In the following year, the editor having returned with the Union army, it was re-established as the Knoxville *Whig and Rebel Ventillator* and was edited by Brownlow until his inauguration as governor. After that occasion he discontinued his connection with the newspaper world. The *Whig*, however, continued to be edited by his son, John Bell Brownlow, from 1865 to 1869 and was the organ of the Brownlow administration in East Tennessee.[11]

As an editor Brownlow wielded a fierce and bitter pen, and because of this fact he was constantly involved in complicated situations. While located at Jonesboro he engaged in a long and violent controversy with a rival editor, Landon C. Haynes. Brownlow's war was of the pen solely, but Haynes resorted to violence. In 1840 the two met on the street in Jonesboro, and Haynes shot Brownlow through the leg. Brownlow was unarmed, but Thomas A. R. Nelson, a bystander, who witnessed the affair, declared that he exhibited the coolest and most determined courage.[12] He succeeded in driving Haynes from the editorial chair, but attacks continued to be made upon the life of the former. On one occasion shots were fired at night into the window of his house, narrowly

[11] The Library of Congress possesses a complete file of the *Whig*.
[12] R. M. Price, *op. cit.*, p. 348.

missing his breast.[13] On another occasion, while returning from a church conference, he was attacked from behind by a miscreant with a hickory club. A blow was
dealt him on the head, fracturing his skull, rendering him
unconscious for several weeks, and doubtless shortening
his days.[14] He always believed, or professed to believe,
that these attempts upon his life were instigated by
Haynes. Whether this is true is of little consequence,
but the fact remains that his severe style of writing and
speaking made for him many vindictive enemies. Matters
were little improved when he removed to Knoxville. There
the mottoes of his paper were "Cry aloud and spare
not" and "Independent in all things, neutral in nothing," and naturally the pursuit of such a policy gave rise
to many unpleasant situations. His chief opponent was
the Knoxville *Register,* an old Whig newspaper, established in 1816, and controlled by some of the most influential men of the city. John H. Crozier, James and William
Williams, and William G. Swan were the chief stock-
holders of the *Register,* and they resented the encroach-
ment of another Whig newspaper. A severe and desperate contest ensued. For years, day after day, both papers teemed with the bitterest denunciations. At one time
the *Register* faction determined to destroy Brownlow's
paper by violence, but this design was abandoned because of the strong defense made by his friends. Finally,
however, he succeeded in making his newspaper the official organ of the Whig party in East Tennessee, but about
the same time the *Register* became a Democratic paper.
The situation was not remedied by this transformation,
and the conflict continued until the suppression of the
Whig in 1862.[15] The *Whig,* however, prospered in spite
of opposition and persecution. Although it carried little
news, it was tremendously popular among a large class

[13] *Ibid.,* p. 347.
[14] *Ibid.,* p. 349. Knoxville Whig, Mar. 13, 1867.
[15] O. P. Temple, *Notable Men of Tennessee,* pp. 274-75.

because of the spicy and biting character of the editorials and personal views of the editor. By the opening of the Civil War it had reached a weekly circulation of ten thousand copies.

Brownlow's other journalistic venture was the publication of the Jonesboro *Review*. In 1847 he became involved in a theological controversy with Frederick A. Ross, a Presbyterian minister and editor of the *Calvinistic Magazine*, a review of substantial influence in East Tennessee. In order to facilitate his attacks upon Ross he established in June, 1847, the Jonesboro *Quarterly Review*, which in December of the same year was changed to a monthly publication.[16] Ross was highly respected, an author of note, and a scholarly gentleman, but as usual Brownlow did not scruple at bringing personalities into the argument.[17] In bitterness and vituperation the *Review* exceeded anything that its editor had then attempted. Grotesque woodcuts were displayed in its pages, picturing Ross "straining at a gnat and swallowing a camel" and attempting to extract "the mote from his brother's eye" while prevented from reaching the brother's eye by a huge "beam" that protruded from his own. Coarse personal abuse was freely used, and the *Review* even went to such lengths as to accuse Ross of being the son of a Negress. A woodcut of this "dusky matron" appeared in one of the issues of the magazine.

On the subject of slavery Brownlow's views in the ante-bellum period, although no less intense, were of a very different nature from those which he later held and expressed. His editorials were bitter against the abolitionists, and on one occasion he issued a very elaborate challenge to the friends of freedom in the North to debate with him the merits or demerits of slavery. This chal-

---

[16] Ross's best known work was *Slavery Ordained of God.*

[17] These magazines were all published later in one volume, *The Jonesboro Review.* There is a copy of this volume in the Library of Congress and also in the Lawson McGhee Library at Knoxville.

lenge was particularly directed to Theodore Parker, but with the exception of a conditional acceptance by Frederick Douglass it was not acted upon until September, 1858, when Abram Pryne, a Congregational minister and editor of an anti-slavery paper in McGrawville, New York, proposed to accept it. The question was reduced to a single proposition, "Ought American Slavery to be abolished or perpetuated," and after satisfying himself that Pryne was "in good standing with his church" and a white man rather than a "gentleman of color," Brownlow agreed to a meeting in Philadelphia. The debate began on Tuesday, September 7, and continued for the remainder of the week. Brownlow, having contracted bronchitis by over-heating himself in a controversy during the previous summer, found himself at the opening of the debate for "the first time in thirty years. . . . without a strong and powerful voice," and was compelled to have his speeches read. Nevertheless his arguments were pointed and powerful. To his own satisfaction at least, he proved from the Bible that slavery was ordained of God. After quoting numerous passages relating to the institution, including the story of Hagar, met by the Angel when fleeing from her mistress, Sarah, he exclaimed,

And last, but not least, the Angel of God arrested a fugitive slave and forced her to return to her lawful owner. High authority this, for apprehending runaway negroes! And when I tell you, as I now do, in all candor, that the Angel of God, on this occasion, was acting in the capacity of a United States Marshal, under the then existing fugitive slave laws of the Old Testament, and arresting a fugitive slave, the anti-slavery portion of you, either think me crazy, or guilty of a profanation of sacred things.[18]

His conclusion was that "American slavery is not only not sinful, but especially commanded by God through

[18] William G. Brownlow and Abram Pryne, *Ought American Slavery to be Perpetuated, a Debate Held at Philadelphia, September, 1858*, p. 79.

Moses, and approved through the Apostles by Christ''
and that ''what God ordains and Christ sanctifies should
command the respect and toleration of even Northern
Abolitionists.''[19]

Personally and in private life Brownlow seems to
have been less cynical and disagreeable than his extravagance of writing and public utterance would lead one to
expect. His friend and biographer, Oliver P. Temple,
described him as a man ''warm-hearted, genial, and de-
lightful . . . far beyond most men, mild, gentle, and good
natured.''[20] This may be true, but it is to be remembered
that the enemies made by his public actions far exceeded
in number the friends made by his amiability and patience
in the family circle. It is also to be remembered that this
genial temper and amiable disposition were clouded and
embittered by his ill treatment in the Knoxville jail and
by the insults which, he contended, were inflicted upon the
members of his family by the Confederate authorities. It
is doubtful if Temple's description would have fitted him
very accurately after 1862. Physically, he was a remarkable specimen of splendid manhood until, in later years,
disease weakened his constitution—a disease which was
greatly aggravated by his confinement in jail. He suffered
terribly from both quinzy and palsy, diseases which
sapped his vitality and darkened his vision at times.

In 1862 he described himself in a characteristic
manner:

I am about six feet high and have weighed as heavy as one hundred and seventy-five pounds—have as fine a constitution as any
man need desire. I have very few gray hairs in my head, and,
although hard-favored than otherwise, I will pass for a man of
forty years. I have as strong a voice as any man in East Tennessee, where I have resided for the last thirty years, and have a
family of seven children. I have been speaking for all that time
and for the last twenty-five years I have edited and published a
Whig newspaper. I have taken part in all of the religious and
political controversies of my day and time. . . . I am known

[19] *Ibid.*, p. 91.   [20] O. P. Temple, *op. cit.*, p. 279.

throughout the length and bredth of the land as the "Fighting Parson"; while I may say, without incurring the charge of egotism, that no man is more peacable, as my neighbors will testify. . . . I have never been arraigned in the church for any immorality. I never played a card. I never was a profane swearer. I never drank a dram of liquor, until within a few years—when it was taken for medicine. I never attended a horse-race, and never witnessed their running, save on the fairgrounds of my own county. I never courted but one woman; and her I married.[21]

This was the man who became the chief executive of Tennessee in 1865. Austere in his habits and almost fanatical in his love and devotion for the Union, he was determined to restore the state to the control of the truly loyal citizens and to bend his efforts toward punishing and impoverishing those who had aided and participated in the rebellion. Although sympathetic and kind to these persons as individuals,[22] he regarded the former Confederates, as a group, as degenerate, dishonest, and corrupt, and was willing to countenance any scheme of his advisers and supporters that would serve to embarrass and humiliate them. Keenly aware of the distress and hardship that the war had caused in East Tennessee, and always out of contact with the ideals and institutions of the other sections of the state, he naturally filled offices with and conferred favors upon the citizens of his own region. With certain notable exceptions, Tennessee suffered little from "carpet-bag" rule in comparison with the other Southern states, but it did suffer from Brownlow rule, which was the domination of East Tennessee Republicanism.

[21] *Sketches of the Rise, Progress, and Decline of Secession*, pp. 18-19.
[22] An instance of Brownlow's attitude toward individual Confederates is illustrated in his treatment of the former governor, Isham G. Harris, who, after the war an exile in Liverpool, desired to return to his family in Tennessee. Brownlow, although a bitter political enemy, pledged his word that Harris should not be molested by the state authorities upon his return, and even exerted his influence with President Johnson to secure a pardon for him.

The gubernatorial election was held on March 4, but the military government was already at an end. Andrew Johnson had left Nashville during the latter part of February to assume the office of Vice-President of the United States to which he had been elected in the preceding November. As the new governor could not be inaugurated until the legislature should convene, on the first Monday in April, an interregnum developed. It was expected by many persons that President Lincoln would appoint Brownlow as military governor to succeed Johnson for this period. The President, however, solved the difficulty by allowing Edward H. East, the secretary of state, to perform the functions of the gubernatorial office until the new civil officers were qualified.[23]

The inauguration occurred on April 5, and was a notable event attended by substantial and elaborate ceremonies. At eleven o'clock committees of both branches of the legislature, after waiting upon the governor-elect, entered the chamber of the House of Representatives in the capitol and announced his arrival. Within a few minutes a brilliant array of military officers ushered him into the chamber. Heading the procession was the massive form of Major-General George H. Thomas, the defender of Nashville, who attracted the attention of all the spectators.[24] Following him were Major-General Rousseau, then commander of Camp Joe Holt, dressed in rich full-dress uniform, and Major-General Milroy, noted for his success as a guerrilla queller, his magnificent form towering aloft like a man of war mast. Brigadier-Generals Donaldson, Towers, and Miller, and last named, com-

[23] J. T. Moore and A. P. Foster, *Tennessee, the Volunteer State*, I, 256.

[24] Brownlow was a great admirer of "the hero of Nashville." During his administration he had life-size portraits of both himself and General Thomas painted and hung in the capitol. A succeeding Democratic legislature placed the portrait of the Governor in a corner and used it as a cuspidor. It was later restored to its place, on the walls of the state library, but the tobacco stains have never been entirely removed, whether from inability or unwillingness it is impossible to say.

mander of the post of Nashville, followed with their respective staffs.[25]   Judge Samuel Milligan of the state supreme court administered the oath of office to the governor, and the delivery of the inaugural address began.

The occasion was at this time exceedingly propitious for an early restoration of civil government and orderly administration to the state.   In a few days the surrender of Lee and the flight of the Confederate Government from Richmond was to relieve the administration from all anxiety on the subject of its tenure.   Likewise the elevation of Andrew Johnson to the presidency of the United States, which was to occur within a short time, placed at the head of the national administration a man friendly to the adoption of measures for the speedy return of the people to the occupations and orderly habits that belong to the time of peace.   Moreover, there was no danger to be apprehended from the returning Confederate soldiers. They were content to accept the verdict of battle and were anxious to return to the pursuits of peace.   As one of them expressed it,

When the last expiring efforts of Confederate obstinacy gave evidence of a rebellion extinct, men with beards on their faces came creeping home from the war, half naked, starved, and bankrupt.   They did not care to talk of bloody scenes, it was over, rest and peace were enough for them.   This is how we felt, but not how we lived, for we did not know the trouble that was in store for us.[26]

The inaugural, as well as the events that had preceded it, however gave unmistakable evidence that the administration would not be disposed to adopt measures in any way favorable or conciliatory to the former Confederates.

The policy that the administration intended to pursue

---

[25] Nashville *Daily Times*, Apr. 6, 1865.

[26] John M. Johnson, *Memoirs of John M. Johnson*, p. 5.   A typewritten copy of the original manuscript is in the State Library at Nashville.

had been clearly forcasted in the events connected with
the nomination and election of the governor. On January 14, in a speech before the Union State Convention, accepting the nomination, he had declared,

I will not speak to you, Gentlemen; but what you will lack in
speaking, if the people should ratify the nomination, I will try
to make up in deeds and acts; and, God being my helper, if you
will send up a legislature to reorganize the militia and transact
other necessary business, I will put an end to this infernal system of guerrilla fighting in the state, in East, Middle, and Western Tennessee, if we have to shoot and hang every man concerned.[27]

This announcement was greeted with "loud and continued applause," indicating clearly that the convention
approved of harsh measures. Again, on February 1,
Brownlow issued, through the columns of his Knoxville
Whig, a threatening and uncompromising announcement:

Those who voted to separate in 1861 are for rejection [of the
new constitutional amendments] now. Let them vote it, putting
their names on the backs of their tickets, and when they have
done so, let them quietly prepare to leave the state. The ratification men are going to prevail, and they are going to govern
the state.[28]

The loyal press in Nashville expressed a similar attitude regarding the measures which seemed necessary.
The *Union,* speaking in terms of high praise for Brownlow, expressed the feeling that there was no longer any
room for equivocation in dealing with the "rebels":

His intimate knowledge of men and affairs in Tennessee will enable him to discriminate as to the method of treating those who
have outlawed themselves by joining in the confederacy; and in
his firmness, decision of character, and independence, we have a
full assurance that the leaders of the rebellion will not go un-
punished of their crimes, if they have the hardihood to again
venture upon the soil of a commonwealth they have betrayed and
among a people upon whom they have entailed untold horrors.
Union men who have suffered will be guaranteed protection.[29]

[27] Nashville *Daily Times,* Jan. 16, 1865.
[28] Knoxville *Whig,* Feb. 1, 1865.   [29] Nashville *Daily Union,* Feb. 9, 1865.

The *Times* characterized him as a man who

has drained the cup of insult and malicious persecution to the bitter dregs, and knows as well as any man living, and better than most men, that perjury, blasphemy, brutality, ingratitude, fanaticism, malignity, and duplicity with which the souls of the partizans of the southern rebellion are deeply imbued.[30]

Again the *Union,* apprehending the danger that lay in granting the suffrage to the former slaveholders, pointed out that,

The old spirit which animated them has not been destroyed with their *divine* institution.   It burns in their hearts with a glow intensified by disappointment and malice.   They cannot and will not forgive their friends and neighbors who have aided in their humiliation.   They will cherish resentment, they will form cliques and parties. . . . If, therefore, the disloyal are allowed to enjoy the right of suffrage, they and their allies will succeed in grasping the power and shaping the future policy of the state, while . . . loyal men who have assisted in the destruction of slavery will be proscribed and punished.[31]

In his inaugural address the governor gave no evidence of disappointing those who had thus placed their confidence in him as a persecutor of rebels.   He was now an old man, palsied in limb, but firm in intellect and, according to the Memphis *Ledger,* still able to ''express more vituperativeness and a scorching hate than any half a dozen men that ever appeared in American politics.'' He was vigorous in his determination to strengthen the supremacy of the national Union.   Quite at variance with his former position, and apparently oblivious of the inconsistency, he now attacked the institution of slavery. It had been, he now declared, a curse to the state of Tennessee, which only the fine soil, excellent climate, and free labor could overcome. He denounced state sovereignty and denied that he was ''one of those men who are alarmed at the powers assumed by the Federal Govern-

---

[30] Nashville *Daily Times,* Feb. 13, 1865.
[31] Nashville *Daily Union,* Mar. 8, 1865.

ment at this time, regarding them as a departure from
their former precedents.'' Finally, lauding the Union, he
expressed his determination to live and die for the principles upon which it was founded:

Who among us, Gentlemen, of our own generation, can estimate
the value of the American Union. Proud, happy, thrice happy
America, the home of the oppressed, the asylum of the immi-
grant, where the citizens of every clime and the child of every
creed, roam free and untrammelled as the wild winds of heaven.
Baptized at the fount of liberty in fire and blood, during our
revolutionary struggle, cold must be the heart that thrills not
at the name of the American Union.[32]

With all of this florid eloquence, however, there was no
promise or offer of reconciliation to the "traitors," as the
Confederates were then regarded.

The legislature was equally determined that the loyal
men should control the state government. This was not
a "carpet-bag" legislature,[33] as it has been frequently
viewed, but rather a native Republican or "scalawag"
body, elected on a general ticket.[34] This method of electing members to the general assembly, whereby the electorate voted for a general "slate" or ticket, submitted by
a state convention and containing the names of the candidates nominated from each county, was unusual in Tennessee though not illegal. It was used at this particular
time to insure the election of members from all the districts, as well as to prevent the election of anyone not
having the endorsement of the convention.[35] It was

[32] Nashville *Daily Times*, Apr. 6, 1865.

[33] Of the twenty-five senators, twenty were natives of the state, and of
the seventy-six representatives, sixty-two were natives. Nashville *Daily
Times*, Apr. 3, 1865.

[34] The legislative ticket received the same majority as that for governor.
The ballot contained the name of the candidate for governor, the names of
the twenty-five candidates for the Senate, and the eighty candidates for the
House of Representatives, and the vote cast for one was cast for all. Four
of the representatives who were elected did not take their seats.

[35] It was claimed by the Brownlow faction that the election of the
governor and legislature was by a majority of *all the voters then in the
state*. According to John Bell Brownlow, ''A little over 120,000 Tennesseans

severely criticized by the Conservatives, but it served the purpose of the Radicals at the time. In addition to the irregularity in the method of its election, the legislature was open to the criticism that its members were, for the most part, men of little experience in legislative procedure. Only five of the senators had ever sat in a previous legislature, and only three of the representatives had the advantage of any earlier experience. The majority of the members were men of mediocrity whom the war had brought into prominence, either in actual service in the field or in some clerical capacity. An examination of the roster of the legislature reveals the presence of few names that were to be found in the newspapers and public records of the ante-bellum period. Some of the members were doubtless men of real ability, but their experience in the war had made them bitter and radical. Following the example of the Governor, they saw in secession a monster which had wrecked the peace and prosperity of the state, and they were determined that its perpetrators should be made to suffer the consequences of their "treason." Under such conditions the members of the general assembly were easily influenced and led by the governor and his advisors. Presumably they were honest, but their radicalism and inexperience caused them to be drawn into the wake of the extreme radical minority. This was unfortunate, for the occasion certainly demanded men of experience and sound individual judgment.

The legislature met, in accordance with the schedule amending the constitution, on April 3. Edward H. East, the secretary of state, in turn called each house to order and read a certified list of the members legally elected. Each house then proceeded to organize itself for the transaction of business. In the senate, D. C. Trewhitt,

went into the rebel army, and those not voting were in that army, in prison, or in their graves.'' Marginal note pencilled in the Library of Congress file of the Knoxville *Whig*, Mar. 8, 1865.

chancellor of the second division of the state, administered the oath of office to the new senators. William H.
Wisener, of Bedford County, then nominated Samuel R.
Rodgers, of Knox, for speaker and he was unanimously
elected. E. P. Cone, of Davidson, was elected as principal
clerk.[36] In the lower house, Edmund Cooper, of Bedford,
and James R. Hood, of Hamilton, were nominated for
speaker on the first day, and six ballots were taken without an election. On the second day, after the seventh
ballot had been taken without result, Cooper withdrew his
name and nominated William Heiskell, of Knox County.
On the eighth ballot Heiskell received a majority of all
the votes cast and was declared duly and constitutionally
elected speaker. J. T. Shelley, of Roane, was elected as
chief clerk.[37]

The conditions under which this legislature assembled
were exciting and tumultuous. Almost immediately after
the session began, returning Confederate soldiers crowded into the city. Although they were as orderly as one
would expect under the circumstances, the administration regarded them as dangerous and seized upon their
presence as a pretext for securing the retention of large
numbers of Federal troops in and around Nashville. The
city was thus given the appearance of a military camp,
with the army supporting the legislature and the administration.[38]

The policy indicated by the governor in his inaugural
address was further borne out in his first message to the
legislature, communicated on the day following the in-

[36] *Senate Journal, 34th Tenn. General Assembly, 1st Session, 1865,*
pp. 3-8.

[37] *House Journal, 34th Tenn. General Assembly, 1st Session, 1865,*
pp. 3-11.

[38] Governor Brownlow wrote to the *Whig* in May: "The town is full
of returning and parolled rebel soldiers and has been for a week. I am
sorry to report many of them are still bitter and defiant rebels, not disposed to calm down and behave themselves. They speak of being 'home
only on a resting spell,' and several of them for disloyal talk and threats
have been arrested and imprisoned." Knoxville *Whig*, May 24, 1865.

auguration. "Secession," he informed the members, "is an abomination which I cannot too strongly condemn, and which you cannot legislate against too strongly." Then followed a long harangue, reciting the evils which secession had brought upon the state:

It has formed odious and unconstitutional military leagues, passed military bills, and inaugurated a system of oppressive taxation without consulting the people, and then, in mockery of a free election, has required them by their votes to sanction its usurpation, at the point of the bayonet under the penalty of imprisonment and death. It has offered a premium for crime, in ordering the discharge of culprits from prison, on condition that they should enter the rebel army, and in recommending to the judges to hold no courts for the trial of offenders. It has stained our statute books with the repudiation of honest northern debts, and has palpably violated the constitution, by attempting through its unlawful extensions to do away with the right of suffrage. It has passed laws making it treason to say or do anything in favor of the government of the United States, or against the so-called Confederate States. It has prostrated and overthrown the whole South in a war whose success is now proven to be utterly hopeless, and which, ere another year rolls around, must lead to the ruin of the common people. Its bigoted, murderous, and intolerant spirit has subjected the people of Tennessee to many grievances. Our people have been arrested and imprisoned; our houses have been rudely entered and shamefully pillaged: our families have been subjected to insults; our women and children have been tied up and scourged, or shot by a ruffian soldiery: our towns have been pillaged; our citizens have been robbed of their horses, mules, grain, and meat, and many of them assassinated and murdered.[39]

Slavery was again denounced and characterized as "the monster institution which has embroiled the government for half a century, and culminated in the most wicked, uncalled for, and bloody war known to the history of our civilized world."[40] Some legislation, he said, was necessary for the protection and government of the emanci-

[39] *Senate Journal, 34th Tenn. General Assembly, 1st Session, 1865,* pp. 19-20.
[40] *Ibid.,* p. 21.

pated slaves, but he preferred to leave the determination
of the character of this legislation to "the good-sense,
prudence, and reflection of the members of the General
Assembly." Attention was called to the need for a more
severe criminal code, in which horse-stealing, house-
breaking, and highway robbery—crimes that were very
prevalent at the time—should be punished by death, and
a solution of the financial problem was suggested in the
form of an increase both in taxation and the bonded in-
debtedness of the state.

Perhaps the most important feature of the message
referred to the elective franchise. "I would urge you,"
he stated, "to guard the ballot-box faithfully and effec-
tually against the approach of treason, no matter in what
character it may come. The loyal people of the state, who
sent you here, expect you to act decisively in the matter,
and to have no child's play in determining the qualifications of voters."[41] A limitation of the franchise, it was
further pointed out, was all the more important in view
of the fact that it was necessary to redistrict the state
and provide for the election of eight congressmen. Only
the limitation of the suffrage, in the opinion of the governor, would restore the state to the union and avert the
inconvenience of military reconstruction.

After the reading of the message the two houses were
left to their own devices. An examination of the proceedings, however, discloses the fact that the members
of the general assembly fulfilled the governor's expectations in good measure. Many of the acts passed during
this session dealt directly with reconstruction, and considerable information as to the state of feeling in the
administration, with regard to a number of important
questions, is to be had from a study of the debates upon
the measures under discussion.

Among the measures introduced and discussed, which

[41] *Ibid.*, p. 23.

illustrate the temper of the administration, was one pro-
hibiting, under the penalty of a fine, the wearing of Confederate uniforms. This act, designed to place a particular humiliation upon the former Confederates by preventing their wearing, in many cases, the only clothing they
possessed, was passed by the lower house but failed in
the more conservative Senate.[42]   Another act sought to
deprive secessionist ministers of the gospel of the right
to celebrate the marriage rites, require them to work on
the roads, pay a poll tax, serve in the militia, and subject
them to various other humiliations. This act passed the
Senate but failed in the House.[43]   Still another bill attempted to forestall the propagation of rebels by forcing
every woman to take the oath of allegiance to the United
States before securing a marriage license.[44]   A bill requiring a test oath for plaintiffs in lawsuits failed in the
Senate by a narrow margin.[45]

Several resolutions adopted during this session were
likewise severe in their denunciation of the former Confederates and their associates. A Senate resolution declared that the acts of the special session of the legislature in 1861 were "treasonable and usurpative, unconstitutional, null and void." Another Senate resolution stig-
matized all those who had voted for separation in 1861 as
infamous, forever fixing "a stain upon them which is in-
delible and must remain upon them forever,"[46] and a
House resolution called for the seizing of all railroad
stock owned by former secessionists.[47]

One of the immediate problems confronting the legislature was that of providing for the Negroes and fixing

[42] *House Journal, 34th Tenn. General Assembly, 1st Session, 1865,*
p. 179.

[43] *Senate Journal, 34th Tenn. General Assembly, 1st Session, 1865,*
p. 116.

[44] *House Journal, 34th Tenn. General Assembly, 1st Session, 1865,*
p. 35.

[45] *Senate Journal, 34th Tenn. General Assembly, 1st Session, 1865,*
p. 119.

[46] *Ibid.,* p. 15.   [47] *Ibid.,* p. 316.

their status. Nothing was effected in this respect during
the session, but the debates and proceedings regarding
the condition of the colored man are illuminating and
suggestive of what was to be done later. Shortly after
the beginning of the session W. Peart of the nineteenth
district read to the Senate a petition "from the colored
people of East Tennessee." This petition stated that the
Negroes, although loyal, were being maltreated. They
were "looked upon with contempt and despised without
any cause." They were left without the protection of the
law, and they demanded that they be given an opportunity
to prosper in the world. They expressed a desire for admission to the franchise, but they were emphatic in their
repudiation of a desire for social equality with the whites,
even requesting that a law be passed forever barring
marriage between members of the white and black
races.[48] The petition was referred to the committee on
freedmen, and no further action was taken upon it.[49]

In the House, however, the Negro question gave rise
to a heated debate between Edmund Cooper and James
R. Hood, who curiously enough had been opponents for
the office of speaker. This debate arose on April 12,
when a bill was introduced to amend the bastardy laws
of Tennessee so as to allow a Negro woman to testify
against a white man as the putative father of her child.[50]
Cooper spoke against the bill. Declaring himself a Tennessean, "to the manor born," and a proslavery man, he
expressed a desire that the Negro should be protected in
his freedom, but he was unwilling to admit that Negroes
were sufficiently educated for such treatment as the bill
contemplated. The speech of Hood in support of the
bill might well have been made by an abolitionist. He

[48] Nashville *Daily Press*, Apr. 15, 1865. The proceedings of the legislature were reported much more fully in the newspapers than in the *Journals*.

[49] *Senate Journal, 34th Tenn. General Assembly, 1st Session, 1865*,
p. 46.

[50] *House Journal, 34th Tenn. General Assembly, 1st Session, 1865*,
p. 50.

had not had, he said, the same advantage as the Senator from Bedford; he was not a Tennessean but an American, not knowing one state from another; but he rejoiced that the car of progress had crushed slavery. He believed that "a man who would co-habit with a nasty, dirty, kinky-haired negro wench was far inferior to the latter." There was little distinction in his mind to be made between the integrity and truthfulness of a white and a black woman who had borne a child by a white man; both labored under the same wrong and had the same feelings.[51] Nothing came of this bill, but, as subsequent events were to show, the speech of Hood represented the views of the majority of the members of the legislature.

The members of the legislature were not slow in giving vent to their feelings against the former Confederates. In the house on April 11 Wines of Montgomery County spoke in favor of a bill offering terms of good treatment to those who would return to their allegiance. Such a course, in his opinion, would be wise and Christian; it would show the Confederates that the administration was not vindictive; and it would affirm faith in Lincoln's policy of conciliation. That such a lenient and conciliatory policy was not approved by the majority of the members was demonstrated by a speech of the Radical leader, James R. Hood, who denounced the bill which Wines had sponsored. Hood expressed decided unwillingness "to pin his faith on Lincoln's sleeve," and declared that any policy which did not contemplate the punishment of the leaders of the rebellion would be disastrous to the state. "Mr. Lincoln may do as he pleases," he added. "So will I. If rebels are permitted to remain in this country, the immigrants from the countries of Europe, as well as those from the northern states will refuse to settle with us."[52]

[51] Nashville *Daily Press*, Apr. 14, 1865.
[52] *Ibid.*, Apr. 12, 1865. This hesitation in doing anything that would

The plea of economic necessity and the desire to effect the speedy industrial rehabilitation of the state were well founded, and this factor contributes in some degree to justifying much of the feeling that was displayed against the former Confederates as a class. With the state impoverished by four years of war, which the secessionist legislature had done its part to bring on, and with the widespread interest in the development of industry and the encouragement of immigration that was being manifested in the post-war period, it is not difficult to see how the Radicals would sedulously avoid any measure that might serve to prevent the state from securing its share of the general prosperity that was current. "We greatly need both men and money to pump up the oil, and dig up the coal, iron, and copper which now lie hidden to the value of hundreds of millions in the bowels of the state and put them to market," said the Nashville *Daily Times*.[53] It was feared, or affected to be feared, by many members of the legislature, as Hood intimated in his speech, that a failure to punish the secessionists would endanger the economic security of the state by turning away immigrants and capital. No such excuse can be made, however, for the treatment of the "rebel" governor, Isham G. Harris, by Governor Brownlow and this legislature. On May 1 a joint resolution was unanimously passed by both houses which, after reciting a long list of the horrors of the rebellion—for which Harris was declared to be responsible—directed the governor "to offer a reward of five thousand dollars for the apprehension and delivery to the civil authorities of the state the afore-

serve to keep capital and labor out of the state seems to have been an important factor in developing the Radical theory. The *Daily Times*, on May 2, 1865, deplored the jealousy against capital from abroad and expressed hope that the legislature would "grant all just and reasonable encouragement to individuals who wish to bring capital and labor into the state for industrial purposes." See also W. B. Hesseltine, "Tennessee's Invitation to Carpet-Baggers", *East Tennessee Historical Society Publications*, IV, 102-15.

[53] Nashville *Daily Times*, May 2, 1865.

mentioned Isham G. Harris.''[54] Nothing but pure vindictiveness was the motive for this measure. Harris,
however reprehensible his acts may have been, was already a fugitive from the state, without money and without friends. There was no possible way in which he
might have constituted a danger to the state at this time.

The most important and most widely discussed problem that came before the legislature was that of regu-
lating the elective franchise, and upon this matter only
was any definite and general legislation enacted. It was
generally agreed that the former Confederates should
be denied the suffrage, but there was some question as
to the severity of the restrictions that should be placed
upon them. Considerable pressure was brought to bear
on the legislature from the outside. The loyal press was
especially severe in its demands. The *Union* declared
that,

The right of suffrage and of holding office should be denied to
those men by law, except upon conditions that will not jeop-
ardize the interests of the state and her loyal citizens. . . .

[54] *Acts, 34th Tenn. General Assembly, 1st Session, 1865,* pp. 147-48. The
Governor's proclamation offering the reward, which appeared on May 3,
was a masterpiece of invective and a typical Brownlow creation. The description of Harris is especially ribald. ''His complexion is sallow, his
eyes are dark and penetrating—a perfect index to the heart of a traitor—
with the scowl and frown of a demon resting upon his brow. The study of
mischief and the practice of crime have brought upon him premature bald-
ness and a gray beard. With brazen faced impudence, he talks loudly and
boastingly about the overthrow of the Yankee army and entertains no
doubt but that the South will achieve her independence. He chews tobacco
rapidly and is inordinately fond of liquor. In his moral structure he is
an unscrupulous man, steeped to the chin in personal and political profligacy
—now about lost to all sense of shame, honor, with a heart reckless of social
duty and fatally bent upon mischief. If captured he will be found lurking
in the rebel strongholds of Alabama, Mississippi, or Georgia, and in female
society, alleging with the sheepfaced modesty of a virtuous man that it is
not a wholesome state of public sentiment, or of taste, that forbids the
indiscriminate mixing together of married men and women.''—*Proclamation
Book,* pp. 2-3, in Tennessee State Archives, Nashville, containing all governor's proclamations from Brownlow to Alf. Taylor. In a message, noted
for its irony, Brownlow later recommended the repeal of this offer on the
ground that ''the state is likely to be called upon, at any day, for this
reward, and in return she would have nothing to show for the outlay.''
—*House Journal, 35th Tenn. General Assembly, 1st Session, 1867,* p. 29.

If they don't like the laws a loyal legislature may provide for their government, let them depart hence. At any rate until they "bring forth fruits meet for repentance" let them have no part in conducting the affairs of Tennessee.[55]

The *Press and Times* was equally harsh in its requirements,

Does anyone dream that the people of the United States will suffer Tennessee to pass into the power of men whose souls and hands are foul with the blood of treason? Never, never, never. By the blood of Shiloh, of Murfreesboro, of Chickamauga, of Mission Ridge, of Franklin, of Nashville, a thousand times no. American integrity, honor, and patriotism will never suffer such injustice and treachery to humanity and freedom to prevail. The loyal men must rule this state. Better another four years war in Tennessee and a Shiloh in every county of the state than that the affairs should pass into the hands of men whose hands are red with the blood of patriots or whose brains devised and plotted the villainy which they had not the courage to execute.[56]

The *Dispatch* opposed the projected limitation of the franchise on the ground that suffrage was a right and that a law for its limitation "might readily become a precedent for proscription on account of the utterance of political sentiments obnoxious to the party in power."[57] Its mild editorials, however, were easily overwhelmed by the radical diatribes of the other papers.

The question as to when, where, and how the line of disfranchisement should be fixed was the subject of a long and vociferous debate in the House. On May 22 Edmund Cooper, chairman of the joint judiciary committee on the franchise, reported from that committee a bill to fix the qualification of voters and to limit the elective franchise. This bill was recommended by the majority of the committee, and it was mild in its terms. It disfranchised only such persons as were exempted from the amnesty proclamation of December 8, 1863, and such

---

[55] Nashville *Union*, May 7, 1865.
[56] Nashville *Daily Press and Times*, May 16, 1865.
[57] Nashville *Dispatch*, June 2, 1865.

"conscious and intelligent traitors in the State of Tennessee as ought not, because of their conduct at present, be admitted to all the privileges of the elective franchise."[58]   A minority of the committee, headed by S. M. Arnell, dissented from the liberal terms of the majority report and introduced another bill that was much more stringent in its limitations.[59]   The debate as to the respective merits of the Cooper and Arnell bills then began.   Although the Radicals won, the debate illustrates the strength of the Conservatives in the house.

Excellent arguments in favor of the Cooper bill were advanced by Steele of Marshall and Gaut of Bradley. They pointed out the necessity of harmonizing the policy of the state with that of the Federal government as expressed in the amnesty proclamation.   Steele painted a dark picture of the future of the state if the minority bill should become a law:

Pass your sweeping disfranchisement bill and you will make the state government a solitude—a despotism.   You by that will exclude the admission of our members to Congress, because of the small vote by which they were elected.   It will practically nullify, so far as Tennessee is concerned, that part of the United States constitution giving representation and votes in proportion to population.   If you do not allow that population to vote, how can you justly claim representation in Congress for it?[60]

Wines of Montgomery attempted to refute the arguments of Steele, but his speech was not convincing.[61]   Cooper defended his bill with great ability and criticized the minority bill in a brilliant legalistic argument.   He denounced the latter bill because it would exclude from the franchise all except those "publically known to have entertained unconditional sentiments from the outbreak

[58] *House Journal, 34th Tenn. General Assembly, 1st Session, 1865,* pp. 191-2.
[59] *Ibid.,* p. 196.
[60] Nashville *Daily Press and Times,* May 25, 1865, gives the speech of Steele; that of Gaut is in the Nashville *Dispatch,* May 27.
[61] Nashville *Daily Press and Times,* May 30, 1865.

of the rebellion to the present time," and, like Steele, pointed out that its passage would result in a reduction of Tennessee's representation in Congress. His chief argument was based upon the contention that the schedule, upon which the minority bill relied for its constitutionality, was not a part of the new amendments to the state constitution, but that it was only a suggestion or direction to some judicial or legislative body as to what the people desired them to do in their judicial or legislative capacity.[62]

Cooper presented sound and judicious arguments, but in eloquence he was surpassed by Arnell, who spoke at great length in defense of his bill. Making no attempt to answer the legalistic arguments of Cooper he attempted to arouse the passions of the members of the legislature by giving a somewhat melodramatic description of the results of secession in the state. It was a species of "waving the bloody shirt," the logical conclusion of which was that those who had brought on secession should be punished by a denial of the privilege of exercising the franchise to them. Describing conditions in Tennessee he said,

The barn is empty; the flocks and herds have been hunted down and killed; the fields are unfenced and unfurrowed; the old homestead stands out on the common and dismally rattles its broken blinds; the "old folks" talk to you in a low hushed tone about their boys in the grave; and it needs no spoken voice to tell you that their wealth has taken to itself wings and disappeared. In the refugee's hut the widow crouches on her low stool and hushes her child to sleep, but with no promise of the father's coming—he died in Georgia or Virginia. Blank despair, gaunt famine are staring her in the face. In vain she tries to hide their spectres with the manly form that stood by her side at the marriage morning, but the recollection of now and then, the sense of loss overcomes her, she breaks down, her eyes swim, and she prays in her agony to the only friend left—the widow's God. Droves of homeless children flock over our streets daily asking you openly for charity—asking you silently, by the dear love of brotherhood and the love of God, for home and education. Our public calamities are even greater than our private misfortunes. . . .

In view of these conditions, which he had described with such emotion, he thought it "just and righteous" that rebels should be disfranchised. They were not his constituents, he said, and as a proof of his contempt for them added,

I represent on the floor no rebel. God helping me, never shall I stoop so low. I represent Union men alone—men who have walked forty miles on foot from guerrilla infested country. I want protection for them.[63]

Arnell's eloquence, together with the Radical predisposition of many of the members, carried the day, and the minority bill was successfully carried through the three readings in the House. It was passed by the House on June 2 by a vote of forty to twenty-two.[64] In the Senate it met with little opposition, and was passed on June 5 by a vote of twenty to one.[65]

The act as passed in its final form was the very embodiment of the spirit of radicalism and proscription. Its provisions were drastic in the extreme. It provided that only those persons might vote who were of lawful age and residence and who had entertained unconditional union sentiments from the outbreak of the war, or who had arrived at the age of twenty-one years since November 4, 1865, or had been honorably discharged from the Union army, or had served as conscripts in the Confederate army, or had voted in the elections of 1864 and 1865. All officers, civil, and military, and diplomatic, of the Confederacy, all persons who had left Federal or state civil offices to aid in the rebellion, and all persons who had left homes within the protection of the United States to

[63] Nashville Daily Union, June 4, 1865.
[64] House Journal, 34th Tenn. General Assembly, 1st Session, 1865, p. 223.
[65] Senate Journal, 34th Tenn. General Assembly, 1st Session, 1865, p. 195.

aid the rebellion should be disfranchised for fifteen years. All persons not included in these categories were denied the franchise for five years, at the end of which they might be re-admitted by petition to the circuit or chancery court, on proof of loyalty to the United States in open court, upon the testimony of two or more loyal citizens. County court clerks were required to keep a registration of voters and issue certificates. No one might vote without a certificate, and even one possessing a certificate, if challenged, must take a prescribed oath. This oath required the challenged voter to swear that he was an active friend and supporter of the Constitution of the United States; that he would heartily aid and assist the loyal people in whatever measures that might be adopted under the Constitution and laws to establish the national authority over every state and territory; and that he would faithfully and heartily support the state constitution and its new amendments. Judges of elections and candidates for office were also required to take this oath, and anyone taking it falsely was declared guilty of perjury.[66]

Shortly after this act was passed the legislature adjourned until October 2.[67] Thus, with the Brownlow administration securely inaugurated, its first phase came to an end.

[66] *Acts, 34th Tenn. General Assembly, 1st Session, 1865*, pp. 32-6.
[67] *Senate Journal, 34th Tenn. General Assembly, 1st Session, 1865*, p. 230.

Chapter V

THE CONSUMMATION OF THE RADICAL ASCENDENCY

Governor Brownlow adjourned the legislature on June 12 and, on the same day, issued a proclamation calling for the holding of an election for congressmen on August 3.[1] Much importance was attached to this election by the administration. In the first place care must be taken that only uncompromising Union men should be elected; otherwise, the Tennessee delegation would in all probability not be admitted at Washington. In the second place, it was generally supposed that the election would afford a convenient opportunity for testing the validity and constitutionality of the recently enacted franchise law. Lastly, it would serve as a referendum upon the policy of the legislature, and the successful election of Union men would result in a tremendous strengthening of the prestige of the administration. Every effort, therefore, was made by the administration and its supporters to push the election to a successful conclusion.

These efforts took the form of executive proclamations, editorials in the administration newspapers, and public meetings which were probably arranged by the Governor—certainly by his henchmen. The proclamations began to make their appearance before the legislature had adjourned. On May 13 the Governor demanded that all "rebels" cease stealing, robbing, and plundering and "betake themselves to honest pursuits." His advice to the leaders of the late rebellion was indicative of the measures that were to follow:

Those leaders who notified Union men, at the beginning of the rebellion, that but one party could hereafter live in East Tennessee, and drove them from their homes, would act wisely to

[1] *Proclamation Book,* p. 10.

quietly and forever withdraw from the country. Intelligent, influential men of wealth, who instigated this rebellion have forfeited all rights to protection and life, and merit the vigorous
and undying opposition of loyal men.[2]

This was followed by another proclamation declaring
that the elective franchise act was the supreme law of
the land and warning all persons against attempting to
vote without first fulfilling its requirements. The Governor was also careful to specify that only loyal men would
be permitted to become candidates in the approaching
election:

All who shall band themselves together for the purpose of de-
feating the execution of said law will be declared in rebellion
against the State of Tennessee and dealt with as rebels. And
I call upon the civil authorities throughout the state to arrest
and bring to justice all persons, who, under pretense of being
candidates for Congress or other office, are travelling over the
state denouncing and nullifying the constitution and laws of the
land and spreading sedition and a spirit of rebellion.[3]

It was thus evident that the Governor intended that the
franchise act should be enforced to the letter in the congressional election.

The newspapers were especially active in this campaign. Those of the administration took particular pains
to point out the necessity for electing a solid Union ticket
to Congress. The *Union* urged that,

Not a voter should be permitted to stay away from the polls, if
proper information, respecting his rights and sense of duty, can
prevail upon him to vote. Let everyone who feels an interest
in a large vote, and the election of a thoroughgoing friend of
the Union and the administration, exert himself to bring out
every voter.[4]

The *Press and Times* avowed that a new rebellion was
manifesting itself in the opposition to the elective franchise law and advocated that stringent action be taken
to counteract such a movement.

[2] *Ibid.*, p. 7.
[3] *Ibid.*, p. 24.
[4] Nashville *Union*, July 19, 1865.

Let no one deceive himself with the belief that the politicians who are so fiercely and vehemently seeking to bring the State government into odium, mean nothing more than discussion and action at the ballot-box. . . . The same editors who used to spew out maudlin blackguardisms against "Massa Andy's *damnasty oath*" and rave at the "government on Campbell's Hill" all join in the hue and cry against Governor Brownlow. . . . Those who used to bray at Andrew Johnson's test oath, now rave against "the abominable franchise law."[5]

Many public meetings and county conventions were held throughout the state during the interval between the adjournment of the legislature and the congressional election. The majority of these meetings approved heartily of the general policy of the administration. At Winchester resolutions were adopted ardently desiring "to return to the 'old paths' and have civil law and authority restored." "We regard the re-establishment of the Federal Union as final," the resolution continued, "and we will stand by it as the only sure guarantee of our peace and prosperity."[6] There was, however, a marked disposition shown in some of these meetings to criticize the elective franchise act because of the severity of its provisions. At Duck River, for example, a Union meeting adopted resolutions approving "the proceedings of our late legislators as a whole" but earnestly recommended "the repeal or modification of the late franchise act, so as to make it in exact keeping with the policy of the general government."[7] At Dresden a meeting was held, addressed by Emerson Etheridge, and extreme resolutions were drawn up, declaring that the Governor and his "self-styled legislature are scarcely less treasonable, revolutionary, and lawless than the original authors of the rebellion."[8] The last named incident was doubtless an

[5] Nashville *Daily Press and Times*, July 11, 1865.
[6] Nashville *Dispatch*, June 10, 1865.
[7] Nashville *Union*, July 11, 1865.
[8] Nashville *Dispatch*, July 23, 1865. For his participation in this meeting Etheridge was arrested and carried to Columbus, Kentucky, by Negro

extreme case, but such accounts of these meetings as have been preserved demonstrate conclusively that there was much disapproval of the new franchise law.   Consequently, as the conventions reflected, much more accurately than the legislature, the sentiment of the people throughout the state, their disapproval indicated that the Radical party was somewhat in advance of the general will in its program.[9]

The Radical minority was confined largely to the eastern section of the state. A suggestive, though somewhat extreme, illustration of its position is found in the following "order":

Special Order No. 1.
In the woods near New Market, Tenn.
July the 24th, 1865.

All damed rebels are hereby notified to lieve at wonce. If found her at the expiration of ten days from the date of this order and no preparations to lieve thrashing mashines will be sit at wonce to thrash all crops with the usual tale hickry withs and cowhides or anything els that may be required for the occasion. We are working by the order that your thieving, God-forsaken, Hell-deserving Rebels issued four years ago— Union men and Rebels cannot live together—which we find not altogether bogus.

We are vary
Respectivly
Old Soldier.[10]

As might be expected the chief issue of the campaign which followed was the elective franchise act. The electorate, while incidentally choosing members of Congress, was in reality discussing and voting upon the action of

soldiers. He was imprisoned there and later tried by court martial.— Nashville *Union,* Nov. 14, 1865.

[9] The so-called Radical party developed in Tennessee during this period. "The term *radical* was applied to such men who were in favor of disfranchising the whites of Tennessee and elevating the Negroes above the majority of white men".—Testimony of A. A. Steele in the contested election case of Sheafe *v.* Tillman, *House Misc. Docs.,* 41 Cong., 2 Sess., No. 143, p. 76.

[10] Copy of the original in the Nelson Papers.

the recent session of the legislature. The results of the election were to show, however, that in some sections at least the governor stood in need of additional support.

In the campaign the Radicals stood upon the legality of the reorganized state government and its subsequent legislation. Their strongest argument was to the effect that only Radicals or uncompromising Union men would be admitted to seats in Congress if elected, or would be able to benefit the state in Washington if admitted. This attitude was well illustrated in the campaign in the Hermitage district, in which the capital of the state was located. The Conservative candidate for Congress in this district was William B. Campbell, formerly governor of the state, who had opposed secession and had entered the Union army, where he had eventually risen to the rank of brigadier-general. He had, however, viewed the new amendments to the state constitution as illegal and invalid[11] and had opposed the elective franchise act. For this attitude he was violently assailed by the Radical party and press. The Nashville *Union* called him a "rebel sore-head, who was not in sympathy with the administration of Johnson" and urged all good Unionists to aid in his defeat.[12] His course was violently assailed by J. O. Shackleford, a Clarksville Radical, and described as "detrimental to the public interest" and the "last struggle of the slaveholders to restore their institutions."[13] Horace Maynard, speaking at the Market House in Nashville, in the course of the campaign defended the Brownlow government as "in all respects a legal, constitutional, rightful government having the highest sanction and authority possible, both of the state and of the national constitution." Hostility to the government, he said, would not prevent Negro suffrage, but would rather hasten its establishment. At the same time, with evident

[11] Nashville *Daily Press and Times*, July 13, 1865.
[12] Nashville *Union*, July 22, 1865.
[13] Letter of J. O. Shackleford to Jerry Frazer, *Tennessee Archives*.

reference to Campbell's attitude, he warned his hearers against attempting another rebellion or listening to politicians "who harp on 'abolitionists' and 'blue-bellied' yankees."[14]

On the other hand, the Conservatives, also staunch Union men, denied most strenuously the expediency and even the constitutionality of the franchise law. In a letter to the *Dispatch* on July 1, "An Original Union Man" from Knox County denounced the act as an outgrowth of a "low feeling of hatred and revenge." With regard to the motives that actuated the legislature in passing the law this anonymous correspondent was equally critical, alleging that "to exclude a few aspiring rebels from office and to retain the offices for themselves were matters of more importance with the majority of the honorable representatives than to heal the wounds of the body politic and restore the government and country to their original beauty and grandeur."[15] A similar sentiment was expressed by Dorsey B. Thomas, a Conservative candidate for Congress, in a speech at Clarksville. This speech cast particular odium upon the framers of the franchise law and characterised their action as "the move of those who wanted office."[16]

The Conservative opposition developed to such strength that the Governor felt called upon to issue another proclamation against it.[17] He had hoped that his administration would be peaceful, he declared in this proclamation, but he was pained to announce his serious apprehensions that a different order of things was soon to be encountered. He then entered upon one of his customary diatribes against the opposition:

The harangues of aspiring politicians denouncing the termination of slavery, the establishment of a free state constitution,

---

[14] Nashville *Daily Press and Times*, July 24, 1865.
[15] Nashville *Dispatch*, July 1, 1865.   [16] Nashville *Union*, Aug. 3, 1865.
[17] Brownlow issued such a large number of proclamations that the opposition newspapers gave him the nickname of "Old Proc."

and the very existence of the government over which I am called
to preside as unconstitutional, spurious, and a usurpation, the
conduct of numerous county officers . . . proclaim, too plainly
to be misunderstood, that the spirit of nullification and rebellion still exist and must be defeated.[18]

The proclamation further defended the state government
as the true "republican form" and gave assurance that
the franchise law would "be enforced on the day of the
election as far as the civil and military authorities can
enforce it."

The reference to the military authorities in this proclamation was no mere rhetorical allusion, for attempts
were actually made by the Governor to secure their services. There was a rumor afloat in June to the effect that
there was being organized a mysterious body known as
"The Blood Faction," and it was alleged that this faction
had a plot under way for calling an election for governor
and members of the general assembly in August, under
the provisions of the Constitution of 1834 as it stood
before the new amendments were added. The administration press professed to believe that "The Blood Faction" was contemplating the overthrow of the Governor
and the administration.[19] It was also "learned" on some
unnamed "authority from Washington" that President
Johnson had been formulating plans for the superseding
of Governor Brownlow by the appointment of Gordon
Grainger as military governor of Tennessee.[20] To secure
the frustration of these two supposed plans, which were
thought to have some connection with the approaching
election, the Governor appealed to General George H.
Thomas for military forces to aid in conducting the election legally.[21] There was of course no foundation for the
rumor that Johnson was contemplating the overthrow of

[18] *Proclamation Book*, pp. 18-23.
[19] Nashville *Daily Press and Times*, June 15, 1865.
[20] Knoxville *Whig*, July 25, 1865.
[21] *O.R.*, series I, vol. XLIX, part II, p. 1093.

the state administration, for he himself had just recently authorized the Governor to call upon General Thomas for troops whenever their presence should be deemed essential to the preservation of order in the state.[22] The troops were secured, however, and dispatched to a number of counties in the state where the Conservative strength was the most extensive, but their presence was unnecessary.[23] The election passed off quietly and without disorder, although the results were somewhat disappointing to the Governor and the Radical party.

The returns showed the election of Nathaniel G. Taylor, Horace Maynard, William B. Stokes, Edmund Cooper, William B. Campbell, Dorsey B. Thomas, Isaac R. Hawkins, and John W. Leftwich.[24] The disappointment of the Governor and the administration resulted from the fact that only three of these, Maynard, Stokes, and Hawkins, were Radicals, while the other five, Taylor, Cooper, Campbell, Thomas, and Leftwich, were elected as Conservatives over Radical opponents. It was

[22] *Ibid.*, p. 1095.

[23] Troops were sent to the counties of Benton, Henry, Weakley, Gibson, Lauderdale, Henderson, Carroll, Humphreys, Dickson, Stewart, Montgomery, Shelby, Fayette, Williamson, Davidson, Sumner, Robertson, Cheatham, Bedford, Lincoln, Marshall, Giles, Maury, Hickman, and Lewis. It will be observed that none of these counties was located in East Tennessee.

[24] Nashville *Daily Press and Times*, Nov. 27, 1865. The whole number of votes cast was 61,768, about two-thirds of the vote of June, 1861. The districts are numbered from the East toward the West. It will be seen from the following table that the decline in the number of votes cast in 1865 as compared with 1861 increases as the districts proceed toward the West—the result of the operation of the elective franchise act.

District	August, 1865	June, 1861
1...	11,345	21,678
2...	12,786	20,625
3...	7,848	18,813
4...	7,918	16,138
5...	8,098	22,043
6...	5,156	17,150
7...	5,131	16,851
8...	3,486	16,787
	61,768	150,085

Senate Journal, 34th Tenn. General Assembly, 2nd session, 1865-6, pp. 167-8.

thus evident that the policy of the Radicals was not supported by the majority of the people in many sections of the state.

Almost immediately after the election returns were in, the Radicals raised the cry of fraud. Letters were received by the Governor from outraged citizens who professed to feel that their rights had been violated by the Conservatives. A communication from the citizens of Meigs County reported that the provisions of the elective franchise law had been almost completely disregarded in that county, and that in scarcely any case had the voters been required to make oath or produce legal proof of loyalty when procuring certificates of registration.[25] Acting upon information thus received the Governor issued a proclamation on August 11 stating that, in his opinion, the franchise act had been misconstrued, evaded, and disregarded, and calling upon the clerks and sheriffs of the various counties to answer certain questions with regard to the manner in which the elections had been conducted.[26] In this manner he discovered that five methods had been used in obtaining certificates of registration. As only two of these methods were legal in his opinion, he proceeded to "throw out and not take into account" the votes of twenty-nine counties in Middle and West Tennessee where he alleged the law had been most "extensively disregarded." "Whatever others may think of my duty," he informed the legislature, "I will not declare in a certificate, or otherwise, that the election was regular in counties and districts when I officially know that it was *not* regular."[27]

The rejected votes came from every congressional district, but the Governor's action changed the result in only one, the sixth. There the Conservative candidate,

[25] Brownlow Papers, State Library.
[26] Nashville *Union*, Aug. 13, 1865.
[27] *Senate Journal, 34th Tenn. General Assembly, 2nd Session, 1865-6*, pp. 168-69.

Dorsey B. Thomas, had been elected over his Radical opponent, S. M. Arnell, by a vote of 2,805 to 2,350.[28] Brownlow, however, threw out the votes cast in Montgomery, Humphreys, Maury, Lawrence, and Stewart Counties, alleging that the registration certificates issued were clearly void, and thereby producing a very different result. By the "corrected" returns the vote stood 1,546 for Arnell to 521 for Thomas. There was some criticism of the Governor's action in the legislature, but a resolution contemplating further discussion of the matter was tabled in the senate by a vote of 34 to 25.[29]

Brownlow defended the legality of his procedure in a letter to the *Whig,* in which he characterized the evasion of the franchise law, which was supposed to have occurred in the election, as a "rebel" scheme directed against the stability of the reorganized state government.[30] Conclusive evidence does not exist to show that there was an organized conspiracy to defeat the policy of the administration at the polls by false registration, but the results of the election certainly demonstrated clearly that there was still considerable opposition to the Radical program in the state. The Boston *Transcript* characterized the result of the election as "the reverse of encouraging to those expecting the Southern whites to repudiate, at the ballot-box, the treason they have supported at the mouth of the cannon."[31]

The Conservatives at the same time were not disposed to surrender their claims without further effort, and they continued the contest in Congress. Thomas made application for his seat in the Thirty-ninth Congress, alleging that the Governor had "disregarded the facts in the returns, and by arbitrary act of power unknown to the law,

[28] It was an interesting coincidence that Arnell himself was the author of the elective franchise act.
[29] *House Journal, 34th Tenn. General Assembly, 2nd Session, 1865-6,* p. 204.
[30] Nashville *Union,* Aug. 19, 1865.
[31] *Ibid.,* quoting the Boston *Transcript.*

issued a certificate to Arnell.'' He further contended that the interpretation placed upon the franchise law by the administration was in direct conflict with the judicial decisions of the state, and to substantiate this claim he cited the recent decision of Judge Smith of the common law and chancery court of Memphis in the case of Sale v. Ware.[32]

The case of Sale v. Ware was one of a number of cases that arose in the state with regard to the validity of the elective franchise act. John F. Sale applied to Ware, the clerk of the Shelby County court, for a certificate of registration. This the clerk refused to issue unless the applicant would undertake to prove that he had been ''publically known to have entertained loyal sentiments from the outbreak of the rebellion in 1861.'' Sale then petitioned Judge Smith for a writ of mandamus which was issued. Thereupon the clerk appeared and moved to dismiss the petition. The facts were admitted and the case proceeded to trial on a question of law. At the trial the court upheld the franchise law, which was the sole point at issue, and dismissed the petition for mandamus.[33]

Thomas contended in his petition to congress, contesting the election, that Judge Smith, although sustaining the ''constitutionality of the law,'' had construed its meaning in a very different manner than that upon which the Governor had acted. However, he was unable to state specifically the manner in which the governor had varied his procedure from that which was declared valid in the case, and the committee on contested elections, to which the matter was referred, took little notice of this allegation.[34] Numerous other documents were produced by Thomas to show that the election in the Sixth District was held according to law and that Brownlow had illegally and arbitrarily changed the result so as to secure

[32] *House Misc. Docs.*, 39 Cong., 2 Sess., No. 6.
[33] *Ibid.*, pp. 24-28.
[34] *House Misc. Docs.*, 41 Cong., 2 Sess., No. 152, p. 162.

the election of the Radical candidate. His efforts were futile, however, for the committee decided against him on a technicality and admitted Arnell along with the other congressmen from Tennessee.[35]

It was evident from the results of this election that, even under the franchise law of 1865, the Conservative Union men would be in the ascendency in Tennessee. This class was composed of solid and substantial Union men whose loyalty was above question, but they were not radical. Their success, therefore did not meet with the approval of the Radical administration. It became necessary then for the Governor and the legislature which he dominated to place further restrictions upon the exercise of the suffrage in the state if the Conservatives were to be kept in the minority. Brownlow was truly alarmed at the situation, and he was quick to perceive that the act of 1865 was in need of amendment or replacement by a more stringent measure. Such was the state of affairs when the adjourned session of the legislature convened on October 4, 1865.

Matters pertaining to the condition of the freedmen engrossed the attention of both houses until the Christmas recess began, but immediately after the re-assembling of the members, on January 8, 1866, the franchise question was called up for discussion. As in the previous session, much pressure was brought to bear upon the legislature from without. The press as usual was especially active. The *Union* averred that "the opinions of rebeldom have not changed" and called upon the Radicals "to fight fire with fire."[36] On January 9 a large group of German-American citizens met in Nashville and issued a statement declaring their belief that rebels were gaining control of Tennessee politics. The continuation of this state of affairs, they said, would drive loyal immi-

[35] *Cong. Globe*, 39 Cong., 2 Sess., p. 4.
[36] Nashville *Union*, Dec. 4, 1865.

grants elsewhere, and "from the rebel yoke" they prayed to be saved.[37] There were also many vague but persistent threats from several sources that only by a more severe treatment of former Confederates would the state secure its readmission into the Union.

On January 24 S. M. Arnell, chairman of the house committee on franchise, reported from that committee a bill to alter and amend the act of June 5, 1865.[38] He spoke at some length in support of this measure, alleging that its passage and enforcement was necessary in order to prevent disciplinary measures from being taken by the Radical party at Washington. The bill was violently attacked by William B. Lewis of Davidson County on the ground that it was inappropriate and unnecessary. There was no evidence, he declared, that the rebels were plotting against the government, and the law would only serve to keep alive and aggravate disloyal sentiment.[39] Harvey Brown of Madison County also attacked the bill with well directed and pertinent arguments.[40] Nevertheless the measure passed the first and second reading in the house. Then it was halted by a filibuster. When the vote was taken on the third reading it was found that a quorum was not present. Twenty-one members had absented themselves, it was supposed as a result of a mutual understanding in order to obstruct the passage of the bill. A disorderly scene ensued. Mullins of Bedford accused the speaker of complicity in the filibuster, whereupon the speaker threw his gavel at his accuser. The entire house rose to its feet, epithets were freely exchanged, and pistols were drawn.[41] The doorkeeper was sent after the absent members, but they eluded his pursuit by submitting their

[37] Nashville *Union and American*, Jan. 16, 1866.

[38] *House Journal, 34th Tenn. General Assembly, 2nd session, 1865-6*, p. 291.

[39] Nashville *Daily Union*, Feb. 6, 1866.

[40] Nashville *Daily Press and Times*, Feb. 1, 1866.

[41] Nashville *Union and American*, Feb. 17, 1866.

resignations.[42]   This incident caused a temporary halt in the franchise legislation.

The Governor then issued a proclamation denouncing the action of those members who had resigned as "factious and revolutionary," and ordered new elections to be held in their respective counties. He especially urged upon the voters of these counties the advisability of returning men who were in accord with his policy and threatened military occupation if this advice was not complied with.[43] In this way he hoped to purge the legislature of all opposition to the franchise act. The elections were held on March 31, but in defiance of the Governor's threats, all but five of the "seceders" were returned by large majorities. On April 10 nineteen of the new members reported to the legislature, which had adjourned from day to day since the filibuster and demanded that they be admitted and qualified as members of the house.[44] As it was generally understood that many of these men had been elected under pledge to their constituents to oppose the franchise act it was confidently expected that their readmission would result in another deadlock. The Radicals held that the pledge "to bolt again" constituted a bar to the readmission of the seceders and the speaker declined to admit them. He did, however, direct the clerk to administer the oath to the three Radicals who had applied for admission, and a quorum was thus secured. This conduct on the part of the speaker was in turn denounced by the opposition press as "factious and revolutionary,"[45] but it was allowed to stand; and it resulted in the passage of the franchise bill in the house on April 12.[46]

[42] *House Journal, 34th Tenn. General Assembly, 2nd Session, 1865-6* p. 403.
[43] Nashville *Union and American*, Mar. 6, 1866.
[44] *House Journal, 34th Tenn. General Assembly, 2nd Session, 1865-6,* p. 425.
[45] Nashville *Dispatch*, Apr. 11, 1866.
[46] *House Journal, 34th Tenn. General Assembly, 2nd Session, 1865-6,* p. 425.

It then remained to secure the passage of the bill through the more conservative Senate. In a message to that body on April 13 the Governor pointed out the necessity for a thorough revision of the existing suffrage laws. As evidence of the inadequacy of these laws he cited the recent election for county officers in which he said that many of the candidates had "openly and publicly based their claims to election upon wounds received and losses incurred in the cause of the rebellion, and were often successful." He also expressed his belief that the returning of the seceding representatives in the March election clearly demonstrated the fact that their constituents were anxious to destroy the state government. These two instances, he alleged, were sufficient to show that "those who, but a few months since, were engaged in the work of destroying all government, and who suceeded in destroying the state government, and only failed to destroy the national government by being overpowered by force of arms, are not yet safe depositories of the elective franchise."[47]

The Governor's election doubtless had its effect upon the Senate, but the specific event that determined the action of that body upon the franchise law was a threatened attempt on the part of the inhabitants of East Tennessee to secede and form another state. The citizens of that section were firm and aggressive in their refusal to be dominated or outvoted by the Conservative sections of the state, and they delivered the ultimatum that the Conservatives should be disfranchised or East Tennessee would secede. In April the "new state" movement was widely agitated, and its instigators even went so far as to call a convention to meet at Knoxville in May to consider plans for its furtherance.[48] In the face of the im-

[47] *Senate Journal, 34th Tenn. General Assembly, 2nd Session, 1865-6,* p. 426.

[48] Nashville *Union,* Apr. 19, 1866; Nashville *Dispatch,* May 6, May 20, 1866.

pact of this movement the Senate cowered and passed the franchise law on May 3.[49]

Under the new law the Radical ascendency was virtually assured. It provided for the perpetual disfranchisement of all citizens, otherwise qualified, who had voluntarily borne arms against the government of the United States in the late rebellion; all who had sought, or voluntarily accepted any office, or attempted to exercise the function of any office under the authority or pretended authority of the so-called Confederate States; and all who had voluntarily supported any government, power, or authority hostile or inimical to the authority of the United States, by persuasion, influence, or in any other way whatsoever. The act further required that all persons other than Union soldiers should prove by the evidence of two legal voters that they were not subject to any of the disabilities mentioned in the act, and, in addition, provided that they must take the iron-clad test oath. In the place of the county court clerk, who had issued certificates of registration under the former law, special commissioners were to be appointed in each county to receive evidence for and against the applicants for certificates and to determine as to the propriety of issuing the certificates. As these commissioners were to be appointed and removed by the Governor at pleasure the new law placed the control of the suffrage absolutely, although indirectly, in his hands.[50] The Radicals had now triumphed in the legislature; only the judiciary remained to check them, and such obstacles as it was able to interpose were soon swept aside.

The administration immediately signified its determination to enforce the franchise law. On May 5, only two days after its enactment, a meeting of the Radicals was held at the capitol. Both the Governor and the secretary

[49] *Senate Journal, 34th Tenn. General Assembly, 2nd Session, 1865-6*, p. 483.

[50] *Acts, 34th Tenn. General Assembly, 2nd Session, 1865-6*, pp. 42-8.

of state were present and made lengthy addresses. The Governor, presiding and speaking from the chair, called attention to the necessity for the appointment of "the right sort of men as commissioners of registration." Fletcher, the secretary of state, spoke in a similar vein:

We want men whom no influence, social, political, or pecuniary, can swerve from a strict performance of duty. If Middle and West Tennessee cannot furnish the material to carry out our behests, why, then we will draw upon East Tennessee. Any means must be resorted to, if necessary, to keep rebels from the polls and out of office.[51]

The Nashville press on the whole supported the law, but there was some criticism of its severity by the *Union and American*. This paper was rapidly becoming the anti-administration organ, and it affected a skeptical attitude toward the Governor's policy regarding the franchise:

It will lead to confusion, and ill-blood, and disgrace. To expect good from it is impossible. Though it may not now be so distinctly seen by the majority, it will soon become visible that it is full of evil, and nothing but evil. Tennessee wants peace on the basis of liberty and constitutional laws. This, sooner or later, the people of the state will have, whatever obstructions may be temporarily thrown in their way.[52]

It was generally anticipated and desired that the franchise law would soon come before the courts in order that its constitutionality might be tested.[53]   Events occurring during the autumn of 1866 hastened the consummation of this desire. In August it was reported that the commissioners of registration were exerting a pronounced and preconceived effort to prevent the registration of the Conservatives. In certain counties, it was said, none but members of the Union League and adherents of the Brownlow administration were allowed to register.[54]   In

---

[51] Nashville *Dispatch*, May 6, 1866.
[52] Nashville *Union and American*, May 6, 1866.
[53] Nashville *Dispatch*, May 4, 1866.
[54] *Ibid.*, Aug. 8, 1866.

November the *Dispatch* printed an editorial saying that:

There are hundreds, perhaps thousands, of men scattered over Middle and West Tennessee, who have heretofore voted with the Republicans, but have become disgusted with the disfranchisement movement begun and carried out by the men who obtained power, not by the will of those they assume to represent, but under circumstances which made the thing they called an election little better than a farce of the broadest character.[55]

With such a situation prevalent it was inevitable that an attempt would be made to defeat the operation of the franchise law in the courts. This attempt was made in the case of Ridley *v.* Sherbrook.[56]   On August 1, 1866 Bromfield L. Ridley of Murfreesboro applied to Freeman Sherbrook, the commissioner of registration for Rutherford County, for a certificate of registration. The applicant affirmed that he was fifty years of age, a free white man, and that, a citizen of Rutherford County for more than twenty years, he had been accustomed to exercise the privilege of voting. He further stated that, although he had taken part in the rebellion, he had been pardoned by President Johnson on July 26, 1865, for all offenses committed against the United States and the state of Tennessee, and that he had committed no crimes since receiving the pardon. He demanded the right to exercise the franchise under the state constitution. Sherbrook refused to issue the certificate unless the applicant could qualify under the provisions of the elective franchise act of May 3, 1866. Ridley then applied to Judge Henry Cooper of the circuit court for a writ of mandamus compelling Sherbrook to issue the certificate. The facts were admitted, and the case came to trial on the sole question of the constitutionality of the elective franchise

[55] *Ibid.*, Nov. 13, 1866.

[56] 3 Coldwell (Tennessee) 56. An earlier attempt to test the constitutionality of the franchise law had been made on July 15 in the case of House *v.* Nesbet, in the circuit court of Williamson County. Judge M. M. Brien, however, held that upon the facts as presented no question of constitutionality might arise. Nashville *Union and American*, July 27, 1866.

act. In an elaborate opinion, regarded by its enemies as the ablest argument that had been advanced upon the subject, Judge Cooper granted the mandamus and held the act to be unconstitutional. He based this decision upon the fact that the law had been passed while several of the members were wrongfully excluded from the legislature:

All the representatives, as I have said, need not be present, but all must have the right to be present. If any material part of them are wrongfully excluded—it would not perhaps be going too far to say (although not necessarily in this case to be so held) if any one of them be wrongfully excluded—the body ceases to be the general assembly, and becomes an unauthorized mob.[57]

The decision was applauded by the enemies of the administration, and it was supported by a statement issued by four prominent attorneys of Knoxville. They stated themselves to be ''fully satisfied that the said 'franchise act' is unconstitutional and ought to be so held by every judicial officer.''[58] The administration, however, was not to be so easily defeated, and Sherbrook appealed to the state supreme court, which was at this time composed of Radical appointees of Governor Brownlow.[59]

The importance of the case was fully realized, and an elaborate array of counsel was employed. Ridley was represented by Edwin A. Keeble, Charles Reedy, Edwin H. Ewing, Robert L. Caruthers, M. S. Frierson, A. O. P. Nicholson, and James E. Bailey, the most prominent and able members of the Middle Tennessee bar. Sherbrook's counsel was not so well known as that of his opponent, but it was capable and had the strong support of the administration. It included William H. Wisener, Sr.,

[57] Nashville *Daily Press and Times*, Jan. 23, 1867.
[58] *Ibid.*, Jan. 7, 1867. The attorneys who signed the statement were John M. Fleming, Thomas A. R. Nelson, John Baxter, and George Brown.
[59] The members of the supreme court at this time were Sam Milligan, Alvin Hawkins, and J. O. Shackleford. Shackleford wrote the opinion in this case.

Eugene Cary, E. H. Otis, J. J. Noah, and Horace H. Harrison. In reality the prosecution of this appeal was an attack upon the administration, and it was so regarded. The administrative organ, the *Press and Times,* openly declared that,

The argument is not merely to set aside an oppressive law. Its ultimate purpose is the complete overthrow of the existing State Government and the amended constitution on which it is based and the restoration of the old one which is more consonant with the feelings of the rebel leaders. . . . The very basis on which the present state government rests is the restriction of suffrage to loyal men and the disfranchisement of the Rebels.[60]

The case came before the supreme court on January 25, 1867. The argument was opened by Edwin A. Keeble for the relator. In an elaborate, ingenious, and eloquent speech he reviewed the legal and constitutional points involved in the case and cited the principal authorities.[61] He was followed by Charles Reedy, who delivered a masterful argument against the constitutionality of the law.[62] Eugene Cary, for the defense, then read a brief argument confined to questioning the power of the lower court to issue the mandamus prayed for in the petition. Edwin H. Ewing then closed for the relator. It will be noted that the defense made little argument in the case as compared with the elaborate speeches of the counsel for the relator. The inference is, though positive evidence does not exist, that the administration was already assured of the success of the case before the judges and that it did not think it necessary to expend the energies of its counsel in the open court.[63]

---

[60] Nashville *Daily Press and Times,* Jan. 28, 1867.

[61] Nashville *Union and Dispatch,* Jan. 26, 1867.

[62] Nashville *Daily Press and Times,* Jan. 26, 1867.

[63] The fervor with which the administration press greeted the decision also gives color to the charge that the court was unduly influenced by the Governor. The *Daily Press and Times,* referring to the decision, exclaimed, ''All honor to a firm, fearless, dispassionate judiciary. It stands forth today as the shining bulwark of the state. A grateful people will appreciate it.''— Nashville *Daily Press and Times,* Mar. 22, 1867.

The decision, which was in favor of Sherbrook, gave color to the above charge. The court merely decided that the elective franchise was not an inalienable right, but that it was only a political privilege which the people acting in their sovereign capacity might restrict, limit, or withhold. The arguments advanced so forceably in the decision of Judge Cooper, that the legislature which passed the law was an illegal body because of the exclusion of certain members, was dismissed with the sole statement that it was "wholly untenable."[64]

The Radicals were now in control of the executive, legislative, and judicial branches of the state government.

[64] Ridley v. Sherbrook, 3 Coldwell 56.

CHAPTER VI

THE NEGRO IN POLITICS

THE ESTABLISHMENT of Negro suffrage and the consequent rise of the freedmen to a position of political prestige were developments that were only gradually accomplished in Tennessee. The ratification of the new constitutional amendments on February 22, 1865, resulted, to use the words of Andrew Johnson, in "formally striking the shackles from the limbs of more than 275,000 slaves in the state,"[1] but it did not admit them to the franchise.[2] Indeed there is no evidence to show that the leaders of the administration contemplated the admission of the Negroes to the ballot-box at any early date. There was a clear distinction in the minds of these leaders between Negro freedom and Negro suffrage. The most of them probably agreed with Brownlow, who, in supporting the amendments, had declared: "To stand by slavery is to stand by rebellion. The nigger is the rebellion and the rebellion is the nigger, and to put down the one we have to get rid of the other."[3] In other words, the emancipation of the slaves in Tennessee was due to a desire to end the war and set the state right with the administration at

---

[1] Nashville *Daily Times and Union*, Feb. 27, 1865.

[2] No satisfactory explanation for the exception of Tennessee from the terms of the Emancipation Proclamation seems to exist. Blaine holds that it was due to the urgent request of Andrew Johnson. "He possessed the unbounded confidence of Mr. Lincoln, who yielded to his views respecting the best mode of restoring Tennessee to the Union and her inhabitants to the national government."—James G. Blaine, *Twenty Years in Congress*, I, 446. Another writer suggests that the omission was due to a provision in the act whereby North Carolina ceded her western lands to the national government, to the effect that "no regulation made or to be made by congress shall tend to emancipate slaves."—William Lloyd Imes, "Legal Status of Free Negroes and Slaves in Tennessee," *Journal of Negro History*, IV, 256. The real reason is doubtless to be found in Lincoln's desire to avoid giving offense to the border slave states.

[3] Knoxville *Whig*, Jan. 11, 1865.

Washington rather than to a design to effect the political advancement of the Negro.

The events accompanying the inauguration of the Brownlow administration gave little indication that there would be any change in this attitude toward the freedmen. It was a well known fact that the Governor himself had been a courageous and almost violent defender of the institution of slavery. In 1858 he had expressed his opinion that:

The condition of the southern negroes has been vastly improved by slavery. I also assert, without fear of successful contradiction, that slavery, only, could have worked that improvement, and that the preservation of the relation of master and slave is essential to the continued improvement and future welfare of the negro race of the South. I assert that "American Slavery" is a blessing; a blessing to the master, a blessing to the non-slaveholders of the South, a blessing to the civilized white race in general, and a blessing to the negro slaves in particular.[4]

Although he had reversed this opinion so far as to favor emancipation by the time that he became governor of the state, his initial message to the legislature gave no evidence that he had acquired a desire to extend political privileges to the former bondmen. He was exceedingly moderate in his suggestions in this message:

I am, myself, the advocate of providing for them [the Negroes] a separate and appropriate amount of territory, and settle them permanently, as a nation of freedmen. In this case, as in most others, it is well to guard against exceptive legislation. The negro has had no agency in bringing on our troubles, and does not merit unkind treatment at our hands.[5]

At the same time the members of the legislature seem to have been of like mind with the Governor, and a resolution was adopted postponing "all bills and resolutions having for their object any legislation upon the colored people of the state, until the meeting of the next session of the legislature."[6]

---

[4] Brownlow and Pryne, *Ought American Slavery to be Perpetuated*, p. 102.
[5] *Senate Journal, 34th Tenn. General Assembly, 1st Session, 1865*, p. 22.
[6] *Ibid.*, p. 55.

During the summer of 1865, however, a change occurred in the attitude of the Governor regarding the question of Negro suffrage. On July 3 he stated his views in the *Whig*:

The Negroes like the Indian tribes will gradually become extinct. Having no owners to care for them and no one owning property in them, they will cease to increase in numbers, cease to be looked after and cultivated, while educated labor will take the place of slave labor. Idleness, starvation, and disease will remove a majority of the negroes in this generation. The better class of them will go to work and sustain themselves, and that class ought to be allowed to vote, on the ground that a loyal negro is more worthy than a disloyal white man.[7]

The Governor was beginning to appreciate the force and value of the Negro vote should the race acquire the franchise. A further change in his attitude was manifested in his opening message to the second session of the legislature on October 3 of the same year:

I am free to admit, that, for the present, we have done enough for the negro, and, although negro voting cannot suit my natural prejudices of caste, there is a class of them I would be willing to see vote at once. A large class, ignorant, docile, easily led by designing men, and not safely to be trusted with political power, I am not willing to see at the ballot-box; but as even these have been faithful among the faithless, if rebels are to be restored to the right of the elective franchise, I would say let us no longer deny these political rights to the slaves. In my judgment a loyal negro is more eminently entitled to suffrage than a disloyal white man.[8]

The Governor had no love for the Negroes. On the contrary he thoroughly despised them. In a letter to the *Whig* in September, 1865, he characterized them as indolent and crazy, criticized their fiddling and dancing, and expressed his complete disapproval of colored soldiers, Negro balls, and the practice of miscegenation.[9]

[7] Knoxville *Whig*, Sept. 27, 1865.
[8] *Senate Journal, 34th Tenn. General Assembly, 2nd Session, 1865-6,* p. 11.
[9] Knoxville *Whig*, Sept. 27, 1865.

His design to admit the Negroes to the ballot-box was influenced by a desire to appease the radical majority that was rapidly gaining the ascendency in Congress and by the threatening attitude that the freedmen were coming to manifest.

The national administration was insistent in its demands that the Negroes be admitted to the franchise. Even Lincoln and Johnson had favored allowing the more intelligent ones to vote,[10] and Congress was more extreme in its demands. The force of these demands was distinctly felt in Tennessee. A. O. P. Nicholson, writing to the New York *Times,* lamented the fact that the radical party in the North seemed to be insistent upon the immediate enfranchisement of the Negroes in the state.[11]

At the same time the freedmen themselves were rapidly becoming a force to be reckoned with. Intelligent Negro agitators had come from other states and were exerting a strong influence upon the members of their race, and the Freedmen's Bureau was protecting them in this activity. On April 6 a petition had been sent to the legislature by a group of Negroes asking for "the legal right to use the elective franchise and to testify upon oath to the truth in the several courts of the state."[12] No action was taken upon this petition and the Negroes became restive. On August 7 a large meeting of colored men was held at Nashville. Nelson Walker, an intelligent and able Negro, was the chairman and guiding spirit of the meeting, and General Fisk, the assistant commissioner of the Freedmen's Bureau in Tennessee, was one of the speakers. A threatening attitude was assumed by those who attended the meeting, and a petition was sent to Congress demanding that the senators and representatives from Tennessee should not be admitted unless the

---

[10] A. B. Lapsey, ed., *The Writings of Abraham Lincoln,* VII, 102. For Johnson's view see note 36, *infra.*

[11] New York *Times,* July 7, 1865.

[12] *House Journal, 34th Tenn. General Assembly, 1st Session, 1865,* p. 35.

legislature should act upon the petition of April 6 before the first of December.[13]

The first action contemplating the admission of the Negroes to political rights was taken in the legislature on October 10, when John Trimble reported from the Senate judiciary committee a bill to render persons of African and Indian descent competent witnesses in all courts of the state.[14] Strangely enough the most intense opposition to this measure came from East Tennessee. Negroes were hated in that region, notwithstanding the fact that over thirty thousand of its citizens had served in the Union armies, and the speeches of the East Tennessee members of the legislature in opposition to the bill resembled the old ante-bellum philosophy of slavery. Benjamin Frazier of Knox County attacked the measure on the ground that it was "forestalling public opinion . . . in advance of the times, and in the face of deep and settled prejudices that should never be disregarded by the servants of the people."[15] To counteract the measure Frazier introduced a resolution calling for the establishment of a colonizing board to aid in sending the Negroes to Liberia. In support of this resolution he set forth a view that "the white man was the original proprietor. The Negro must always remain a hewer of wood and a drawer of water. His black skin and tainted blood will hang like an incubus upon his aspirations and efforts."[16] DeWitt Clinton Senter, also of East Tennessee, opposed the measure on the ground that it was inexpedient and would endanger the harmony and unity of the Union party in the state.[17]

John W. Bowen of Smith County took issue with Senter on this point and declared that the Union party of

[13] Nashville *Union*, Aug. 10, 1865.

[14] *Senate Journal, 34th Tenn. General Assembly, 2nd Session, 1865-6*, p. 43.

[15] Nashville *Daily Press and Times*, Oct. 21, 1865.

[16] Nashville *Union and Dispatch*, Dec. 12, 1865.

[17] Nashville *Daily Press and Times*, Oct. 25, 1865.

the United States was pledged to the policy of protecting
the emancipated slaves. "To oppose the principles of
this bill," he said, "is to oppose the great Union party
of the nation. The harmony of that party demands its
passage."[18] There was the usual outside pressure upon
the legislature. The Nashville *Union* advocated the bill
because it would serve to keep the Negroes out of the
Federal and Freedmen's Bureau courts, a distinct advantage to the whites.[19] After two weeks of desultory discussion, however, the bill passed the third reading in the
Senate and was sent to the House of Representatives.[20]

In the House there was much opposition to the bill,
especially from the representatives from East Tennessee.
H. P. Murphy of Johnson County delivered a long speech
in opposition to the bill, asserting that the Negroes and
whites could never live together on an equal basis. The
Negro, he alleged, was a distinct race and there would
always be friction between him and the whites. He therefore advocated that the United States should purchase
land in Africa, South America, or elsewhere, and colonize
the Negroes there.[21] The result of this opposition was
that the House judiciary committee to which the bill had
been referred reported unfavorably to its enactment. Two
reasons were given by the committee for this action; that
the majority of the people of the state were opposed to
the measure, and that legislation in favor of Negro
testimony would be premature at this time.[22]

The action of the judiciary committee called forth
the most strenuous protests from the friends of the bill,
especially from the administration press. The *Daily
Press and Times* viewed the matter with distinct alarm.
"Nothing is more certain," it stated, "than that no con-

[18] *Ibid.*, Oct. 25, 1865.
[19] Nashville *Daily Union*, Oct. 22, 1865.
[20] *Senate Journal, 34th Tenn. General Assembly, 2nd Session, 1865-6,*
p. 70.
[21] Nashville *Daily Union*, Dec. 2, 1865.
[22] Nashville *Daily Press and Times*, Nov. 22, 1865.

gressional delegation will be received at Washington from any state which refuses to allow Negro testimony. On this point congress and the president are in perfect harmony.''[23] Three members of the judiciary committee, headed by S. M. Arnell, submitted a minority report demanding the passage of the law in the interest of justice and humanity,[24] and William B. Lewis of Davidson County spoke at great length on the advantage to be derived from its passage in saving the state from inconvenience of the Freedmen's Bureau courts.[25] The pressure was so great that on January 23, 1866, a motion to reconsider the bill was passed.[26] After a slight amendment had been effected the bill passed the House on the next day.[27] The first step in the advancement of the emancipated slaves to political equality had been made.

By this time the Governor had become thoroughly committed to the policy of Radicalism. He professed to believe that the state was in great danger of being retaken by the rebels and that the support of the congressional Radicals was necessary to avert the horrors of another rebellion. Speaking at the opening exercises of the Fisk Freedmen's School on January 9, he said,

I advise the teachers, male and female, to be exceedingly prudent and cautious, and to do nothing offensive to the predominant party here. If General Thomas should take his soldiers away you would not be allowed to occupy this place a week. Our high civil and military functionaries may travel through the South hurriedly, and otherwise, and may go back to Washington and report that all is well and reconstructed, and those of you who are green enough to believe it, can believe; but pardon me when I tell you, that I don't believe a word of it.[28]

[23] *Ibid.,* Nov. 22, 1865.
[24] *House Journal, 34th Tenn. General Assembly, 2nd Session, 1865-6,* p. 162.
[25] Nashville *Daily Union,* Dec. 2, 1865.
[26] *House Journal, 34th Tenn. General Assembly, 2nd session, 1865-6,* p. 286.
[27] *Ibid.,* p. 295.
[28] Nashville *Union and American,* Jan. 10, 1866. The ''high civil and military functionaries'' was a reference to General Grant, Carl Schurz, and

In March he openly avowed his Radicalism. In a speech before the German Union League of Knoxville, he said,

I announce to you that if Andy Johnson is to lead the way in reconstruction with the Democratic Party at his back, I go the other way. I go with the Congress of the United States, the so-called radicals, I do not fear to side with them. The name of radical has no terrors for me. I have been known as a "damned blue-light whig" and a "damned lunatic," and I think it cheap if they will now let me off by calling me a "damned radical."[29]

In accordance with the Radical policy of the administration the legislature, now completely under the Governor's control, passed another law on May 26 granting still further privileges to the Negroes. It provided that all persons of color should have "the right to make and enforce contracts, to sue and be sued, to be parties and give evidence, to inherit, and to have full and equal benefits of all laws and proceedings for the security of persons and estates," and "should not be subject to any other or different punishments, pains, or penalty, for the commission of any act or offense, then such as are provided for white persons committing like acts or offenses."[30]

Tennessee thereupon became an attractive state for Negroes, and hundreds of those who had been taken South to avoid the Union armies now returned. An observer reported in April that they were coming in large numbers:

When I left Selma, Alabama, last fall, a constant stream of them, of all ages and conditions, were pouring through that city on their way, as they always told me, to Mississippi or Tennessee. Many were transported free by our government, while many were on foot, trudging hopefully but painfully toward their old homes from which they had been taken to escape our armies.[31]

others who had recently been on investigating tours in the South. Grant's report, in particular, was quite favorable to the South.

[29] Nashville *Daily Union*, Mar. 28, 1866.
[30] *Acts, 34th Tenn. General Assembly, 2nd Session, 1865-6*, p. 65.
[31] *Senate Ex. Docs.*, 39 Cong., 1 Sess., No. 43.

Even more hopeful conditions were in store for these refugees as well as for the Negroes that were already in the state, for the Governor's next move was to give them the suffrage. In September he attended the southern loyalist convention which met at Philadelphia for the purpose of foiling President Johnson's reconstruction policy. During the course of the convention he made a speech in which he stated his intention to extend the elective franchise to the Negroes of Tennessee at the earliest possible convenience.

We have but one more law to pass, and that is a law enfranchising the negroes, and we will do it next winter. We have two reasons for doing this: it is necessary for sixty or seventy thousand votes to kick the beam to weigh down the balance against rebellion. The second reason is because it is proper, just, and we will simply be returning to where we were in 1833. The negroes used to vote in Tennessee. Old Jackson, and John Bell, and Felix Grundy used to treat them with liquor, and electioneer with them for votes. John Bell once beat Felix Grundy for congress in the Nashville district, by a few votes, and would not have done so but for the negro vote.[32]

The Conservative *Union and American* greeted this announcement with ridicule and sarcasm. In an editorial entitled "The Two Faces of Brownlow," it pointed out the inconsistency between his attitude in the debate with Pryne and this speech at a "black and tan convention."[33] The Radical *Press and Times,* on the other hand, supported his demand for Negro suffrage and referred to the great advantages that were to be derived from granting it:

Our friends in Tennessee have the strongest reasons which could possibly be presented to them to establish impartial suffrage during the present session of the legislature. If they fail to do it, a tedious, protracted, and violent struggle must immediately take place, in which the rebels will receive all the help that a perfidious President can give them. The power is now in

[32] Nashville *Union and American,* Sept. 16, 1866.
[33] *Ibid.,* Sept. 14, 1866.

Top: THE SOUTHERN LOYALISTS' CONVENTION AT PHILADELPHIA IN 1866—
"PARSON BROWNLOW" PASSING THROUGH THE RANKS OF THE NORTHERN
DELEGATION IN INDEPENDENCE SQUARE. FROM AN ENGRAVING IN HARPER'S
WEEKLY.

Bottom: "PARSON BROWNLOW" ENTERING THE KNOXVILLE JAIL AS A
PRISONER OF THE CONFEDERATE AUTHORITIES IN 1861. FROM AN ENGRAVING
IN PARSON BROWNLOW'S BOOK.

our hands, and every consideration of statesmanship and humanity appeals to us to use it for the protection of all who love the
union.[34]

The second adjourned session of the legislature convened on November 5, 1866.[35] In his initial message the
Governor again discussed the question of Negro suffrage.
He violently criticized the intention of the President to
extend the franchise to the colored race only gradually,[36]
and utilized his accustomed argument against antagoniz-
ing the Radical party in Congress. "I think we should
now, without great and controlling reasons," he added,
"sever ourselves from that great national party, whose
wisdom and courage saved the life of the nation, and
rescued the loyal people of Tennessee from the hand of
the oppressor." Negro suffrage, in his opinion, was
"bound to follow as one of the great results of the rebellion," and he thought that "all of this great outcry
against a negro voting in any contingency" came "from
a lingering sentiment of disloyalty in the South."[37]

No action was taken upon this portion of the measure
until after the Christmas recess was over, but in January,
1867, W. A. Garner of Lawrence County introduced a
bill in the lower house providing for Negro suffrage.[38]
This bill passed the third reading on February 6 and was
thereupon sent to the Senate.[39] There it was slightly
changed but was passed on February 25.[40] The lower

[34] Nashville *Daily Press and Times*, Nov. 14, 1866.

[35] It should be noted that the Fourteenth Amendment had been ratified
by an extra session of the legislature on July 19, 1866.

[36] Johnson gave this view in a letter to George L. Stearns of Boston, on
October 3, 1865. "If I were in Tennessee," he wrote to Stearns, "I
would try to introduce negro suffrage gradually; first those who served in
the army; those who could read and write, and perhaps a property qualification for others, say $200 or $250. It would not do to let the negroes
have universal suffrage now; it would breed a war of races."—Nashville
Dispatch, Oct. 27, 1865.

[37] *House Journal, 34th Tenn. General Assembly, 3rd Session, 1866-7,*
pp. 16-17.

[38] *Ibid.*, p. 179.   [39] *Ibid.*, p. 243.

[40] *Senate Journal, 34th Tenn. General Assembly, 3rd Session, 1866-7,*
p. 355.

house concurred in the changes made in the bill by the Senate, and the measure became a law on the following day. This bill, which was entitled "An Act to Alter and Amend an Act Passed May 3, 1866," granted the franchise to the Negroes indirectly. It provided that "every male inhabitant of the state, of the age of twenty-one years, a citizen of the United States, and a resident of the county where he may offer his vote, six months next preceding the day of election, shall be entitled to the privilege of the elective franchise," subject to certain exceptions and qualifications.[41] None of these exceptions and qualifications applied to the Negroes, however, and as they had been made citizens of the United States by the adoption of the Fourteenth Amendment, the emancipated slaves were thus admitted to the ballot-box.

The more intense section of the Conservative press bitterly assailed the law. The Memphis *Appeal* was especially severe:

It would be better for the whole black breed to be swept away by a pestilence. This may sound harsh but it is true. . . . If one had the power and could not otherwise prevent that curse and inconceivable calamity, in many of the southern states, it would be a solemn duty for him to annihilate the race. The right to vote might just as safely be given to so many South American monkeys as to the plantation negroes of Mississippi and Louisiana.[42]

The more thoughtful and designing Conservatives, however, saw in the new law a powerful instrument that might be utilized to their own advantage. The Lebanon *Herald* thought "that if proper steps are taken, the great bulk of the negro votes can be turned against the radicals."[43]

In a speech at Winchester on March 4, 1867, A. S. Colyar followed the advice of the Lebanon editor and made a strong appeal for Negro votes. He asserted:

[41] *Acts, 34th Tenn. General Assembly, 3rd Session, 1866-7*, pp. 27-33.
[42] Memphis *Appeal*, Feb. 26, 1867.   [43] Lebanon *Herald*, Feb. 27, 1867.

Any appliance will be used, and every conceivable device resorted to to prejudice the freemen against their former masters, and it will be well for us to see that [sic.] he is not misled. Fortunately, notwithstanding the late war, in which it was confidently predicted there would be a war of races, there is the best possible feeling between the two races. They [the Negroes] know very well that slavery was established, not by us, but by the people from whom we are descended; that we did not make them slaves, and that we were their best friends when they were slaves, and that we have been by no means unmindful of their interest since they were freed.[44]

This speech was circulated widely among the freedmen by the Conservatives as campaign propaganda. At the same time Edmund Cooper, a Conservative candidate for Congress, made a similar appeal. Speaking at Shelbyville he said that he had always expressed doubts as to the wisdom of admitting Negroes to the ballot-box, but that, as the law had been enacted, he would regard the colored men as his constituents in the campaign.[45]

The Negro thus came to occupy a favored position in the political situation in the state. Both parties desired his vote, and he was in a position to demand terms of them. The "Negro in politics" had become a reality, and Negro suffrage was a two-edged weapon that might be turned against its fabricators.

Elections were to be held for both governor and congressmen in the fall of 1867, and the Radical and Conservative parties alike exerted themselves to secure the support of the recently enfranchised Negroes. In the end the Radicals were successful, but the Conservatives made a strenuous effort to enlist the aid of the blacks. The first attempt of the Conservatives to utilize the Negro strength was made at Nashville on April 1, when members of that race were invited to participate in the county convention held for the purpose of selecting delegates to the state Conservative convention. This attempt was

[44] Nashville *Daily Press and Times*, Mar. 11, 1867.
[45] Nashville *Union and Dispatch*, Apr. 4, 1867.

unsuccessful. The *Press and Times* sarcastically called it "Moses Johnson's April Fool Meeting" and described it as a "signal failure to inveigle the colored population into the ranks of the Conservative party."[46] This description was not entirely correct, for some of the Negroes did join with the Conservatives.

A colored convention met at Nashville on April 6, in spite of the attempts of the Radicals to prevent it, and resolutions were adopted supporting the Conservative program. In a speech before the convention, John Williams, a Negro, strongly condemned the Radicals because they were proposing to silence all the blacks who would not vote the Radical ticket. The tone of the convention was decidedly Conservative. "Believing that the spirit and tendencies of radicalism are unfavorable to our aims," its resolutions read, "we take our stand with the true union conservatives of Tennessee and invite our race throughout the state to do the same."[47]

When the state Conservative convention met at Nashville on April 16 it adopted a very conciliatory attitude toward the Negro voters. "Our colored fellow-citizens" were declared to be "entitled to all rights and privileges under the constitution and laws of the United States and the state of Tennessee." Even a speech by John Williams was loudly applauded.[48] The nomination of Emerson Etheridge for governor, however, was extremely ill-advised and it contributed greatly towards alienating the support of the Negroes. Etheridge was a former slaveholder who had bitterly resented emancipation. In a speech at Trenton on April 19, only three days before his nomination he had assumed a very unfriendly attitude toward the blacks:

The negroes are no more free than they were forty years ago, and if any one goes about the country telling them that they

---

[46] Nashville *Daily Press and Times*, Apr. 2, 1867.
[47] Nashville *Union and Dispatch*, Apr. 7, 1867.
[48] *Ibid.*, Apr. 17, 1867.

are free, shoot him; and these negro troops, commanded by low and degraded white men, going through the country ought to be shot down.[49]

It was scarcely to be expected that the Negroes would support a man who was so unfavorable to their interests, and thus the Conservatives, in the nomination of Etheridge, contributed to the alienation of the Negro vote from their party.

A more compelling factor in alienating the Negro vote from the Conservatives was the organization of the so-called Union Leagues. As early as February, 1867, the Radicals were active in this work, and the *Union and Dispatch* called attention to it in an editorial:

We are informed that the radicals are now very busy in the work of initiating our colored fellow-citizens into the radical leagues. They are, we learn, required to take an oath upon admission, the exact purport of which has not been disclosed; but the object of it is understood to be the support of the radical ticket at the ballot-box and the radical revolutionary authority in general. The proceedings are held in secret, and the political ritual is particularly confined to the "loyal tycoons who manipulate the party wires."[50]

These Union Leagues were very active in arranging Negro mass meetings and in promoting sentiment in favor of the Brownlow administration. A number of mass meetings were held in April, usually under the direction of the league members. On April 3 a meeting at Chattanooga endorsed Brownlow for governor. Thomas King, a Negro, spoke in terms of strong denunciation of the "copperheads." To vote for this party, he said, was only sharpening a knife to cut the Negro's throat:

When Brownlow went into office he commenced to labor unceasingly for the elevation and education of the colored race. To him we owe the privilege of casting our votes today, and the

[49] Nashville *Daily Press and Times*, Apr. 19, 1867.
[50] Nashville *Union and Dispatch*, Feb. 15, 1867.

colored man would be an ingrate indeed who would not cast his vote for the savior of his political and educational freedom.[51]

At Jonesboro a meeting was held under the direction of the Reverend Amos J. Beman, a Connecticut minister who was attached to the educational service of the Freedmen's Bureau. Resolutions were adopted to the effect that:

We tender our heartfelt thanks to Governor Brownlow for his noble and patriotic course in the administration of the laws of the state, and his devotion to liberty and justice, as applied to us and our race, and we will, as an evidence of our deeply felt gratitude for those generous acts, give him our undivided support in the election in August next, for the position which he now occupies.

The actions and proceedings of the Radical legislature were also endorsed, and it was agreed to oppose all those whom "we find arrayed with those who would forever make us the hewers of wood and the drawers of water."[52]

On April 14 there was a "grand pow-wow" of Negroes at the capitol in Nashville. It was opened with a speech by Abraham Smith, praising the Radical administration of the state:

If it had not been for the radicals we would be slaves today, and our prayers should ever ascend to God for the grand cause. The radicals fought four years to free you, and the rebels fought four years to enslave you. All the radicals in the Tennessee legislature voted to give you the right of suffrage, and the rebels voted against it. To vote for a conservative is to vote for the chains of slavery to be riveted to your necks.

Resolutions were offered endorsing Brownlow for governor and others severely criticizing Andrew Johnson:

We deeply regret the transmorphoses of our once beloved "Moses" into the slave-catching "Pharaoh" of ancient Egypt, and that the dynasty of our glorious republic should be so

[51] Nashville *Daily Press and Times*, Apr. 6, 1867.
[52] *Ibid.*, Apr. 9, 1867.

tarnished by "His Ascendency" as chief executive of the nation.[53]

Under such conditions it soon became evident that the Negroes would support the Radical candidates almost without exception at the elections in August. The Conservatives were greatly disappointed at this development, and they made some efforts to intimidate the Negroes. In Franklin County, a Conservative stronghold, threats were made against Negroes who might dare to vote the Radical ticket,[54] and at Memphis it was said that those who would not support the Conservatives would lose their jobs. At the latter place about fifty of them were driven from their homes for voting the Radical ticket, but this amounted to little in a population of several thousands of Negroes.[55] This was done, according to the Knoxville *Whig,* by a very low class of Conservatives:

That class of conservative editors who now talk of proscribing negroes are men who would never be able to employ more than one or two servants, and who did not always pay them their just dues. Such rebels as own property and pay their store accounts and pay the negroes for their labor, are not the people who have made these threats to "starve" the negro. But a poor devil, who has no meat and bread to feed his own starving children, makes a great noise about starving radical negroes.[56]

The Negroes who had been threatened in Franklin County sent a request to the Governor, asking that a supply of Colt revolvers and ammunition be sent to them. The request was complied with, and there was little further attempt made to molest them in the exercise of the elective franchise.[57]

The election returns indicated that the Radicals had been eminently successful in their measures designed to

[53] Nashville *Union and Dispatch,* Apr. 14, 1867.
[54] Letter of J. W. Brown to Governor Brownlow, Brownlow Papers.
[55] Knoxville *Whig,* Sept. 18, 1867.
[56] *Ibid.,* Sept. 18, 1867.
[57] Letter of J. W. Brown to Governor Brownlow, May 21, 1867, Brownlow Papers.

secure the Negro vote. Brownlow received 74,484 votes, while Etheridge, his opponent, received only 22,584.[58] A Radical congressional delegation was also chosen. As Brownlow had received only 23,353 votes in 1865, and as the elective franchise had not been greatly extended to whites since that time, it would seem that his majority was largely increased by the votes of the freedmen. This was the view taken by the Conservatives at least. The Paris *Intelligencer,* commenting on the election, said,

The untutored and illiterate fanatics of East Tennessee and the ignorant and superstitious Africans of Middle and West Tennessee have united and elected Brownlow governor for the next two years. The uninformed, non-reading whites of the mountains and the blacks of the other sections of the state have alike been made the miserable dupes of this foul oligarchy.[59]

The contest to secure the Negro vote was repeated in 1868, when the presidential election was approaching. In March the Governor announced his intention to oppose those who were demanding "a white man's government":

I cannot but regard all such movements as alike inexpedient, unjust, and mischievous. I will enter upon no sectionalizing conspiracy to proscribe northern men. I will not consent, for one, that fraud and oppression shall be practiced upon the colored man.[60]

At the same time the legislature, mindful of the events that occurred in Memphis during the recent election, passed a law that the state should "guarantee to any man the right to go to the polls and vote without fear or molestation." The act provided further that,

No person shall be allowed to make contracts with work-hands or others in their employ, that will, or is intended to, keep them from going to the polls on election days; nor shall they, or any party, have the legal right to claim that any contract has been

[58] *American Annual Cyclopedia, 1867,* p. 709.
[59] Paris *Intelligencer,* Aug. 12, 1867.
[60] Address of Governor Brownlow to the loyal people of Tennessee, Nashville *Union and Dispatch,* Mar. 20, 1869.

violated because parties or individuals in their employ have left their work to go and vote on election days in their county.[61]

This renewed activity on the part of the administration was made all the more necessary because of two factors: the criticism of the Governor by certain Radical Negroes who thought that he had not gone far enough in his efforts to secure political and economic equality for the members of their race, and by the presence, in alarming proportions, of the Ku Klux Klan which had been recently organized for the purpose of counteracting the influence of the Union Leagues among the Negroes.

There was a distinct disposition on the part of the more advanced Radical Negroes to find fault with the Brownlow administration. A group of these recalcitrants held a meeting at the court house in Nashville on July 7, and a speech, abounding in carping criticism, was delivered by Randall Brown, one of their number.

You all, gentlemen, voted for Brownlow. What has he done for you? He may be a clever man; I hope he is, but what has he done for us? He has been governor a long time. He has appointed about one hundred and twenty men to office, and he has never put a colored man in office.[62]

On the other hand the activities of the Ku Klux Klan made it very necessary for the administration to take active and immediate steps to prevent that organization from detaching the Negro vote from the Radicals. As a means of preventing such a consummation the administration determined to continue in effect the disabilities under which the former Confederates had labored since the close of the war. In his message to the legislature on July 27, 1868, the Governor gave unmistakable evidence that such was his intention.

I have been appealed to by prominent men of both political parties, to urge upon you the propriety of removing political

[61] *Acts, 35th Tenn. General Assembly, 1st session, 1867-8,* pp. 86-7.
[62] Nashville *Daily Press and Times,* July 9, 1869.

disabilities formerly imposed upon a large class of rebels. The conduct of that class of people has been, and still is, such that I do not feel justified in making this recommendation. They have a military organization in this state, whose avowed object is to trample the laws under foot and force the party in power to enfranchise themselves and their sympathizers. I cannot stultify myself by yielding to this request, accompanied with threats of violence.[63]

The chief aim of the Conservatives was to prevent the Negro from voting at all, and it was to this end that the Ku Klux Klan was organized. There was some effort made, however, to secure the Negro vote for Seymour and Blair. Edwin H. Ewing and A. S. Colyar canvassed Middle Tennessee in the interest of these candidates, but they were contemptuously characterized by the Governor as "rebel gas pipes and blow hards."[64] At the same time he issued an appeal to the colored citizens of the state, through the columns of the Knoxville *Whig*, warning them against any activity that might attempt to seduce them to vote for the Democratic candidate for president.[65]

In the presidential campaign the Radicals were again successful, and the electoral vote of Tennessee was cast for Grant and Colfax. A comparison of the popular vote in that election with that cast in the gubernatorial election in 1867, however, seems to indicate that the activity of the Conservatives and the Ku Klux Klan had not been entirely misspent. Grant received almost twenty thousond votes less than Brownlow had received, while Seymour received only four thousand more than Etheridge had received in 1867. As the decrease in the number of Radical votes cast was not accounted for by a corresponding increase in the vote of the Conservatives, it is reasonable to suppose that this increase was due in large

[63] *Senate Journal, 35th Tenn. General Assembly, Extra Session, 1868,* p. 10.
[64] Knoxville *Whig*, Aug. 26, 1868.
[65] *Ibid.*, Sept. 2, 1868.

HORATIO SEYMOUR AND HIS FRIENDS!

HOW DEMOCRATS TREAT THE COLORED MAN!

"Remember this: that the bloody, and treasonable, and revolutionary doctrine of public necessity can be proclaimed by a MOB as well as by a Government."

These were the words of Horatio Seymour, Presidential candidate of the Rebel Democracy, delivered on the Fourth of July, 1863, in the city of New York.

On the thirteenth day of July, 1863, the Democratic MOB, thus appealed to, attacked the office of an Assistant Provost Marshal, charged in part with the execution of a conscription ordered by President Lincoln. Gettysburg, Vicksburg, Port Hudson, and other fields, had rendered necessary the refilling of the Union armies.

The MOB by whom the Provost Marshal's office was destroyed held the city for several days, growing in numbers, brutality, licentiousness, and treason with each hour's sway. This seditious riot was the reserve of Lee's army, and had evidently been organized to act in concert as to advance on Philadelphia. His early defeat, however, prevented the consummation of the conspiracy, of which Horatio Seymour's words, quoted above, are the key-note. Rebel agents were leading the mob, and actively inciting it to greater atrocities Just before it broke out, Clement L. Vallandigham, the leader of the Northern Rebels, who had been sent South beyond the Union lines on account of seditious speeches and acts, ran the blockade at Wilmington, N. C., reached the British port of Nassau, and sailed immediately, with a party of Confederate agents, for Halifax, Nova Scotia, avowing on the voyage that his object was the direction of riots to be fomented in Northern cities, and designed to aid projected military movements of the Confederacy He arrived about the twenty-eighth of June, 1863. At that date the Rebel army, under Lee, was occupying the Cumberland Valley, in Pennsylvania. The Copperhead, Vallandigham, left Halifax for Boston. Attempts to incite riots were made there immediately after his arrival. They failed In New York Horatio Seymour, acting in concert with Lee in Pennsylvania, and Vallandigham in Boston and Canada, advised the MOB that it was lawful for them to resist the Government The MOB bettered the bloody instructions; and, during the time in which they held sway, burned, destroyed, and plundered private property to the amount of ONE MILLION THREE HUNDRED AND SIXTY-SIX THOUSAND THREE HUNDRED AND SEVENTY-NINE DOLLARS, ($1,366,379,) besides destroying public property to a large extent. The fury of the Democratic rioters was chiefly turned upon prominent Republicans, and especially upon the unoffending colored people of the city. The buildings of the COLORED ORPHAN ASYLUM was burned to the ground, and its inmates brutally outraged. A majority were only saved from murder by the exertions of the Metropolitan Police, under the command of a Republican Superintendent, Mr. Kennedy. The publication office of the *Tribune* was gutted, the house of Mayor Opdyke, a Republican, was plundered. All leading Union men's lives were threatened, their residences attacked, robbed, and in many instances, burned Everywhere the NEGROES were assailed, hung on trees—in one instance burned alive—beaten to death, without regard to sex or age. It was only by the greatest exertions of the military and police that the lives of any of these unoffending citizens were saved. During the prevalence of this reign of terror, FIFTEEN HUNDRED (1,500) PERSONS were murdered and maltreated, only ONE HUNDRED AND SIXTY-SIX (166) of whom were white persons Fifteen soldiers were killed, and seventy-two wounded. Seventy-six white civilians (rioters) and three females were also killed. About one-half of these were known to be rioters. The balance of those known to be killed and wounded were colored persons many of them being women and children

In the midst of this carnage, Governor Seymour arrived. On the fourteenth of July, the second day of the riot, he addressed the congregated assassins and Democrats in front of the City Hall. They stopped in their bloody and seditious brutalities to listen to the following speech

"MY FRIENDS: I have come down here from the quiet of the country to see what was the difficulty; to learn what all this trouble was concerning the draft. Let me assure you that I am YOUR FRIEND. [Uproarious cheering.] YOU HAVE BEEN MY FRIENDS—[Cries of 'Yes, yes!' 'That's so!' 'We are, and will be again!']—and now I assure you, my fellow-citizens, that I am here to show you a test of my FRIENDSHIP. [Cheers.] I wish to inform you that I have sent my Adjutant General to Washington to confer with the authorities there, AND TO HAVE THIS DRAFT SUSPENDED AND STOPPED! [Vociferous cheers] I ask you, as good citizens, to wait for his return; and I assure you that I will do all that I can to see that there is no inequality and no wrong done to any one. I WISH YOU TO TAKE GOOD CARE OF ALL PROPERTY, AS GOOD CITIZENS, AND SEE THAT EVERY PERSON IS SAFE. The safe keeping of property and persons rests with you, and I charge you to disturb neither. It is your duty to maintain the good order of the city, and I know you will do it. I wish you now to separate as good citizens, and YOU CAN ASSEMBLE AGAIN WHENEVER YOU WISH TO DO SO. I ask you to leave it all to me now, and I WILL SEE TO YOUR RIGHTS. Wait until my Adjutant returns from Washington, AND YOU SHALL BE SATISFIED. Listen to me, and see that there is no harm done to persons or property, but retire peaceably."

Major General JOHN A. DIX, then commanding in New York, knew his man, and, when SEYMOUR made an enquiry about troops, replied: "I BEG TO LET YOU KNOW THAT I HAVE TROOPS ENOUGH AT MY COMMAND TO TAKE CARE, NOT ONLY OF THE RIOTERS, BUT OF YOU."

Let it be remembered that Horatio Seymour, Democratic candidate for President, encouraged the New York rioters by recognizing them, while their hands were red with loyal blood, as " HIS FRIENDS!"

Let it be remembered that no leading Democrat was injured by them!

Let it be remembered that Vallandigham, who was charged by Jeff. Davis to incite riots in the North, nominated Horatio Seymour in the recent Democratic Convention!

Let it be remembered that this same Vallandigham is a candidate for Congress, in the interest of the new Rebellion, threatened by Seymour, Blair, Wade Hampton, Fort Pillow-Forrest & Co.!

Let it be remembered that all the New York rioters, now living, will vote for SEYMOUR and BLAIR, and against GRANT and COLFAX!

Let it be remembered that the rebels who deserted their country's flag, and tried to destroy, through bloody rebellion, this FREE REPUBLIC, will vote for SEYMOUR and BLAIR, in the hope of winning at the ballot-box what they lost on the field—the continued enslavement of the colored man, and the triumph of those who claim that this Government was not established for ALL MEN, but for the WHITE MAN'S benefit only

Let it be remembered that every colored voter who acts with the Democracy sustains the party that sustained slavery, desires caste to be established by his own disfranchisement, and upholds the New York Democratic murderers and rioters, who killed so many members of his own race!!

FACSIMILE OF A POSTER USED BY THE RADICALS DURING THE PRESIDENTIAL CAMPAIGN OF 1868.

measure to the fact that great numbers of Negroes remained away from the polls.[66]

The election of 1867 marked the climax of the Negro
in politics; that of 1868 the beginning of the return of the
Conservatives to power in Tennessee.

[66] Grant received a popular vote of 56,766; Seymour, 26,311. *American
Annual Cyclopedia, 1868,* p. 725.

CHAPTER VII

THE ACTIVITIES OF THE FREEDMEN'S BUREAU

THE SOCIAL and economic consequences of emancipation in Tennessee were perhaps of equal importance with the entrance of the Negroes into politics, and, in point of time, they antedated the latter problem by a period of four years. Immediately upon the advent of the Union armies in the state in 1862 slaves began to seek the camps for protection, subsistence, or mere gratification of idle curiosity. Some were fleeing from their masters; others had been left on plantations whence their owners had been driven by the Union forces or the Confederate conscription acts. Some came of their own volition; others were enticed by the overzealous activities of abolitionist soldiers. The number of these refugees was not so great in Tennessee as in some of the other Southern states, but those who came were penniless, ignorant, and inexperienced in directing the labor of their own hands. Believing the Union army to be an army of emancipation, and filled with unbounded confidence in the Northern soldiers, they sought with the latter the protection that had been formerly afforded by their masters.[1] It therefore became necessary to devise at once some plans for the relief of these childlike blacks who had so implicitly entrusted themselves to the Federal commanders.

The first systematic efforts for the relief of the Negroes who had been rendered destitute by the rebellion occurred in the fall of 1862 when General Grant appointed Colonel John Eaton as superintendent of Negro affairs in his department. Eaton was a young chaplain of an Ohio regiment, a native of New Hampshire, and had for-

[1] Paul S. Peirce, *The Freedmen's Bureau, A Chapter in the History of Reconstruction*, p. 1.

merly served as superintendent of schools in Toledo. Under his direction a contraband camp was established in West Tennessee, where the Negroes were employed in gathering and marketing the corn and cotton crops and in cutting wood for the government steamers on the Mississippi River. All the refugees were well provided with food, clothing, shelter, and medicine, and the proceeds of the crops were placed to the credit of the government.[2] This experiment proved to be the nucleus of a very extensive system, and, according to General Grant, it was the effort from which the Freedmen's Bureau originated.[3]

In his work Colonel Eaton was aided materially by the activity of certain benevolent societies, the most important of which was the Western Sanitary Commission with headquarters at St. Louis.[4] This society had been organized originally for the purpose of improving the sanitary conditions in the army camps and caring for the health and general comfort of the soldiers. Its agents, however, seeing the hardships and privations that were being experienced by the refugee Negroes, with whom they came into contact, speedily turned their attention to this class as well as to the soldiers. Under the sanction of the President and the secretary of war the Commission shortly thereafter extended its relief to Negroes living in the Mississippi valley. Hospitals were improved, supplies were distributed, and Negro recruits were given advantage of the same sanitary improvements and hospital service as was afforded to the white soldiers.[5]

Colonel Eaton co-operated with the benevolent societies in the work of affording relief to the freedmen.[6] In

[2] *House Ex. Docs.*, 39 Cong., 1 Sess., No. 11, p. 19.

[3] Ulysses S. Grant, *Personal Memoirs*, I, 424.

[4] ''Annual Report of the Western Sanitary Commission for the Years Ending July, 1862, and July 1863,'' *North American Review*, XCVIII (1864), 519-30.

[5] *Ibid.*, p. 520.

[6] The term *freedman* came to be used in Tennessee after January 1,

accordance with instructions from the secretary of war in 1863 he chose local school superintendents and a general educational officer, established sewing and other industrial schools, and introduced a large and effective school system. He appointed a general officer charged with the control of property and detailed assistant superintendents to supervise the registration of Negroes, contracts for labor, location of camps, and the care of the infirm, vagrant, and idle Negroes on plantations. In November, 1863, a surgeon was detailed as a medical director and inspector of freedmens' hospitals, camps, and colonies. These officials were generally efficient, and Eaton's efforts, though brief, were notably successful.[7]

During the same year Adjutant-General Lorenzo Thomas was sent to organize Negro troops in the Mississippi valley. After learning something of the social and industrial conditions there, he appointed commissioners to superintend the leasing of plantations and the enforcement of contracts. Terms of leasing and hiring of Negroes were prescribed, wages were fixed, and provisions were made for the humane treatment of the freedmen.[8] After the fall of Vicksburg General Grant found the number of idle and destitute greatly increasing, and he issued a series of orders culminating in a detailed and comprehensive plan for the care of the Negroes and the regulation of their labor. Camps for the unemployed were established at all military posts, and officers were designated to distribute supplies, provide employment, and supervise contracts.[9] Later Adjutant-General Thomas supplemented this by an order forbidding Negroes to remain idle, advising women and children to stay on plantations controlled by Federal troops, promising

1863, when the Emancipation Proclamation went into effect, although the slaves were not freed in that state until two years later.

[7] H. M. Doak, "The Development of Education in Tennessee," *American Historical Magazine*, VIII, 84. See also Peirce, *op. cit.*, pp. 15-17.

[8] *American Annual Cyclopedia, 1863*, p. 428.

[9] Frank Moore, *Rebellion Record*, VIII, 479.

protection to Negroes, and permitting the occupants of plantations to employ them in any capacity best suited to their ability.[10]   These orders embody the main features of the policy that was adopted for this region in 1863. For a time, Adjutant-General Thomas was pleased with the results of this policy, but, as it was soon evident, his measures had been premature.

It will be recalled that after Bragg's disaster at Chattanooga in December, 1863, the danger of a permanent Confederate occupation of Tennessee disappeared. This situation afforded an opportunity for more extensive relief work among the freedmen, and on February 4, 1864, under the direction of the adjutant-general, colored refugee camps were established at Nashville, Clarksville, Gallatin, and Columbia. All Negro refugees capable of bearing arms were to be put in the army, and all others, including women and children, were to be required to perform such labor as might be suited to their several conditions. This included work in the army as teamsters, wood-choppers, and cooks and work on the plantations and farms. The arrangement was not very successful. There was abundant graft and corruption practiced, and the conditions among the freedmen were not greatly improved.[11]

Complaints were entered against the administration of the campus, and on June 2, 1864 the Senate appointed Thomas Hood and S. W. Bostwick as special commissioners to investigate and report on the condition and treatment of colored refugees in Kentucky, Tennessee, and Alabama.[12]   These commissioners found the camp at Nashville, in charge of Captain Ralph Hunt, ''wholly destitute of anything tending to the reasonable comfort of its most unfortunate inmates.''   From the testimony which they took it appears that Hunt was engaged in the

[10] *Ibid.*, p. 479.
[11] *Sen. Ex. Docs.*, 38 Cong., 2 Sess., No. 28, p. 1.
[12] *Ibid.*, p. 2.

most extensive and flagrant corruption. He had five horses for his own private use. He had taken brick from the commissary to build himself a storehouse, had it hauled with government teams, and had the building work done by colored refugees at government expense. He had had large quantities of food and coal carried from the commissary to the home of a Mrs. Mason where he boarded. Poor and insufficient clothing was furnished to the refugees, and the children were not placed in school. Ninety-six thousand dollars was due to the Negroes for work on the government fortifications at Nashville and other places, but they had been given no certificates and hence had no claim on the government.[13] Conditions were found to be satisfactory at Clarksville and Gallatin,[14] but "the most flagrant and enormous abuse of colored men and women" was reported at Columbia, where slaves were reported as having been surrendered to their masters by whom they were whipped and extraordinary favors were granted to secessionists. Hood and Bostwick were of the opinion that "the entire course followed by General Rousseau has done great injustice to the policy of the government."[15]

No action was taken upon this report, but it afforded unmistakable evidence of the presence of disorder and confusion in the administration of relief to colored refugees in Tennessee. This confusion was further complicated by the fact that the whole matter of organization and administration of camps, leasing of plantations, and employing of Negroes had been transferred from the war department to the treasury department on March 3, 1863.[16] The number of benevolent societies had also increased, and, although they usually co-operated with the military commanders, their presence and activities necessarily made for a division of responsibility. In the

[13] *Ibid.*, pp. 4-8.
[14] *Ibid.*, pp. 9-10.   [15] *Ibid.*, pp. 17-18.
[16] *United States Statutes at Large*, XII, 820-21.

spring of 1865, therefore, three sets of functionaries, military commanders, treasury agents, and representatives of benevolent organizations, were attempting to deal with the problem of abandoned and confiscated lands, fugitive Negroes, and white refugees. To meet these conditions and to provide for a better co-ordination of effort in dealing with the freedmen, Congress passed an act, on March 3, 1865, creating in the war department "a bureau of refugees, freedmen, and abandoned lands," commonly called the Freedmen's Bureau.[17]

To this new bureau was committed the supervision and management of all abandoned lands and the control of all subjects relating to refugees and freedmen from the rebel states or from any other district embraced in the operations of the army. It was to continue "during the present war of rebellion and one year thereafter."[18] At its head was a commissioner, appointed by the President with the advice and consent of the Senate. In like manner an assistant commissioner might be appointed for each of the ten states declared to be in insurrection. The commissioner was required to make an annual report to the President and special reports as often as was deemed necessary. The assistant commissioners were ordered to make quarterly reports to the President and special reports as required. The secretary of war was authorized to direct such issues of provisions, clothing, and fuel as he deemed needful for the immediate and temporary shelter and supply of the suffering refugees and freedmen. Under the direction of the President the com-

[17] *House Ex. Docs.*, 39 Cong., 1 Sess., No. 11, pp. 40-41.

[18] In February, 1866, a bill was passed by Congress enlarging the powers of the bureau and continuing it until congress should order otherwise. President Johnson vetoed the bill, and the Senate failed to pass it over his veto. On July 16, 1866, an act was passed, over the veto of the President, extending the existence of the bureau to July 16, 1868. On July 6, 1868, another act was passed, over Johnson's veto, continuing the bureau for one year after July 16, 1868. Other acts were subsequently passed, extending certain phases of the organization, and it was not entirely abolished until June 30, 1872.—Peirce, *op. cit.*, pp. 54-74.

missioner might set apart for the use of loyal freedmen
and refugees such tracts of land in the insurrectionary
states as were abandoned or as should be acquired by confiscation, sale, or otherwise. Of these tracts of land not
more than forty acres might be leased to every male citizen, whether refugee or freedman, and the lessee was to
be protected in the use and enjoyment of the land for a
term of three years. He was to pay an annual rent not ex-
ceeding six per cent of the value of the land as appraised
for taxation in 1860, and at the expiration of the term of
three years he might, upon paying the appraised value,
purchase the land and receive such title as the United
States government could confer.[19]

Upon the urgent request of the President, General
Oliver O. Howard, commander of the army of the Tennessee, came to Washington and accepted the position
of commissioner.[20] In accordance with the provisions of
the act he divided the territory under his jurisdiction into
ten districts, each in charge of an assistant-commissioner.
Brigadier-General Clinton B. Fisk was assigned to the
district embracing Kentucky and Tennessee with headquarters at Nashville.[21]

The appointment of General Fisk was a wise and excellent choice. A native of New York, he had grown up
in the free soil state of Michigan, and at the outbreak of
the war was living in St. Louis. There he recruited a
regiment of Missouri volunteers and after six months of
distinguished service as its colonel was promoted to the
rank of brigadier-general. He had been prominently
identified with freedmen's affairs during the war, and he
was a man of education, ability, and good reputation.
An ardent Methodist, imbued with the spirit of missionary activity, he saw in the recently emancipated Negroes
an opportunity for social and spiritual service, but he

[19] *United States Statutes at Large*, XIII, 507.
[20] *House Ex. Docs.*, 39 Cong., 1 Sess., No. 11, p. 40.
[21] *Ibid.*, p. 46.

was free from the bigotry and self-righteousness that characterized the labors of so many of the Northern missionaries of the period. Honest and austere, a total abstainer whose aversion to drink and profanity stood in vivid contrast with the readiness with which his associates took to both, he was well liked personally in Tennessee even by those who were not disposed to regard his office with approval. Upon hearing of his appointment Andrew Johnson is said to have exclaimed, "Fisk ain't a fool, he won't hang everybody,"[22] and the Nashville *Dispatch* characterized him as "universally recognized as the best man that could have been placed in this somewhat embarrassing position."[23]

During the summer of 1865 circulars of instruction were sent by General Howard to the assistant-commissioners outlining their duties. These officials were to supply the wants and guarantee the freedom of the Negroes and to facilitate the work of relief and education that was being carried on by benevolent societies and state authorities. They were enjoined to guard carefully the unity of the family relations and to designate officers for recording marriages of freedmen. Where necessary they were to adjudicate difficulties between the Negroes themselves or between Negroes and whites. They were to instruct the freedmen as to their duties, to aid them in securing titles to their land, to endeavor to remove the prejudices of the former masters, and to introduce a practical system of compensated labor. All able bodied Negroes and refugees were to be compelled to work, but Negroes must be allowed to choose their employers. The old system of overseers and all substitutes for slavery were prohibited, and contracts between employers and laborers were to be approved and enforced by bureau officials.[24]

[22] Alphonso A. Hopkins, *The Life of Clinton Bowen Fisk*, p. 94.
[23] Nashville *Dispatch*, Sept. 2, 1866.
[24] *House Ex. Docs.*, 39 Cong., 1 Sess., No. 11, pp. 45-6.

Rations were to be issued to those who were not employed by the government and had no means of subsistence, upon the following scale:

Pork or bacon, 10 ounces, in lieu of fresh beef; fresh beef 16 ounces; flour and soft bread, 16 ounces twice a week; hard bread, 12 ounces, in lieu of flour or soft bread; corn meal, 16 ounces, five times a week; beans, peas, or hominy, 10 pounds to 100 rations; sugar 8 pounds to 100 rations; vinegar 2 quarts to 100 rations; candles, adamantine or star, 8 ounces to 100 rations; soap, 3 pounds to 100 rations; salt, 2 pounds to 100 rations; pepper, 2 ounces to 100 rations.

Women and children were allowed, in addition to the foregoing rations which was for adults, roasted rye coffee at the rate of ten pounds or tea at the rate of fifteen ounces to each one hundred rations. Children under fourteen years of age were given half rations.[25]

For purposes of administering the Freedmen's Bureau act the state of Tennessee was divided first into three sub-districts, Nashville, Memphis, and Chattanooga, and later into five, Pulaski and Knoxville being added in 1867.[26] These sub-districts were in charge of army officers detailed for the purpose. In Middle and West Tennessee the sub-districts were further sub-divided into agencies, usually coinciding with the counties, in charge of civilians designated as superintendents and appointed by the assistant-commissioner.[27] In the reports these superintendents were frequently referred to as "agents."

All civilian agents were appointed without any stated salary being specified, but they were authorized to collect a fee of fifty cents for each contract made and registered by them and such costs as the civil law allowed to the regular courts in cases adjudicated by them. They were also authorized to expend so much of the proceeds from fines and forfeitures as might be required to procure

[25] *Ibid.*, p. 47.
[26] *Report of the Secretary of War, 1868*, p. 1057.
[27] *Sen. Ex. Docs.*, 39 Cong., 2 Sess., No. 6, p. 127.

books and stationery for office use. The agents were allowed to retain all costs in cases adjudicated by them, but all fines, after the expenses for stationery and absolute necessities were deducted, were to be remitted to the office of the assistant-commissioner at Nashville. Later the fee for each single contract was increased to one dollar, and a fee of twenty-five cents was allowed for each additional laborer included in the contract.[28] In order to punish crimes and to secure the administration of justice for the freedmen the superintendents held courts in which were tried all cases arising between freedmen and between freedmen and whites. The warrants, writs, and executions of these courts were served by civil officers, except in some counties where they would not act, and in these by officers appointed by the superintendents. From these courts either party had the right to appeal to the assistant-commissioner at Nashville.[29]

There appears to have been a genuine desire on the part of both Radicals and Conservatives in Tennessee that the Negroes should be required to work, and that they should be properly disciplined. Even the Governor was exceedingly critical of the idleness and tendency toward vagrancy manifested by the freedmen,[30] and this view was shared by the more thoughtful of his friends and supporters. In May, 1865, James A. Rogers of Brownsville wrote to him demanding legislation that would force the Negroes to assume a more peaceful attitude and more gainful pursuits:

I think the legislature ought to pass a law requiring negroes to work faithfully for those who are using them on registered farms and have complied with the requirements of the law. It will never do to suffer them to roam about at will, go where they please, work or let it alone as they please. A negro must have some one to manage him, and he must be required to respect and obey his employer. Far better have the last vestige of them

[28] *Ibid.*, p. 127.
[29] *Ibid.*, p. 127.   [30] Knoxville *Whig*, Sept. 27, 1865.

removed from our midst. . . . Those under twenty-one years of age should be hired out to their former masters.[31]

The demand for legislation of this type was rendered all the more imperative by the large increase in Negro population which the state had recently received. From Alabama, Georgia, and Mississippi came hundreds of Negroes at the close of the war. Some of them had accompanied the Federal armies to the North, but a large proportion of them remained to be cared for in the state. To this end camps had been organized under military auspices, and their inmates had become the regular recipients of government clothing and rations. There was, consequently much idleness and discontent among this class of refugees.[32]

General Fisk set himself to work immediately to remedy this situation. He succeeded in breaking up the camps and in supplying the freedmen with work at good wages. This he effected mainly by associating the planters and freedmen with his sub-agents in commissions organized for the purpose of settling local disputes, making labor contracts, and removing from the military courts questions that would otherwise have to be adjudicated by military officers.[33] In his instructions to the sub-assistant-commissioners and superintendents he was careful to warn them against too much supervision of the affairs of the freedmen. Contracts for the current year were not to be interfered with except to compel, if necessary, both parties to comply with the provisions in good faith. No fixed rate of wages was to be prescribed for work by the bureau, and persons could make any trade or agreement satisfactory to themselves so long as no advantage was taken of the freedmen. Only in the latter

[31] Letter of James A. Rogers to Brownlow, May 15, 1865, Brownlow Papers.
[32] *House Ex. Docs.*, 39 Cong., 1 Sess., No. 11, p. 31.
[33] *Ibid.*, p. 31.

instance should any interference be made by the bureau officials.[34]

In his advice to the freedmen General Fisk was equally insistent upon honesty and industry. In an address before a colored mass meeting in Edgefield, on October 6, he urged upon them the necessity of performing faithfully every honorable contract:

If you agree to work for a man one month for ten dollars, do it. Do not quit him because another party offers you twelve dollars a month. We will advance you in every way we can. Do not expect us to do all, nor half, but put your shoulders to the wheel and do for yourselves.[35]

Also in every possible way he attempted to prevent collisions between the bureau officials and the whites in the state. When the state courts excluded Negro testimony the bureau acquired jurisdiction in all cases where Negroes were concerned. He announced, however, that where judicial officers and civil magistrates of the counties would act as agents of the bureau no interference would be made. Even where the bureau assumed jurisdiction the proceedings of its tribunals were governed by the laws of the state except where such laws made a distinction on account of color.[36]

From all indications it appears that General Fisk met with notable success in the administration of the Freedmen's Bureau in Tennessee during the first year of his tenure of office. In one month's time, September 1 to October 1, the number of rations issued per month decreased from 3,785 to 2,984. By the end of October seventy-five schools had been established for the freedmen with 264 teachers and an enrollment of 14,768 pupils.[37] In his report to General Howard, on February 14, 1866, he described the continual improvement of af-

[34] Nashville *Daily Press and Times*, Sept. 18, 1865.
[35] Nashville *Union*, Oct. 6, 1865.
[36] Nashville *Daily Press and Times*, Sept. 18, 1865.
[37] *House Ex. Docs.*, 39 Cong., 1 Sess., No. 11, p. 31.

fairs in the state. There had been a steady advancement in industry, good order, and the administration of justice. Emigration from the towns to the plantations had been large, and only a few dependents remained in the state to whom rations were being issued. Even among the latter class the freedmen themselves were doing valuable work in charitable and relief organizations. "The Nashville Provident Association" had a coal and wood depot, a soup house, and a physician, and it relieved the suffering poor without regard to distinctions of color. "The Freedmen's Association for the Relief of the Poor" was alleged to be feeding, in addition to members of its own race, many widows whose husbands had fought to perpetuate slavery.[38]

With regard to agricultural conditions he was equally optimistic:

Through the rich agricultural districts preparations are being made for vigorous industry during the present year; fences are being rebuilt, plantations stocked with teams, implements, and seeds; and a determination manifested generally to redeem waste places, repair the desolation of war, and again place the commonwealth on the high road to prosperity.[39]

Considerable disappointment was experienced, however, by the freedmen with regard to the Negro testimony bill. As long as the legislature refused to admit their testimony in the courts of the state all Negroes committing offenses against the municipal ordinances of Nashville and Memphis were tried in the "freedmen's courts," and all fines were used for the relief of the suffering and destitute freedmen and refugees.[40] On May 25, however, the legislature passed a law declaring persons of color competent witnesses in state courts, giving them full and equal benefit of the laws, and relieving them of all punishments and penalties except those prescribed for

[38] *Sen. Ex. Docs.*, 39 Cong., 1 Sess., No. 27, p. 13.
[39] *Ibid.*, p. 14.
[40] *House Ex. Docs.*, 39 Cong., 1 Sess., No. 70, p. 211.

white people in similar cases.[41] After this law was enacted
the assistant-commissioner issued an order abolishing the
freedmen's courts, and thereafter the agents "simply
advised and instructed the freedmen in their rights and
the methods of maintaining them in the civil courts."[42]
This law was received with enthusiasm by the bureau
officials at first, for the freedmen's courts had become
somewhat inconvenient for them.[43] The Nashville *Dispatch* also approved the law and was of the opinion that
"the negro need have no fears that he will not be protected in all of his rights as fully under our civil courts
as under that anomaly known as the freedmen's court."[44]
Unfortunately, however, the expectations of the Negro
testimony law were not fulfilled. The abolition of the
freedmen's courts put an end to the fines which had furnished such ample support for the destitute, thus placing the burden of their relief entirely upon the government, while at the same time the Negroes failed to secure
the desired treatment in the state courts. Freedmen were
convicted upon the slightest testimony, and the assistant-commissioner   reported   that   "negro   testimony
wherever introduced, is taken, as they say, 'for what it
is worth,' and in some districts it is *not offered* (another
term for excluded)."[45] With regard to these courts the
same official wrote in 1868, "in the large cities, and in
East Tennessee, and occasionally in Middle Tennessee
justice has been impartially administered in matters
arising out of contracts; but the enforcement of the laws
in criminal cases has been very imperfect."[46]

The abolition of the freedmen's courts also interfered
seriously with the contract labor system. This system
had worked with success in the state. Under its terms

[41] *Acts, 34th Tenn. General Assembly, 2nd Session, 1866,* p. 65.
[42] *Sen. Ex. Docs.,* 39 Cong., 2 Sess., No. 6, p. 128.
[43] *House Ex. Docs.,* 39 Cong., 1 Sess., No. 70, p. 211.
[44] Nashville *Dispatch,* May 27, 1866.
[45] *Sen. Ex. Docs.,* 39 Cong., 2 Sess., No. 6, p. 128.
[46] *Report of the Secretary of War, 1868,* p. 1057.

contracts were made for one year, thus serving to fix the
freedmen in permanent homes, keep the families together,
and give stability to the business enterprises of employers. While the bureau courts were open few complaints
were entered and they were usually settled in equity.
When the civil courts assumed this jurisdiction, however,
the complaints multiplied, and it was reported that employers frequently took advantage of the freedmen by
turning them away after the crops were "laid by."[47] The
bureau was so seriously crippled by this transfer of jurisdiction as to render many of its former duties superfluous.
In October, 1866, J. R. Lewis, who had succeeded General
Fisk as assistant-commissioner in September, reported
to General Howard that,

The bureau in Tennessee has become simply the almoner of the
government bounty. The last clause of the 14th section of the
last bureau bill[48] is shorn of its authority in this state. "The
courts of the state and of the United States are not disturbed
in the peaceable course of justice" and the state is "fully restored to its constitutional relations to the government" and
"duly represented in the congress of the United States." Hence
the power of the bureau is so limited that it can do little toward
stemming the tide of injustice toward the freedmen.[49]

In spite of these difficulties, however, the condition of
the freedmen in the state appears to have been greatly
improved during the year 1866. Colonel Palmer, the sub-
assistant commissioner at Memphis, reported in August
that the condition of the Negroes in West Tennessee was

[47] *Sen. Ex. Docs.*, 39 Cong., 2 Sess., No. 6, p. 130.
[48] The act of July 16, 1866, provided that, until a state was restored in
its constitutional relations to the government of the United States, the
bureau should guarantee "the right to make and enforce contracts, to sue,
be parties, and give evidence, to inherit, purchase, lease, sell, hold and
convey real and personal property, and to have full and equal benefit of
all laws and proceedings concerning personal liberty, personal security,
and the acquisition, enjoyment, and disposition of estate, real and personal," to "all citizens of such state or district without regard to race or
color, or previous condition of slavery."—*United States Statutes at Large*,
XIV, 176-77.
[49] *Sen. Ex. Docs.*, 39 Cong., 2 Sess., No. 6, p. 135.

Top: SCENE IN THE OFFICE OF THE FREEDMEN'S BUREAU IN MEMPHIS. FROM AN ENGRAVING IN HARPER'S WEEKLY.

Bottom: UNIONISTS OF EAST TENNESSEE SWEARING BY THE FLAG. FROM AN ENGRAVING IN HARPER'S WEEKLY.

"generally good." They were working well, and he was making every effort to "encourage them and cultivate good feeling between the blacks and whites."[50] Large sums were expended on school buildings at Nashville, Memphis, Chattanooga, Clarksville, Tullahoma, Springfield, Gallatin, Spring Hill, Smyrna, Shelbyville, and other points.[51] The crop conditions were good in 1866, and this factor added materially to the relief of the Negroes. The report of the assistant-commissioner was especially optimistic in this respect:

It is believed that with justice there will be very little suffering among the freedmen in the coming winter, except among the old, the sick, the widows and orphans, especially about the crowded towns. The crops will furnish subsistence for the entire population, except perhaps in meat. Much more cotton has been planted this season than ever before; it will however, produce not more than half a crop. The corn crop in East and Middle Tennessee is at least an average crop, and will perhaps make up in those localities for the failure in the rest of the state. The wheat has produced about half a crop. Tobacco will be fully an average and more planted than usual. Hogs have suffered from hog cholera, and there will probably be less than one half the usual amount of pork. The total amount of land under cultivation will not fall short of that of 1860.[52]

In January, 1867, General W. P. Carlin was appointed to succeed Lewis as assistant-commissioner.[53] One of his first acts was to discharge a large number of incompetent agents who had been allowed to drift into office during the administration of Lewis and to fill their places with new men. Following this the fee system was abolished and the agents were placed upon a regular salary.

[50] Nashville *Dispatch*, Aug. 18, 1866.

[51] *Sen. Ex. Docs.*, 39 Cong., 2 Sess., No. 6, pp. 131-2. This action was made necessary because of the recent destruction of a large amount of school property. In the Memphis race riots alone, May, 1866, school buildings to the value of $37,800 were destroyed. Schoolhouses at Tullahoma, Shelbyville, Dechard, Athens, and Brentwood had also been burned.

[52] *Ibid.*, p. 130.

[53] *Report of the Secretary of War, 1867*, p. 687. Kentucky was detached and erected into a separate district on June 12, 1866.

This innovation resulted in the development of a better attitude towards the bureau on the part of the people of the state, as the agents no longer made charges for the services that they rendered.[54]   In May Carlin issued an order forbidding officers and agents of the bureau to use the influence of their official positions to secure the nomination and elections of candidates to office.   Chaplain Lawrence who had been guilty of this procedure was forced to resign immediately, and orders were also issued compelling any agent or officer of the bureau who might become a candidate for a civil office to resign his position likewise.

For his action thus exerted in the interest of reforming the administration of the bureau Carlin was bitterly denounced by the Radical press in the state.   The *Press and Times* characterized him as "a bolter and disorganizer, who out of mere revenge, would sell out the district to the Etheridge party."[55]   Such criticism was very unjust, for the assistant commissioner had taken especial precautions to make provision for the relief of any freedmen who might be discharged from their employment as a consequence of voting the Radical ticket.   On June 29 he issued orders to Colonel Palmer at Memphis to the following effect:

It is your duty and that of your agents, to instruct the freedmen in your subdistrict to vote as they may please, whatever the immediate consequences may be.   All freedmen who may be driven from their crops or turned out of their employment in consequence of their political action, will be provided for by the bureau agents until they can find employment for themselves.[56]

Throughout the entire period of its existence in Tennessee the bureau adhered to this policy officially, and in this respect its action stood in marked contrast to that of the Radical reconstructionists.   Its avowed purpose

[54] *Ibid.*, p. 688.
[55] Nashville *Daily Press and Times*, Mar. 14, 1867.
[56] *Ibid.*, July 2, 1867.

was the social and political rehabilitation of the Negro
race. Its efforts were exerted to secure fair and just
treatment of the blacks and the proper enforcement of
their contracts, but social equality was not one of its
aims. Its officials encouraged the Negroes to exercise
the elective franchise and to avail themselves of their
political rights, but it was the uniform policy of Generals
Fisk and Carlin to guard against the use of the bureau
as a political machine. If the subordinate officials prosti-
tuted their positions to such an end, their acts were without the consent and against the advice of the assistant
commissioners.

In his attempt to prevent idleness and to encourage
industry among the freedmen, Carlin's policy was similar to that of General Fisk. In August, 1867, there was a
great demand for labor in the state, but the Negroes
showed little disposition to accept employment. The assistant commissioner thereupon issued orders to the effect that those who had been offered work and had refused it should be given no further aid by the bureau.[57]
It was the view of General Carlin that this reluctance to
work on the part of the Negroes was largely inspired by
certain Radical agitators and irresponsible persons who
were seeking to exert an evil influence upon the freedmen. In this view he was not greatly mistaken, for, as
events were subsequently to show, the actions of this class
of persons was destined to bring disastrous results to
both the freedmen and the bureau.

In February, 1867, the legislature had enacted a law
providing that separate schools, maintained at state expense, should be provided for the Negroes.[58] This separation of the races was vigorously attacked by John
Ogden, a professor in Fisk University,[59] in an address

[57] *Ibid.*, Aug. 9, 1867.
[58] *Acts, 35th Tenn. General Assembly, 2nd Adjourned Session, 1866-7,*
p. 39.
[59] Fisk University, chartered in 1867, was the outgrowth of a school
established for the freedmen in Nashville by the American Missionary Asso-

before the state teachers association in November. The adoption of such a measure he characterized as an attempt to "pander to wicked prejudices," and, referring to the type of educators which he represented, he said:

We do not presume to draw the distinction. We only ask for equal justice and impartial representation. The law should make no distinction or it provides for oppression. It should not even allow the exercise of a partiality, even though the school may desire it. But let these schools be peaceably provided for by law, and nothing be said about color or caste; and mark my word, in less than fifty years this needless prejudice will be dead. But legislate for it and you make it respectable, and will provide for its continuation. It must die sometime and the sooner the legislature strikes the blow the better. If it hurts somebody, let somebody get out of the way.[60]

An especially reprehensible class of ministers and teachers from the North, many of them attached to the bureau educational service, encouraged the Negroes in schemes of social equality and discourtesy to the whites.[61] The assumption of a defiant attitude by the blacks as a result of this encouragement brought down upon them outrages which the bureau was powerless to prevent. In the events which followed the status of the bureau was confused in the popular mind with that of the Union League with which it had no connection. At the same time severe economic disorders followed in the wake of this confusion.

The so-called Southern outrages reached their height in Tennessee in 1868. In all sections of the state the freedmen suffered. There were no outrages in the eastern section of the state,[62] but the cold weather and poor

ciation of New York and the Western Freedmen's Aid Commission of Cincinnati in 1866. It was named for General Fisk who had provided an abandoned army barracks for its first classes. An account of the opening exercises of the school appears in the Nashville *Union and American*, Jan. 10, 1866.

[60] Nashville *Daily Press and Times*, Nov. 15, 1867.
[61] Knoxville *Whig*, Sept. 27, 1865.
[62] *House Ex. Docs.*, 40 Cong., 2 Sess., No. 329, p. 36.

housing conditions among the freedmen in that region led to much distress and privation.[63] In Middle and West Tennessee there was a virtual reign of terror in which the freedmen were the chief victims. Some of the outrages were the acts of the newly organized Ku Klux Klan, but others were perpetrated by lawless bands of individuals having absolutely no connection with the "Invisible Empire." It was usually impossible, however, to distinguish between these two classes of outrages.

In January George E. Judd, the sub-assistant commissioner at Pulaski, reported "general complaints of unfairness among employers."[64] At the same time Michael Walsh at Nashville reported "considerable excitement in Humphreys County over 'yellow jackets,' 'red caps,' etc.," and said that, as a result of this situation, most of the colored people were reluctant to make contracts for the year.[65] In March J. C. McMullen at Clarksville said that "the general tenor of all the reports of agents in this sub-district is terror and oppression to the freedmen and violence and contempt for law on the part of the whites."[66] On March 18 J. W. Newton, an educational missionary at Somerville, wrote to his superior, the Reverend D. Burt, superintendent of education for Tennessee that,

No justice whatever is shown to the freedmen. There is more or less shooting done here every night. . . . No Union man, black or white, is safe here. My labors are crippled. I can hold no temperance meetings, and the people are afraid to come out nights. There is some interest manifested upon the subject of religion, but the night meetings have been interrupted of late by the excitement that prevails.[67]

At Mount Pleasant a colored school conducted by a Miss Allison was broken up, and she and her assistant were ordered to leave town. The assistant, S. A. Graham,

[63] *Ibid.*, p. 28.
[64] *Ibid.*, p. 28.
[65] *Ibid.*, p. 29.
[66] *Ibid.*, p. 38.
[67] *Report of the Secretary of War, 1868,* p. 158.

a former Federal soldier, unwisely applied for board at a "rebel" house. This was regarded as an insult, and he was set upon by a mob of young men who warned him that "no damned yankee or Northern man should stay in that place and teach Negroes."[68] In June Lieutenant-Colonel Joseph W. Gelray was sent upon a tour of inspection through Rutherford, Marshall, and Maury Counties. He wore his uniform at Murfreesboro and was twice ordered off the sidewalk. He reported that there was no hope for a better state of affairs, and expressed the opinion that another war would result from the prevalent disorder. His report added,

It is generally understood by those who ought to know best, and who live here in their midst, that it is the intention of the farmers and planters who have been working their lands on shares to drive the Negroes away as soon as the crops are harvested, so as to avoid paying the colored laborers their share of the income from the crop. Their spirit toward the colored laborers is perfectly devilish and exhibits itself in the most infernal outrages upon their persons and interests that was ever heard of in any community laying the slightest claim to any civilization or Christianity.[69]

The colored schools were singled out as targets for especial abuse. During the year J. W. Newton, a teacher at Somerville, was cruelly beaten and his life threatened. At Saulsbury a teacher named Frost was abused and punished at night by a party of disguised men. At Pocahontas William S. Halley was maltreated in a similar way. Schoolhouses at Wartrace, Carthage, and other places were burned by incendiaries.[70]

The foregoing accounts of the outrages perpetrated in the state are drawn from the reports and correspondence of the officials of the bureau in Tennessee. Due allowance must be made for the bias and exaggeration that are necessarily attendant upon such sources of in-

---

[68] *Ibid.*, p. 161.
[69] *Ibid.*, p. 170-75.   [70] *Ibid.*, p. 1058.

formation, but the fact still remains that the bureau was seriously restricted and hindered in its activity and usefulness by these conditions. Moreover, the fact that such importance was attached to these conditions in the reports demonstrates that the officials of the organization were on the defensive. At the same time, the political conditions, both state and Federal, in Tennessee were rapidly becoming such as to render many of the former duties and functions of the bureau either superfluous or nugatory. The interest shown by the Brownlow administration in the freedmen resulted in their securing the greater proportion of the rights and privileges which the bureau was supposed to guarantee to them. Likewise, the restoration of the state to its constitutional relations with the Federal government and the consequent withdrawal of the United States troops from its soil served to remove the most important instrument upon which the bureau could rely for protection and the enforcement of its decrees.

Thus, little by little, the duties and activities of the Freedmen's Bureau in Tennessee were contracted. The admission of the freedmen to the state courts took away its judicial powers. The Negro education act usurped much of its control over colored instruction. The amnesty acts and the presidential pardons restored the most of the "abandoned lands" to their owners,[71] and the return of good times and prosperity solved the refugee problem.[72] No rations were issued after August 20, 1867,

[71] When the bureau was established in Tennessee there were 355,751 acres of "abandoned lands" in the state. Nashville *Dispatch*, Sept. 2, 1866. By November 1, 1867, all but 27,986 acres had been restored to the former owners.—*Report of the Secretary of War, 1867*, p. 622.

[72] N. R. Wilkes, an attorney of Columbia, wrote to Mrs. William H. Polk, on March 3, 1869, "Our farmers have made money this year, and financially the country is looking upward. Columbia is improving rapidly, and its continued prosperity and advancement are confidently predicted by all, provided the political horizon will only clear away the clouds."—Letter in William H. Polk Papers, North Carolina Historical Commission, Raleigh, N. C.

except to the sick in the hospital at Nashville and the inmates of the orphan asylum at Memphis,[73] and thus the bureau ceased to be "the almoner of the government bounty." Finally, the presence of the hostile Ku Klux Klan rendered the position of the agents and officials of the bureau exceedingly precarious. By the spring of 1869 the Freedmen's Bureau in Tennessee had become the mere shadow of its former existence, and an order was issued from Washington calling for its disbanding on May 1. Brevet-Major L. N. Clark was appointed and retained as superintendent of education in Tennessee, but all other activity came to an end.[74]

It is extremely difficult to make an accurate estimate or appraisal of the work of the Freedmen's Bureau in Tennessee. The whites of the state doubtless derived little benefit from it, and they were usually bitter in their denunciations of its activity. One of the members of this class described it, many years after the war, in particularly critical terms:

The freedmen's bureau was the principle judicature of the land. These courts were presided over in most instances by some campfollower of the meanest type, and who seems to have been elected for his known meanness and hatred of the Southern people. His principle associates and advisers were the meanest Negroes in the neighborhood and their testimony was sufficient to rebut any evidence that could be produced, and the militia stood ready to execute any judgment that his Honor would make. Almost daily, white men, women, and children were torn from their homes and brought by guards before the presiding officer of this august tribunal to answer some information filed by Negroes and frequently to face as witnesses his former slaves. In every instance, I may say, the result was a judgement for money or other penalty imposed and not infrequently ended by sending the accused to a loathsome and vermin-infested jail to await the law's delay. If all the meanness enacted by the freedmen's bureau and Brownlow's militia in Sumner County could be reduced

---

[73] Nashville *Daily Press and Times*, Aug. 9, 1867. See also the *Report of the Secretary of War, 1868*, p. 1058.

[74] Nashville *Daily Press and Times*, Apr. 27, 1869.

to writing it would form a library more extensive than Mr. Carnegie has ever conceived.[75]

The foregoing description was evidently and obviously written with much bias and prejudice. Equally biased and prejudiced is the description of conditions in the same county given in the report of J. R. Lewis, the assistant-commissioner of the bureau, in 1866:

Sumner County is governed by Ellis Harper, the notorious guerrilla chief, who has a band of armed men so strong that any opposition to him by Union men or freedmen would be perfectly futile. Their strength in numbers is unknown, but it is known to be a powerful band, who perpetrate outrages so numerous and revolting as to strike terror to all unorganized and unprotected citizens, whether white or black, who entertain Union sentiments. . . . The civil authorities, whether leagued with them or not, do not attempt to bring the parties to justice, so the civil law is virtually a farce. . . . They take the law into their own hands, 'Harper's law,' and on the most trivial pretexts, inflict the most brutal and summary punishments.[76]

It is evident that a correct impression of the achievements of the Freedmen's Bureau is not to be secured from reading the criminations and recriminations of its respective detracters and supporters. Sumner County was no more "governed by Ellis Harper" than were the freedmen's bureau courts controlled by "the meanest Negroes in the neighborhood." A more accurate appraisal of the work of the bureau must be sought in the statistics of its relief activities.[77] From June 1, 1865, to September 1, 1866, the bureau issued 518,102 rations to the freedmen and refugees of Tennessee and Kentucky.[78] From September, 1866, to September, 1867,

[75] George B. Guild, "Reconstruction Times in Sumner County," *American Historical Magazine*, VIII, 356.

[76] *Sen. Ex. Docs.*, 39 Cong., 2 Sess., No. 6, p. 128.

[77] All statistics for the first year, June, 1865—September, 1866, include both Tennessee and Kentucky.

[78] *Report of the Secretary of War, 1866*, p. 713. In addition to this, 84,586 rations were issued by Major Tracy from the commissary at Chattanooga, without consultation of the assistant-commissioner.—*Sen. Ex. Docs.*, 39 Cong., 2 Sess., No. 6, p. 135.

there were issued 48,173 rations in Tennessee,[79] and during the next year 25,852 rations were issued in the same state.[80] From October 1, 1865, to August 31, 1866, the bureau hospitals in Kentucky and Tennessee treated 13,667 freedmen with only 479 deaths.[81] From September 1, 1866, to June 30, 1868, the hospitals in Tennessee treated 2,523 freedmen with 108 deaths.[82] In November, 1866, the bureau was maintaining in Tennessee 42 schools with 125 teachers and an enrollment of 9,114 pupils.[83] By the end of the scholastic year this had increased to 154 teachers and an enrollment of 9,451 pupils.[84] In June, 1868, there were 120 schools with 161 teachers and 8,246 pupils.[85] The total expenditure of the bureau during the six months, January 1 to June 30, 1867, for schools, asylums, construction and rental of school houses, and transportation of teachers was $13,208.21.[86] When it is remembered that the colored population of Tennessee was estimated at only 300,000 in 1866,[87] it will appear from these figures that the opportunity afforded to each freedman for securing some sort of aid from the bureau was of some consequence.

Whatever the whites might think or say about the bureau, all evidence tends to point to the fact that its work was a godsend to the freedmen. It provided the food which kept many of this class from starvation, and it provided medical treatment and hospital care for those who could not have secured it otherwise. It laid the foundations of Negro education, both elementary and secondary, in the state.[88] It protected the Negroes in

[79] *Report of the Secretary of War, 1867*, p. 640.
[80] *Report of the Secretary of War, 1868*, p. 1027.
[81] *Ibid., 1866*, p. 725.
[82] *Ibid., 1867*, p. 631; *1868*, p. 1024.
[83] *Ibid., 1866*, p. 748.   [85] *Ibid., 1868*, p. 1058.
[84] *Ibid., 1867*, p. 688.   [86] *Ibid., 1867*, p. 653.
[87] *Sen. Ex. Docs.*, 39 Cong., 2 Sess., No. 6, p. 126.
[88] Fisk University, an outgrowth of one of the bureau schools, has become one of the leading Negro institutions for higher learning in the world.

their legal and constitutional relations, and it laid the basis for their economic independence.

By 1869 the Negro's "hard-times" were virtually at an end. The Columbia *Herald* spoke of the great success of free labor in Maury County,[89] and the Nashville *Press and Times* asserted that those who "have nothing but health and hands find ready contracts everywhere."[90] With regard to the condition of the freedmen the *Press and Times* was very optimistic:

Their moral and industrial habits do not fall below the expectations of their best friends. Their desire to accumulate land is strong. It does not appear that more than seven or eight per cent of them had the means to purchase land and enter upon its successful cultivation at the close of the war, but since then this proportion has been considerably increased, perhaps doubled, and goes on strongly augmented. . . . A great number who entered upon the year's work with a fair share of means, good soil, and did not attempt to do too much at once, managed to discharge all their obligations, to lay in a sound stock for the coming year, to increase their facilities for producing, and to add numerous comforts to their households, and are making arrangements for more extended efforts in the future.[91]

The Freedmen's Bureau, with all of its evils and shortcomings, had much to do with making this situation possible.

[89] Columbia *Herald*, Sept. 10, 1868.

[90] Nashville *Daily Press and Times*, Jan. 7, 1869. This newspaper recorded the instance of a colored man in Tipton County, who had rented a farm of thirty acres. He and his family had worked the farm for the year, 1868. He had raised 60 barrels of corn, valued at $180.00; 80 bushels of wheat, valued at $160.00; 2000 pounds of tobacco, valued at $140.00; and five bales of cotton, worth $300.00, making a total of $780.00 for his year's work. In addition to this he had two mules, a horse, and a cow. He had paid his rent in hay and potatoes, and he had enough oats, turnips, potatoes, and hay to last his family and stock for a whole year.

[91] Nashville *Daily Press and Times*, Jan. 7, 1869.

Chapter VIII

THE KU KLUX KLAN

In the preceding chapters attention has been called to the presence of a secret and mysterious order, in Tennessee, known as the Ku Klux Klan. The activities of this organization constitute an important phase of the Reconstruction period in every Southern state, but they are doubly significant in Tennessee, as that commonwealth was the place of their origin. According to William Garrett Brown, a prominent authority on the place of the South in American History,

The Ku Klux movement was an outgrowth of the conditions that prevailed in the Southern states after the war. It was too widespread, too spontaneous, too clearly a popular movement, to be attributed to any one man or any conspiracy of a few men. Had it existed only in one corner of the South, or drawn its members from a small and sharply defined class, some such explanation might serve. But we know enough of its extent, its composition, and the various forms that it took, to feel sure that it was neither an accident or a mere scheme. It was no man's contrivance, but an historical development. As such it must be studied against its proper background of a disordered society and a bewildered people.[1]

The foregoing statement might well be applied to the situation in Tennessee. The Ku Klux Klan originated in that state as a harmless social organization, but in response to the exigencies of the local situation it quickly transformed itself into a political order which, in the extent of its operations and the force of its activity, might be compared with the *Tugendbund* or the *Carbonari* of continental Europe.

Only a brief space is necessary for relating the details connected with the origin of the Ku Klux Klan. In

[1] William Garrett Brown, *The Lower South in American History*, p. 195.

Pulaski, a typical Tennessee small town, there were in 1866 many young men who found time hanging heavily upon their hands. The reaction which followed upon the cessation of the excitement of army scenes and service was intense, and there was nothing to relieve it. They could not engage at once in business or professional pursuits. In the majority of cases, perhaps, business habits were demoralized, and there was no capital that could be diverted to mercantile or agricultural enterprises. There was accompanying this condition a total lack of the amusements and social diversions which prevail where society functions in a normal manner.[2] To relieve the ennui that was occasioned by this irksome existence, it occurred to six of these young men to organize a club or society of some sort. Thus, by accident as it were, John B. Kennedy, J. R. Crow, Frank O. McCord, Richard B. Reed, John C. Lester, and Calvin Jones brought into existence one of the most picturesque and powerful movements in all American history.

The first meeting of the projected club was held in the law office of Judge Thomas M. Jones, the father of one of the members, in May, 1866.[3] At this time a temporary organization was effected by the selection of a chairman and a secretary. Two committees were appointed, one to select a name for the new society and the other to prepare a set of rules for its government and a ritual for the initiation of new members. The club then adjourned to meet again in the following week for the purpose of hearing and acting upon the reports of these two committees. It so happened, in the meantime, that one of the leading spirits in the proposed order was invited to occupy a large residence situated on the outskirts of Pulaski dur-

[2] J. C. Lester and D. L. Wilson, *Ku Klux Klan, Its Origin, Growth, and Disbandment*, p. 52.
[3] *Ibid.*, p. 53. D. L. Wilson, in "The Ku Klux Klan, Its Origin, Growth, and Disbandment," *Century Magazine*, VI, 399, gives the time as June, 1866.

ing the temporary absence of its owner on a business trip to Mississippi. This young man invited his comrades to join him there, and, without the knowledge or consent of the owner, the place of meeting was changed from the law office to the residence.[4]

Much speculation has been indulged in with regard to the source from which these young men drew the idea for their organization. It has been suggested that their plan was an imitation of the medieval German *Vehmgericht* as described in Goethe's *Goetz von Berlichingen*. This novel had been made available in the South through the medium of Sir Walter Scott's translation, and it was widely read along with Scott's *Anne of Geierstein* and other such romances, but there is no direct evidence that its plot was in the minds of the founders of the Ku Klux Klan. It is much more likely that the name of the Klan was derived by accident from a convenient Greek word and that its structure and organization were products of the same impulse that has led to the Alpha Sigma Sigma, the snipe hunt, and various other forms of hazing in small towns rather than an adaptation of the features of a medieval German tribunal.

The committee found it difficult to select a name which would be suggestive of the character and objects of the society, and they reported at the next meeting that they had been unable to make a selection. They did, however, mention several names which had been under discussion. Among these was the word "Kukloi" from the Greek word *kuklos,* meaning band or circle. At the mention of this word, someone is said to have shouted "Call it Ku Klux." "Klan" was added to complete the alliteration. The weird potency of the name Ku Klux had its influence upon the members, and the original plan was so modified as to make everything connected with the order harmonize with the name. The recommendations of

[4] Lester and Wilson, *op. cit.,* p. 54.

THE SPOFFORD HOUSE, PULASKI, TENNESSEE, WHERE THE MEETING WAS HELD
THAT ADOPTED THE NAME AND PRESCRIPT OF THE ORIGINAL KU KLUX KLAN.

the committee on rules and ritual were made to conform with the new idea, and the following officers were provided for, a Grand Cyclops, or president; a Grand Magi, or vice-president; a Grand Turk, or marshal; a Grand Exchequer, or treasurer; and two Lictors, as outer and inner guards of the "Den" as the place of meeting was designated.[5]

The one and only obligation exacted from the members was that they maintain a profound and absolute secrecy with reference to the order and everything pertaining to its existence. As a means to this end each member was required to provide himself with the following outfit, a white mask for the face, with orifices for the eyes and nose; a tall fantastic cardboard hat, so constructed as to increase the wearer's apparent height; and a gown or robe of sufficient length to cover the entire person. No particular color or material were prescribed, these being left to the individual's own taste and fancy. Each selected what would be in his judgment the most grotesque and fantastic. Flashy patterns of "Dolly Varden" calicoes seem to have been used most frequently.[6]

The events conected with the initiation of a new member were ridiculous and ludicrous to the extreme. After the candidate had answered a number of absurd questions to the satisfaction of those present and had assumed the obligation of secrecy, he was placed blindfolded before the "royal altar" and his head was adorned with the "regal crown." The royal altar was a large mirror, and the regal crown was a large hat bedecked with two enormous donkey ears. In this garb the candidate was placed before the mirror and directed to repeat the couplet:

> O wad some power the giftie gie us
> To see oursel's as ithers see us.

[5] *Ibid.*, p. 57.   [6] *Ibid.*, pp. 57-59.

When this act was completed the bandages were removed from the eyes of the initiate, and he was greeted with an outburst of boisterous laughter from those surrounding him. This usually completed the initiation.

It so happened that both the name and the ritual which were selected were readily adaptable to the accomplishment of the plan which the order later adopted—that of inspiring fear in the hearts of the superstitious Negroes and of suppressing the carpet-bagger instigators that were at work among the blacks. The majority report of the congressional investigating committee, as well as the accounts of some of the United States military officers, would suggest that the Ku Klux Klan was designed as a conspiracy against the Federal government and that it was, from the beginning, a lawless order. It is difficult to see how this could be true, for the people of Pulaski were not noted for their lawless or belligerent character, and moreover the constitution of the order was definite and specific in its declaration of allegiance to the United States government.[7] In reality this Ku Klux Klan, in its original form, was nothing more than an organization born of the same impulse and conditions that have led to the snipe hunt and other hazing devices in the Southern country towns, and it was probably as harmless a piece of fooling as any to be found inside or outside of colleges past or present.[8]

Had it not been for the abnormal and disordered condition of affairs in Tennessee at the time and the peculiar fitness of a secret organization of this type for a prominent place in those distressing times, the Klan would doubtless have had nothing more than a mere local and ephemeral existence such as was contemplated for it by its originators. As it was, however, it became, in response to the peculiar civil, social, and political conditions that

[7] Preamble of the *Original Prescript* of the Ku Klux Klan. Reproduced in Lester and Wilson, *op. cit.*, pp. 135-50.

[8] William Garrett Brown, *op. cit.*, p. 201.

AN ORIGINAL KLANSMAN WEARING AN ORIGINAL ROBE. BELIEVED TO BE
THE ONLY ORIGINAL ROBE IN EXISTENCE. SPECIALLY POSED BY R. J.
BRUNSON, PULASKI, TENNESSEE, MARCH 25, 1924. COPYRIGHTED BY MR.
AND MRS. W. B. ROMINE AND REPRODUCED BY THEIR PERMISSION.

prevailed in the South, a powerful order, and it was "as much a product of these conditions as malaria is of a swamp and sun heat."[9]   According to Frank Tannenbaum, who certainly cannot be numbered among the friends of the Ku Klux Klan,

It became a reflex of the vindictiveness of Northern politicians and of the unscrupulous carpet baggers who swooped down upon the South as a vulture upon a wounded and stricken victim.   It was a desperate act of self assertion and self defense.   It was an attempt to rescue for the South the remnents of a civilization that was being subverted by coarser hands and without regard for the feelings of an outraged and unhappy community. . . . It drove the carpet bagger across the Mason and Dixon's line and uprooted his evil influence.[10]

The origin of the Ku Klux Klan is relatively unimportant when compared with its transformation from a social order into a political organization.   This transformation occurred, for the most part, in 1867.[11]   Conditions in Tennessee were at this time exceedingly propitious for the organization of a militant order of this nature.   Brownlow was constantly hurling imprecations of the most intense nature against the "rebels."   He and his legislature had succeeded effectively in excluding this class from the ballot-box, and now they were conferring the suffrage upon the Negroes.

The events connected with the gubernatorial contest in 1867 contributed still further to the dissatisfaction and humiliation of the former Confederates.   Although it was a foregone conclusion that they would not be allowed to vote,[12] this class supported the Conservative candidate,

---

[9] Lester and Wilson, *op. cit.*, p. 50.

[10] Frank Tannenbaum, *Darker Phases of the South*, p. 6.

[11] This transformation really began with the great growth which the Klan experienced in the fall and winter of 1866.   It did not become manifest, however, until the spring of 1867.   Lester and Wilson, *op. cit.*, p. 70.

[12] An attempt was made to secure the suffrage for a large portion of this class in July.   John C. Gaut issued a circular stating that the elective franchise act did not take from the county courts the power to appoint election officials.   This would have made it possible for former Confed-

Emerson Etheridge, who was favorable to their interest
and who advocated the repeal of the franchise acts. In
the old practice of "stumping the state," Etheridge, an
able and fluent orator, would have been more than a match
for Brownlow, who was at this time suffering from both
pleurisy and palsy. The Governor, however, induced the
legislature to pass a militia act, authorizing him to organize, equip, and call into service a volunteer force composed of one or more regiments from each congressional
district. He was made commander-in-chief and was authorized to call out this force "whenever in his opinion
the safety of life, liberty, property, or the faithful execution of the laws required it."[13] When the campaign began Brownlow issued an order calling for the enlistment
of troops to serve for a period of three years unless sooner
discharged.[14] The chief duties of these troops, many of
whom were Negroes,[15] would be to appear at the various

erates to vote in counties where the officials were Southern sympathizers.
Brownlow, however, issued a proclamation assailing the circular as "seditious and rebellious" and ordered the state guards to arrest Gaut or any
of his assistants who might attempt to interfere with the enforcement of the
elective franchise act.—Nashville *Union and Dispatch*, July 6, 1867.

[13] *Acts, 34th Tenn. General Assembly, 2nd Adjourned Session, 1866-7,*
p. 24. The Radical press was very active in supporting the Governor in his
attempts to get this law passed. There was much talk about "lawlessness"
among the "rebels." The following editorial is typical: "We entreat the
legislature to send speedy aid to the suffering loyalists in West Tennessee
before they are murdered and driven from their homes. When the assassination of loyal civil officers is styled 'retributive justice' by the leading
rebel journals, the state government should protect the lives of all true
men against the assaults of desperadoes."—Nashville *Daily Press and
Times*, Feb. 5, 1867.

[14] Printed circular in the files of the adjutant-general's office, Tennessee
State Archives.

[15] Letter book "A," adjutant-general's office, contains several copies of
commissions issued to the commanders of Negro companies. One of the
most notorious of these companies was that organized by Captain Thompson
McKinley of Gallatin.

General Joseph A. Cooper was placed in command of the state guards.
Twenty-one companies were enlisted, but some of them did not contain
over fifty men. By special act, congress appropriated 10,000 stand of
arms. These were stored at Indianapolis, and only 2,000 stand were ever
shipped to Tennessee. As soon as the election was over the larger portion
of the troops were mustered out and disbanded. The remaining companies

places of public speaking under the pretense of protecting the state government against "rebel assaults." In
a proclamation the Governor declared, "I do not consider
it the duty of the state guards to stand quietly by and
hear men excite the mob spirit by denouncing the Federal and state government, counselling resistance to the
courts and setting aside their decisions."[16] This allusion
to the decisions of the courts had reference to the recent
case of Ridley v. Sherbrook, where the elective franchise
act had been upheld, the court declaring that improper
registration or voting would be "resistance to the courts
and setting aside their decisions." After this proclamation Brownlow remained quietly at home, leaving Etheridge to conduct his campaign as best he could.

Every possible obstacle was placed in the way of the
Conservative candidate. When he spoke at Franklin,
Sumner's company of Negro militia stood threateningly
by.[17] At Greeneville he was forced to defend himself
against Horace Maynard with his umbrella.[18] At Rogers-
ville there was a bloody riot when it was announced that
he would speak, resulting in a battle lasting twenty minutes, two persons killed, and seven mortally wounded.[19]
During his speech at Elizabethton a pistol was drawn,
cocked, and pointed at him, while Horace Maynard went
to the Methodist Church and spoke to "nearly all the
darkies and leaguers."[20] The election which followed was
described by the Conservative press as a "hideous
farce.[21] There was a regiment of troops at the polling
place at Memphis. At Knoxville the Negroes "received
all the consideration." At Gallatin Conservative tickets
were torn from the hands of the voters. At Fayetteville

were organized into a battalion with John T. Roberson as Major.—Report
of the Adjutant-General, 1867, in Brownlow Papers.
[16] *Proclamation Book,* 1867.
[17] Nashville *Union and Dispatch,* July 11, 1867.
[18] Nashville *Daily Press and Times,* July 26, 1867.
[19] Nashville *Union and Dispatch,* July 26, 1867.
[20] *Ibid.,* July 30, 1867.   [21] *Ibid.,* Aug. 4, 1867.

certificates of registration were issued by John Cary to Negroes under twenty-one years of age, and at the polls two hundred Negroes had guns.[22] Needless to say, Brownlow was elected by a large majority.

The violent abuse and incrimination that was heaped upon the defeated candidate by the Radical press contributed to increase the anger of the former Confederates. The *Press and Times* was especially ribald in gloating over the defeat of the Conservatives, stating that "Etheridge is at his home in Dresden, surrounded by a lot of drunken rebels, and cursing Brownlow with awful volubility from sunrise to sunset."[23] and that "Etheridge pours forth such a pile of terrific oaths daily over his unexpected defeat that the old women of Dresden gather them up in baskets and use them for kindling. They burn like sulphur matches."[24]

The Conservatives were naturally indignant over the defeat of their candidate, but their indignation was increased by the knowledge that this result had been accomplished by the aid of Radical speakers "imported" from the North. A correspondent in Coffee county wrote to the *Press and Times* in January that "so sure as there is a God in Heaven, if the radicals inundate the state with Northern speakers this year, the conservatives will do the same, and just as sure as this is done, so surely and certainly it will end in blood."[25] In February the Boliver *Bulletin,* a Conservative paper, stated,

The foul mouth radicals of this woe-befallen state are going to have a powerful time this coming summer. In order to win advocates to their lawless clan, they are going to import a dozen or more of the spoon-lifting, eel-skinning fraternity of the North and have them stump every county of the state. Among them will be Fred Douglass, the negro orator. Nigger Douglass and Beast Butler to stump Tennessee. Good Lord, deliver us.[26]

[22] *Ibid.,* Aug. 4, 1867.
[23] Nashville *Daily Press and Times,* Aug. 16, 1867.
[24] *Ibid.,* Aug. 19, 1867.
[25] *Ibid.,* Jan. 25, 1867.   [26] Bolivar *Bulletin,* Feb. 10, 1867.

This prediction was not wholly fulfilled, as Douglass and Butler did not stump the state, but much valuable assistance did come to the Radicals from Northern organizers of the so-called Union Leagues.

The Union League was an organization sponsored among the freedmen by the Northern Radicals. Its ostensible purpose was to inculcate the principles of loyalty and good citizenship among the Negroes, but its real purpose was to secure the votes of this class for the Radical Republican party. It is said to have been composed of the most disorderly element of the Negro population, led and controlled by white men of the basest and meanest type. They met frequently, went armed to the teeth, and uttered, and in many cases executed, the most violent threats against the persons, families, and property of men who had served in the Confederate army.[27] The league made its appearance in the state soon after peace was declared in 1865, but with the admission of the Negroes to the ballot box it began to increase both in numbers and influence. In April, 1867, it had six councils in Weakley County alone,[28] and it was reported to exist in "nearly every county in East Tennessee."[29]

Such were the conditions that existed in Tennessee in the spring and summer of 1867. The former Confederates were disfranchised, while the votes of the Negroes were freely received at the ballot box. The militia act had provided for a "trainband, booted and spurred, to ride down the last vestige of the liberty left to the people of the state."[30] The Union Leagues were encouraging the Negroes in acts of discourtesy and even deeds of violence against the whites. General Forrest was receiving as "many as fifty letters a day" from old soldiers and

[27] Lester and Wilson, *op. cit.*, p. 80.
[28] Letter of A. H. Walker to A. J. Fletcher, Apr. 10, 1867, Brownlow Papers.
[29] Knoxville *Whig*, Dec. 4, 1867.
[30] Nashville *Union and Dispatch*, Jan. 25, 1867.

friends who were suffering under the disordered conditions, whose friends and relatives were being murdered, whose wives and daughters were being assaulted, whose barns, gins, mills, dwellings, and other property were being destroyed by the prowling marauders.[31] The situation in which the former Confederates were placed was virtually unbearable. "The state was in the iron grasp of the Brownlow regime."[32] The Governor professed to fear an uprising, and one might have occurred if the solution of the difficulty had not appeared from an unexpected source—the Ku Klux Klan, for it was at this time and in response to these conditions that this body was transformed into a militant organization whose purpose was to restore the state government to the white democracy.[33]

The Ku Klux Klan had experienced a rapid growth during the first few months following its organization at Pulaski. Rash, imprudent, and bad men, however, had wormed themselves into the order, and the ties that bound the local dens together were entirely too weak for the work that was now contemplated. It became necessary, therefore, to effect a complete reorganization on a basis corresponding to the existing size and purpose of the Klan; to bind the isolated dens together; to secure unity of purpose and concert of action; to hedge the members by such limitations and regulations as were necessary to restrain them within proper limits; to distribute power among prudent men in the local dens and exact from them a close supervision of those under their charge. With

[31] *House Ex. Docs.*, 42 Cong., 2 Sess., No. 22, p. 80.

[32] Marshall S. Snow, in the St. Louis *Republic*, Feb. 28, 1913. Snow was a young New Englander, who came to Tennessee in 1866 as principal of the Nashville high school.

[33] In his testimony before the congressional investigating committee General Forrest assigned four reasons for the transforming of the Klan into a militant organization: animosity between Union and Confederate soldiers, opposition to the Union Leagues, apprehension of violence from the Negroes, and fear of danger from the Brownlow militia. *House Ex. Docs.*, 42 Cong., 2 Sess., No. 22, p. 81.

this purpose in view, the Grand Cyclops of the Pulaski den sent messages to all dens of whose existence he had knowledge, requesting them to choose delegates to meet in a convention at Nashville in the early summer of 1867. This convention assembled at the Maxwell House early in April. So great was the secrecy surrounding its meeting that, in spite of the presence of Federal troops in the city, and of Federal officers in the hotel itself, the delegates were able to assemble, adopt a plan of organization, select and administer an oath to a leader, adjourn, and leave the city without attracting the attention of the authorities.[34]

At this meeting a complete reorganization of the Ku Klux Klan was effected. Few changes were made in the administration of the local units or Dens, but they were bound together in a more formidable hierarchy. The territory represented at the convention, which included the greater portion of the late Confederacy, was designated as The Invisible Empire. This region was under the jurisdiction of a Grand Wizard and ten Genii. The Empire was subdivided into Realms, coterminous with the several states, each ruled by a Grand Dragon and eight Hydras. The Realms were divided into Dominions, corresponding to the congressional districts, and each governed by a Grand Titan and six Furies. The Dominions were divided into Provinces, coinciding with counties, each ruled by a Grand Giant and four Goblins. As formerly the local units were known as Dens. The officers of the Den included a Grand Cyclops and two Night Hawks, a Grand Magi, a Grand Monk, a Grand Exchequer, a Grand Turk, a Grand Scribe, a Grand Sentinel, and a Grand Ensign. The members of the body politic were designated and known as Ghouls. The Genii, Hydras, Goblins, Furies, and Night Hawks were staff officers, and the gradation and distribution of authority was perfect.

[34] Lester and Wilson, *op. cit.*, p. 84.

Except in the case of the Grand Wizard the duties and functions of each official were rigidly and minutely specified.[35] The duty of the Grand Magi was to preside at all meetings of the Den during the temporary absence of the Grand Cyclops. The Grand Monk presided in the absence of both of these officials. The Grand Exchequer had charge of the revenue of the Den. It was the duty of the Grand Turk to notify all Ghouls of meetings of the Den. The Grand Scribe had charge of the correspondence, the Grand Sentinel was the doorkeeper, and the Grand Ensign was charged with the duty of preserving and protecting the Grand Banner. The tribunal of justice consisted of a Grand Council of Yahoos, for the trial of elective officers, and a Grand Council of Centaurs, for the trial of Ghouls and non-elective officers. General Nathan Bedford Forrest was chosen as Grand Wizard.[36]

A constitution or prescript was adopted at the Nashville convention in 1867. This was the so-called original prescript. Where and how it was printed, and by whom it was written, no one now knows. A copy was sent, without notice or explanation, from Memphis to the Grand Cyclops of each Den. It must have been printed in a small printing office, for in the last pages the supply of asterisks ran out and other characters were adopted. Only one copy of the original prescript is known to be in existence. It is in the possession of Dr. Walter L. Fleming, to whom it was given by Ryland Randolph of Tuscaloosa, Alabama, who was the Grand Giant of one of the Provinces.[37]

[35] *Prescript of the Ku Klux Klan Adopted at a Convention of the Order Held in Nashville*, April, 1867. Reproduced in Lester and Wilson, *op. cit.*, pp. 135-50.

[36] The reasons for the selection of General Forrest for this position are not known. Susan Lawrence Davis, in her untrustworthy *Authentic History of the Ku Klux Klan, 1865-1877*, p. 81, says that the selection was made at the suggestion of Captain William Richardson and with the approval of General Lee. In view of Lee's well known abhorrence of anything resembling guerrilla warfare, this statement does not seem tenable.

[37] Lester and Wilson, *op. cit.*, p. 37.

In some respects the original prescript was found to be defective, and in 1868 the "Revised and Amended Prescript" was adopted. Thomas Dixon says that this later prescript was written by General George W. Gordon, but he gives no authority for this assertion, which, in the absence of documentary evidence, is quite worthless.[38] The copies of this prescript were printed secretly in the office of the Pulaski *Citizen* by Laps D. McCord and L. W. McCord, sons of the proprietor of the office. The manuscript was delivered to these boys by unseen persons, and to these persons the printed copies were returned for circulation.[39] When the order was disbanded in 1869, strict directions were given that all documents pertaining to its existence should be destroyed, and only three copies of the "Revised and Amended Prescript" are known to have survived. One of these is in the library of Columbia University, one in the archives of the state of Tennessee, and one in the library of the University of North Carolina.[40]

No material changes in the Klan's method of operation were made as a result of the reorganization. A few new features were added, and some of the old methods were slightly modified, but the essential features remained the same.[41] The status of the Ku Klux Klan in Tennessee, however, was completely transformed. It now began to appear in public and consequently brought itself within the cognizance of the Brownlow government. From this time on the history of the Invisible Empire in Tennessee becomes identified with that of the state government. A struggle ensued between the two, which in the end proved disastrous for the former.

It is impossible to estimate accurately the size of the

[38] Thomas Dixon, "The Story of the Ku Klux Klan," *Metropolitan Magazine*, XXII, 667.

[39] "Ku Klux Klan, Prescript . . .", *American Historical Magazine*, V, 4.

[40] J. G. deR. Hamilton, *Reconstruction in North Carolina*, p. 459.

[41] Lester and Wilson, *op. cit.*, p. 91.

Klan or the extent of its operations in the state. "It probably did not exceed the League in numbers," according to J. M. Beard, who estimated its membership in 1866 at one hundred thousand.[42] This estimate, however, is so clearly a conjecture that it may be disregarded. A newspaper reporter stated that General Forrest placed the number of Ku Klux in Tennessee at forty thousand, but Forrest afterwards denied that he had made such a statement.[43] A later estimate places the number at seventy-two thousand.[44] None of these estimates are accurate or trustworthy. Such records as were kept were destroyed, and there were numerous Dens of which no records were kept and of which little was known. The number of Klansmen in the state will most likely remain a mystery.

It is no less difficult to determine the extent of the operations of the order. Judging from the accounts in the Radical *Press and Times,* it would appear that hundreds of armed and disguised men rode nightly in every county of the state. The Conservative papers were inclined to minimize the importance of these accounts. When it was suggested that the United States troops be called upon for assistance, the *Union and Dispatch* said,

If the Klan in Tennessee be anything like the formidable and bloodthirsty combination that takes so much room in the *Press and Times,* the paltry force of regulars here would hardly be a match for the ghostly cavaliers, could they be found. The probability is that the whole thing will end in smoke and the "bullet read" never get beyond the sublime imagination of the Grand Cyclops, while the regulars will do their fighting in the shadows.[45]

The Ku Klux Klan seems to have made its first public appearance in Tennessee on the night of July 4, 1867. An order had been issued by the Grand Dragon of the Realm of Tennessee to the Grand Giant of each Province

---

[42] J. M. Beard, *K. K. K. Sketches,* pp. 90, 94.
[43] *House Ex. Docs.,* 42 Cong., 2 Sess., No. 22, vol. xiii, p. 32.
[44] Washington *Post,* Aug. 13, 1905.
[45] Nashville *Union and Dispatch,* Nov. 22, 1868.

in the state that a general parade be held in the capital town of the Province on this night. The parade at Pulaski has been described by those present.

After nightfall they assembled at designated points near the four main roads leading into town. Here they donned their robes and disguises and put covers of gaudy material on their horses. A skyrocket sent up from some point in the town was the signal to mount and move. The different companies met and passed each other on the public square in perfect silence; the discipline appeared to be admirable. Not a word was spoken. Necessary orders were given by means of whistles. In single file, in death-like stillness, with funeral slowness, they marched and counter-marched throughout the town. . . . This marching and counter-marching was kept up for about two hours, and the Klan departed as noiselessly as they came.[46]

At a tournament, at Columbia on November 10, "four of the mysterious order" appeared, "two of them attired in flowing robes of scarlet, the others in robes of deepest black, and all wearing ugly black masks. They bore a white flag with 'Ku Klux' printed upon it in consumptive looking black letters, alongside a cross of like color."[47]

During the year 1868 the columns of the *Press and Times* teemed with editorials and news accounts describing the appearance and "outrages" of the "Ku Klux." In January a Union man and four Negroes were taken from a plantation near Lynnville, carried to the woods, and severely beaten.[48] In the same month, a colored tanner, William Wesley, was taken from his home, near Lewisburg, beaten with pistols, and warned against exercising the elective franchise or attending conventions.[49] At Dixon Springs a Republican candidate for sheriff was ordered to leave the town.[50] In March it was reported that "there are in Rutherford County at least

[46] Lester and Wilson, *op. cit.*, p. 93.
[47] Nashville *Union and Dispatch*, Nov. 10, 1867.
[48] Nashville *Daily Press and Times*, Jan. 15, 1868.
[49] *Ibid.*, Jan. 30, 1868.   [50] *Ibid.*, Feb. 7, 1868.

four hundred men, well organized, who are determined to drive every negro from the polls and force all Union men to leave the country."[51] At Columbia a desperado, who had murdered a Conservative, was taken from the county jail and lynched by the Ku Klux.[52] On March 5 one hundred Klansmen marched down Church Street in Nashville, "all mounted on caparisoned horses with their faces heavily masked, while some of them were fantastically rigged out with feathers after the style of a Comanche or Flathead Indian."[53] At Carthage a school house was burned, and the teachers were notified "in a bloody handwriting, with a coffin at the head [of the paper], that they should suffer death unless they went North where they belonged."[54]

On April 19 the Reverend L. Lincoln, a discharged Union soldier and a Baptist minister, was taken from the house of a friend in Marshall County, brutally murdered, and his body thrown into a sink hole.[55] In July William Holley, a native Tennessean, teaching in a colored school in Hardeman County, received the following notice:

Hidden Recess
Unterrified's Retreat
Klan of Vengeance Eternity

William Holley:
    Villian away ! ! !
Ere another moon wanes, unless thou art gone from the place thy foul form desecrates, thy unhallowed soul will be revelling in the hell thy acts have made hot for thee. William, eat heartily and make glad thy vile carcass, for verily the "Pale Riders"

[51] *Ibid.*, Mar. 3, 1868.

[52] *Ibid.*, Mar. 4, 1868.

[53] *Ibid.*, Mar. 6, 1868. It is interesting to compare this account with that of the Conservative *Union and Dispatch:* "At about mid-night a body of thirty horsemen, wearing black masks and dressed in somber habiliments of the Ku Klux, made their appearance on Church Street, but moved silently along, giving no indication whatever of anything but peaceful intentions."—Nashville *Union and Dispatch*, Mar. 6, 1868.

[54] Nashville *Daily Press and Times*, Apr. 27, 1868.

[55] *Ibid.*, Apr. 29, 1868.

will help in thy digestion. You and your friends will sleep an unwaking sleep if you do. Dare you eat?

The Sacred Serpent has hissed for the last time.

Beware ! ! !

K. K. K.[56]

It is to be observed that the foregoing accounts were given by persons bitterly hostile to the Ku Klux Klan. In many cases the stories are interesting only as an indication of the capacity of these people for exaggeration and prevarication. On the whole, they are to be taken as evidence of a state of feeling that existed against the Klan in some quarters rather than as a correct and accurate account of its actviity. The editorials of the Radical papers were scarcely less inflammatory than the news items. The *Press and Times* characterized "the kind of people who join the Ku Klux Klan" as young men, brought up in idleness, with no reflective powers and no purpose in life except drinking whiskey; plantation overseers, with no property, education, intellectuality, or humanity; and townsmen without work.[57] With regard to the Klan, the same paper said that "the intelligent Christian people of Tennessee do not sympathize with the murderous ruffians whom we have described; nor do the honest soldiers of the rebellion who fought the battles of the rebel cause, participate in their nefarious and cowardly practices."[58]

In an editorial entitled "Mosby, Old Saddles, and the Ku Klux Klan," the Knoxville *Press and Messenger* said,

Mosby has been buying old saddles in Washington. This means blood. Anarchy, treason, ruin, and every woe is to follow this apparently simple business transaction. The invincible Stanton, a prisoner in the war department, haunted by the ghosts of the brave soldiers, his insatiable ambition murdered, has become nervous and informed old Ben Wade, that "Mosby's Guerrillas" were to be seated in the same "old saddles" that their chief has purchased. Then the Ku Klux Klans are spreading all over

[56] *Ibid.*, July 14, 1868.
[57] *Ibid.*, Feb. 26, 1868.   [58] *Ibid.*, Feb. 26, 1868.

the South.   We are a done for people—the Ku Kluxes are upon
us.   We caution the inhabitants of the land of Lincoln and the
people who feed on the savory cod, that they cannot resist Mosby,
the Old Saddles, and the Ku Klux Klan.[59]

The Knoxville *Whig,* speaking of those Ku Klux who
had been sending threatening letters to the Governor,
said in its characteristic manner,

We alike despise the threats and the threateners, and we say to
them and to all who are backing them up, that if they want to
bring on another war, to go ahead and do so.   Johnson will not
always be President, to protect and encourage them; but Grant
or some other equally sound man will occupy the chair now dis-
honored by the accidental occupant, and mark what we say, if
the Union army is ever compelled to come down here again to
suppress another slaveholders' rebellion, they will make clean
work of it.[60]

The Nashville *Banner* was disposed to defend the Ku
Klux Klan, but it was a voice crying in the wilderness:

In its birth and origin, the Ku Klux Klan is but the natural
result of an utter disregard of law and order and of the peace
of society on the part of those constituted to make the laws and
execute them in the state.   We hold to the opinion that the Ku
Klux organization has much more to justify its action than the
radical oligarchy (which is mainly responsible for it) has for
the outrages it has committed against the people of Tennessee.[61]

Whether these acts of violence were really committed,
or, if they were, whether their perpetrators were real
Klansmen or only imposters masquerading under their
insignia, is of little consequence.   It is sufficient that these
exaggerated accounts came to the notice of the Governor.
Already infuriated by the opposition that a certain element had offered to his regime, he immediately adopted
measures to punish the enemies of his administration with
great severity.   His first attempt was unsuccessful, but

[59] Knoxville *Press and Messenger,* Apr. 2, 1868.
[60] Knoxville *Whig,* Apr. 15, 1868.
[61] Nashville *Banner,* Aug. 18, 1868.

others followed, resulting in the most stringent anti-
Ku Klux act that the United States has ever witnessed.

The first attempt of the administration to deal with
the problem presented by the Ku Klux Klan occurred on
February 1, 1868, when the legislature passed an act providing that a sheriff, instead of being restricted to his
own county in raising a force to put down an uprising,
might "recruit said force by the employment of any loyal
citizens in the state."[62] This act was designed to secure
the enforcement of the laws in counties where the population was "disloyal," but it failed in its purpose as the
sheriffs were themselves frequently in connivance with,
or under the intimidation of, the Klan. The indignation
of the Governor at this check in his program is expressed
in a private letter to a friend in Philadelphia, in which he
said, "We want another war to put down the rebellion.
After that is fought, reconstruction will be easy in the
Confederacy. We will only want a surveyor-general and
a land office, with a deputy in each county, and a large
amount of hanging."[63]

In June, however, an event occurred which gave the
administration an opportunity to adopt more severe
measures. While S. M. Arnell, a member of Congress
and the author of the unpopular elective franchise act,
was visiting his home in Columbia the Ku Klux, with
"pistols and rope in hand," made an unsuccessful attempt upon his life, and he appealed to the Governor for
military aid.[64] As the militia act had been allowed to
expire earlier in the year, no state troops were available,
and Brownlow appealed to General George H. Thomas,
commander of the Department of the Cumberland, requesting a company of Federal troops to aid in the en-

[62] *Acts, 35th Tenn. General Assembly, 1st Session, 1867-8*, pp. 34-38.
[63] Letter of Brownlow to Ferdinand J. Dreer, June 22, 1868, in Library
of Congress.
[64] *Senate Journal, 35th Tenn. General Assembly, Extra Session, 1868*,
p. 5.

forcement of the state laws. Thomas replied that "the state of Tennessee being in full exercise of all the civil functions of a state, the Military authority of the United States cannot legally interfere except in the aid and support of the civil authorities."[65] He thus declined to send the troops and suggested that the Governor put in force the act for the protection of sheriffs passed in February. As this act could not be satisfactorily enforced, Brownlow was desperate. It was absolutely necessary that something should be done to repress the activity of the Ku Klux Klan, else this organization would succeed in frightening all Negroes from the polls in November and thus carry the state for Seymour and Blair. Such a result might alienate the support of the congressional Radicals and seriously impair the cordial relations of the state to the Federal government. Moreover, the discovery of a "Ku Klux Klan oath" by the metropolitan police of Memphis[66] served to convince him that the order was contemplating mischief to the administration. He therefore called an extraordinary session of the legislature to meet on July 27, 1868.

In his opening message to the legislature, the Governor called especial attention to the Ku Klux situation:

[65] *Ibid.*, p. 6.

[66] The discovery of this oath created great consternation for a time, but it was later shown to be spurious. Memphis *Avalanche*, Apr. 14, 1868. The "oath," printed in the Memphis *Bulletin*, Apr. 7, 1868, was couched in especially strong language. The Ku Klux initiate was represented as standing before a human skull and swearing, ". . . should I ever, by sign, word, or deed betray a secret or a member of the brotherhood may the skull upon which I now look be a counterpart of mine, and I hope that all the social relations which I now enjoy may be sundered, that honesty in men or virtue in females may not be known to my family or generation, and that all who own my name may be branded as dogs and harlots. . . . I further swear that I will, under any and all circumstances, bear true allegiance to the South and her interests as interpreted by the supreme cyclopean council, and when I receive its orders, should I be even in the embraces of my wife, I will leave her to obey them. I further swear that all Radicals and negroes, who have placed themselves opposite to the interests of the owners of the soil of Tennessee, shall forever be my enemy, and that under no circumstances will I have any connection with them . . . than to welcome them with bloody hands to hospitable graves."

This dangerous organization of ex-rebels now ramifies almost every part of the eleven states that once constituted the Southern confederacy and has already grown into a political engine of oppression so powerful and aggressive as to call forth an opposition, several notable military orders. Organized upon the same basis and having the same dark designs in view, that found a fit culmination in Booth's assassination of Abraham Lincoln, it works in secret, mid signs, symbols and pass words, hatching plots to scatter anarchy and permanent disorder wherever it may have an existence.[67]

As a remedy for this situation, Brownlow requested that the legislature reenact the militia law of 1867.

The action of the Governor was the subject of much criticism. The *Union and Dispatch* denounced the message as "the gauge of battle thrown to an exasperated people" and "a movement in the interest of the radical candidate for President."[68] The Gallatin *Examiner* said,

We have but one reply to make to the atrocious message of Brownlow. If he wishes war, he will find our entire population ready for it. If peace, he can have it. The fearful responsibility rests upon him and his legislature. If war is the decision we can promise to make it short and sharp.[69]

The legislature was soundly criticized by the Knoxville *Press and Herald,*

Their follies have ruined the state. They have brought its reputation so low that the once proud Tennessean blushes to tell where he hails from. The people of Tennessee, as all now see and feel, in their office holders and members of the legislature have been afflicted with plagues similar to those of the frogs and lice of Egypt, and they are panting to be delivered from their oppressors as did the Israelites of old.[70]

So extensive and vigorous was this criticism that William B. Stokes felt called upon to reply to it. In a speech at the capitol he warned the people against resistance to the

[67] *Senate Journal, 35th Tenn. General Assembly, Extra Session, 1868,* p. 7.
[68] Nashville *Union and Dispatch,* July 29, 1868.
[69] Gallatin *Examiner,* Aug. 1, 1868.
[70] Knoxville *Daily Press and Herald,* Aug. 8, 1868.

government of the state. In such an attempt, he said, they would be defeated just as they were in the Civil War. "You can never get control of this government by force. You cannot cut down the white and black loyalists without war, and you are not prepared for that."[71]

On July 28 "so much of the governor's message as referred to the calling out of the militia and to the suppression of the Ku Klux Klan" was referred to the committee on military affairs.[72] While this committee was making an extended investigation a number of events occurred, showing that the legislature was far from conciliatory. On August 1, B. F. Cheatham, Nathan Bedford Forrest, William B. Bate, John C. Brown, Joseph B. Palmer, William B. Quarrels, Thomas B. Smith, Bushrod R. Johnson, Gideon J. Pillow, S. R. Anderson, George W. Gordon, and George Maney, all prominent military officers of high rank in the late Confederacy, met at the capitol and issued a statement, denying that they were hostile to the state government, or that they entertained a desire for its overthrow by revolutionary or lawless methods. Moreover, they expressed a belief that there was no organization, public or secret, in the state with such a purpose, and they thought that the peace of the state did not demand military organization for its preservation.[73] In a letter to a member of the state legislature, General Thomas expressed a feeling that this event afforded "some hope of a peaceable and amicable adjustment of the difficulties now threatening the peace and welfare of the state."[74]

The legislature was of a different mind, however, and when petitions began to be presented, asking for the repeal of the elective franchise acts, they were not favor-

[71] Nashville *Union and Dispatch*, Aug. 1, 1868.
[72] *Senate Journal, 35th Tenn. General Assembly, Extra Session, 1868*, p. 6.
[73] Nashville *Daily Press and Times*, Aug. 2, 1868.
[74] Nashville *Union and Dispatch*, Aug. 11, 1868.

ably received. On August 4 the Governor submitted for
the consideration of the legislature a letter from Judge
John M. Lea. This letter called upon the Governor and
the legislature to complete the reconstruction of the
state by the adoption of an amendment to the constitution conferring the right of suffrage upon "every man,
white or black, being a citizen of the United States and
a citizen of the county wherein he may offer his vote, six
months next preceding the day of election."[75] Such a
settlement, according to Judge Lea, would cause peace
to reign throughout the state:

Ku Klux organizations would be compelled to disband; Loyal
Leagues would cease to exist; the people would look to the law
for protection, and not count on any help from secret associa-
tions; and our Presidential canvass, conducted, it might be with
warmth, would be the most quiet and peaceable that ever took
place in the country.[76]

The attitude of the legislature towards such a proposal
is shown in the debate that followed the reading of this
message. Such a decided opposition manifested itself
towards entertaining any proposition to repeal the franchise acts that the whole matter was laid on the table.[77]

In this action the legislature was encouraged and supported by the action of an extreme Radical convention
which met in Nashville in August. This convention endorsed the course of the Governor in calling the extra
session for the purpose of "protecting defenseless loyal
men from the wanton violence of the Ku Klux banditti
and others, aided and encouraged by wealthy rebels;"
opposed the repeal of the elective franchise law; and
called upon the legislature to pass an efficient militia law
that would enable the Governor to meet any emergency.[78]

[75] *Ibid.*, Aug. 5, 1868.
[76] *Ibid.*, Aug. 5, 1868.
[77] *Senate Journal, 35th Tenn. General Assembly, Extra Session, 1868,*
pp. 50-51.
[78] Nashville *Daily Press and Times,* Aug. 20, 1868.

Similar resolutions were adopted by a Radical convention at Knoxville on August 26.[79]

On August 25 D. G. Thornburgh, chairman of the House committee on military affairs, reported a bill to organize and equip a state guard. The bill passed third reading in the House on August 26, and was transmitted immediately to the Senate.[80] Meanwhile, however, the proposed law was denounced by petitions and editorials from all sections of the state. The Knoxville *Press and Messenger* declared,

We need no militia. We need no soldiers of the regular army to keep the peace in this state. We are law abiding and intend to be. There is no use for any militia, even to bring to justice the two hundred and fifty thieves, murderers, and violators of female chastity that Brownlow has turned loose upon the country by his wholesome pardons.[81]

The Governor, it was said, was intending to use the militia to aid in carrying the state for Grant in the forthcoming Presidential election. The Knoxville *Press and Herald* expressed the hope ''to see the bloodthirstiness of Governor Brownlow checked at every point, and an era of reason and sobriety once more prevail in the government of the state.''[82] Even the Radical *Press and Times* was skeptical as to the propriety of passing such a severe law as the House committee had reported. It was feared that such procedure would necessitate the presence of Federal troops in the state to put down the terrific opposition that the law would engender and thus defeat the purpose of the law itself.[83]

In the Senate, however, more moderate counsel prevailed, and the House bill was modified to some extent.[84]

[79] Nashville *Union and American*, Aug. 28, 1868.

[80] *House Journal, 35th Tenn. General Assembly, Extra Session, 1868*, pp. 148-9.

[81] Knoxville *Press and Messenger*, Aug. 20, 1868.

[82] Knoxville *Daily Press and Herald*, Sept. 8, 1868.

[83] Nashville *Daily Press and Times*, Aug. 31, 1868.

[84] *Senate Journal, 35th Tenn. General Assembly, Extra Session, 1868*, p. 198.

As it was finally enacted the law authorized the Governor
to organize, equip, and call into service a volunteer force
to be known as "the Tennessee State Guards." He was
also authorized to declare martial law in any county
where, upon the evidence of the judge, attorney-general,
senator, representative, and ten men of good character,
it should appear that "the laws cannot be enforced, and
the good citizens of the county or counties cannot be protected in their just rights on account of rebellion or insurrection, or the opposition of the people to the enforcement of the laws." In such counties the Governor was
authorized to quarter troops and to assess and collect
from those counties a sum sufficient for the payment and
maintenance of the state guards so employed.[85]

On September 2 the committee on military affairs submitted a lengthy report, embodying the results of its investigation of the Ku Klux Klan situation in the state.
This report, containing thirty-eight printed pages, was a
long catalog of outrages that purported to have been committed by members of the Klan. In the opinion of the
committee conditions in the state were such as to demand
a resort to severe measures. The report stated:

The committee, after summoning a great many witnesses before
them, are satisfied that there exists an organization of armed
men going abroad, disguised, robbing poor negroes of their fire-
arms; taking them out of their homes at night, hanging, shooting, and whipping them in a most cruel manner, and driving
them from their homes. Nor is this confined to colored men
alone; women and children have been subjected to the torture
of the lash; and brutal assaults have been committed upon them
by night prowlers, and in many instances the persons of females
have been violated, and when the husband or father complained,
he has been obliged to flee to save his own life.[86]

Depredations were found to have been committed
practically all over Middle and West Tennessee and in

[85] *Acts, 35th Tenn. General Assembly, Extra Session, 1868,* pp. 23-24.
[86] *Senate Journal, 35th Tenn. General Assembly, Extra Session, 1868,*
p. 131.

some parts of East Tennessee. Particularly was this
true in the counties of Maury, Lincoln, Giles, Marshall,
Obion, Hardeman, Fayette, and Gibson. As the greater
portion of the testimony taken by this committee was
given by agents of the freedmen's bureau, it is of little
value as accurate evidence of the activities of the Ku Klux
Klan, but it served to convince the committee "that a
resort to some measures that will correct evils of such
enormity is an absolute necessity," and "that no further
evidence is necessary to convince every thoughtful mind
that more than ordinary means are requisite, under existing circumstances, to secure peace and protection to persons and property."[87] The committe therefore recommended "that the governor should be invested with full
powers to call out such military force as may be required
to secure obedience to the laws" and "that ample means
should be placed at his disposal to see that the laws are
faithfully executed."[88]

Acting upon this recommendation the legislature
passed "an act to preserve the public peace," commonly
known as the Ku Klux act. This was one of the most
severe pieces of legislation ever inscribed upon an American statute book. It provided,

That, if any person or persons, shall unite with, associate with,
promote or encourage, any secret organization of persons, that
shall prowl through the country or towns of this state, by day
or by night, disguised or otherwise, for the purpose of dis-
turbing the peace, or alarming the peaceful citizens of any portion of this state, on conviction by any tribunal of the state,
shall be fined five hundred dollars, imprisoned in the state pen-
itentiary not less than five years, and shall be rendered infamous.[89]

The same punishment was provided for any witness who
should refuse to obey a summons, or who should appear
and refuse to testify; for any prosecuting attorney who,

[87] *Ibid.*, p. 187.   [88] *Ibid.*, p. 168.
[89] *Acts, 35th Tenn. General Assembly, Extra Session, 1868*, p. 19.

THE KU KLUX KLAN

having been informed of a violation of the law should refuse to prosecute; for any officer, clerk, sheriff, or constable who should refuse to perform any of the duties imposed upon him by the act; for anyone who should write, publish, advise, entreat, publicly or privately, any class of persons to resist any of the laws of the state; for any person who should make threats with the intention of intimidating or preventing any elector or person from exercising the elective franchise; for anyone who should attempt to break up an election in the state; and for anyone who should feed, lodge, entertain, or conceal in the woods or elsewhere any person known to be a violator of the act. The law further provided that no prosecutor should be required on indictments and that no indictment should be held insufficient for want of form; that when any process should be returned unexecuted, for any cause whatever, to the court from which it was issued the clerk should issue an *alias capias* to the said county; and that if the inhabitants of such county should permit such defendent to be or live in said county, they should be subject to an assessment of not less than five hundred or more than five thousand dollars, at the discretion of the court. All inhabitants of the state were authorized to arrest offenders under the act without a warrant. Every public officer, in addition to his regular oath, must swear that he had never been a member of the Ku Klux Klan. In addition to this, it was provided that damages might be assessed upon the following scale: for entering the house or residence of any officer at night, in a hostile manner or against his will, ten thousand dollars; for killing any peaceable individual in the night, twenty thousand dollars; and all other injuries to be assessed in proportion.[90]

On September 16 the Governor, acting under the authority thus conferred, issued a proclamation against the

[90] *Ibid.*, pp. 19-23.

Ku Klux Klan and called upon all good, loyal, and patriotic people, both white and black, to raise companies
and report to him at Nashville.

I propose to meet them [the Ku Klux] with such numbers and
in such a manner as the exigency shall demand, whatever may
be the consequences. I will not be deterred from the discharge
of my duty herein by threats of violence from rebel speakers or
rebel newspapers, nor by any other means of intimidation.[91]

Notwithstanding the force of this proclamation, it did
not meet with the desired response, and the Governor was
forced to rely upon the assistance of Federal troops for
a time.

On September 1 a legislative committee composed of
William H. Wisener, Thomas A. Hamilton, and J. H.
Agee, was sent to Washington to importune the President for aid. Johnson referred this matter to the secretary of war, General Schofield, who directed General
George H. Thomas to send such forces into Tennessee as
would be necessary "to execute the laws, preserve the
peace, and protect the law abiding citizens of the state."
General Thomas thereupon ordered a regiment of in-
fantry to proceed to Tennessee where, upon the advice of
the Governor, it was distributed over the counties where
the Ku Klux were supposed to be the most dangerous.
The headquarters of the regiment with three companies
were sent to Columbia, and one company each was sent to
the county seat of Franklin, Bedford, Lincoln, Marshall,
Wayne, Rutherford, and Giles counties respectively.[92]
This action contributed to the success of the Republican
presidential ticket in the state.

The conditions in the state militia in 1867 had not been
attractive,[93] and for this reason there was no great desire

[91] *Proclamation Book*, pp. 116-19.
[92] *Report of the Secretary of War, 1868*, pp. xxxi-xxxiii.
[93] A private in the militia wrote to the governor, on June 12, 1867,
"We have never had a change of diet, which you know is contrary to the
laws of nature, hygiene, and army regulations. We draw meal, bacon,
sugar, and coffee, and occasionally a small quantity of beans, salt, and

on the part of able-bodied men to enlist in the state guards. An additional campaign was therefore necessary in order to induce enlistments. During the winter of 1868-9 the columns of the *Press and Times* were again filled with accounts of "Ku Klux outrages." In Giles County it was reported that Negroes had been driven away from their homes for voting for Grant.[94] In Overton County Mike Strohmeir was notified to cease collecting revenue.[95] In Bedford County Negroes were constantly whipped, robbed, and threatened.[96] In almost every county in Middle Tennessee it was "reported" that various and sundry "outrages" had been committed upon Negroes and Union men.

To meet this situation the Governor issued another proclamation, on January 20, 1869, calling upon "all good and loyal citizens to enter the ranks of the state guards, be mustered into service, and aid in suppressing lawlessness."[97] This proclamation met with the desired response, and on January 25 Brigadier General Joseph A. Cooper was placed in command of all the state forces. On February 20 the Governor issued his last proclamation, stating that there were over sixteen hundred state guards in the city of Nashville. At the same time he proclaimed martial law over the counties of Overton, Jackson, Maury, Giles, Marshall, Lawrence, Gibson, Madison, and Haywood, and directed General Cooper "to distribute these troops at once and continue them in service until we have unmistakable evidence of the purpose of all parties to keep the peace."[98]

soup, all of which is deficient in quantity and inferior in quality, which we have to carry daily one mile for lack of water."—Brownlow Papers. James H. Sumner, captain of a company of Negro militia, wrote to the adjutant-general, on July 29, 1867, with regard to his troops, "They are laying on the ground at night in the dew. I want blankets, coats, tents, drawers, and shirts. The men are to go on a march in one or two days and have not the things to go with." Letter in the files of the adjutant-general's office.

[94] Nashville *Daily Press and Times*, Nov. 13, 1868.
[95] *Ibid.*, Jan. 12, 1869.   [97] *Ibid.*, Jan. 21, 1869.
[96] *Ibid.*, Jan. 14, 1869.   [98] *Ibid.*, Feb. 21, 1869.

General Cooper, thereupon, mobilized the state guards and prepared for an active campaign against the Klan.[99] His precautions, however, were unnecessary for the Ku Klux Klan was a dying order in Tennessee. On February 20 Brownlow resigned his position as chief executive in order that he might take his seat in the United States Senate to which he had been elected by the preceding legislature. His successor, DeWitt Clinton Senter, almost immediately began to extend promises of conciliation to the Conservatives. The Brownlow regime was at an end. "Law and order meetings" began to spring up in the various counties, and, with its arch-enemy departed, the Ku Klux Klan gradually disappeared from the state.[100]

At the same time the Invisible Empire ended its existence. In March, 1869, the Imperial Wizard issued a proclamation in which he recited the legislation that had been directed against the Klan, and stated that the organization had, in large measure, accomplished the objects for which it was brought into existence. In time of danger, he said, it had afforded protection and security to many people and in many ways it had contributed to the public welfare. But the members of the Klan had violated positive orders, and others, under the name and disguise of the organization, had assumed to do acts of violence for which the order had been held responsible. Therefore, he directed that the organization heretofore known as the Ku Klux Klan be dissolved and disbanded.[101]

Thus lived, and so died this strange order. Its birth was an accident; its growth a comedy; its death a tragedy. It owed its existence wholly to the anomalous condition of society and civil affairs in the South during the years immediately succeeding the unfortunate contest in which so many brave in blue and gray fell, martyrs to their convictions.[102]

[99] General Order Book, Tennessee State Guards, pp. 30-31. State Archives.
[100] Nashville *Daily Press and Times,* Feb. 10, 1869.
[101] Lester and Wilson, *op. cit.,* p. 129.
[102] *Ibid.,* p. 129.

CHAPTER IX

THE RESTORATION OF TENNESSEE

THE COLLAPSE of the Confederate administration and the consequent restoration of the authority of the Federal government in the state of Tennessee have been described in another chapter. It is to be remembered, however, that these events, although they were quickly followed by the reorganization of the state government, did not restore the commonwealth to its constitutional relations with the Union. During his administration as military governor, Andrew Johnson had been active in his efforts to end the insurrection in the state; he had exerted himself to maintain the supremacy of the Federal laws; and he had "earnestly labored to restore the state to its former proud position in the Union."[1] It was not until the end of his administration, however, that the terms of the presidential "ten per cent" plan of reconstruction had been complied with,[2] and thus the task of guiding the state back into the Union was left to his successor. The events attendant upon this task constitute one of the important phases of the Brownlow administration.

Events moved with rapidity in the early part of the year 1865, and there was every indication that the state would experience an early restoration to its former position in the Union. In a dispatch to the President on January 13, announcing the action of the Union convention recently held at Nashville, Johnson expressed confident hope,

Thank God that the tyrant's rod has been broken. Without some reverses in arms, the state will be redeemed and the foul blot of slavery erased from her escutcheon. I hope that Tennessee will not be included in the bill now before congress and will

[1] Nashville *Times and Union*, Feb. 27, 1865.
[2] February 22, 1865.

be made an exception if the bill passes. All is now working well, and if Tennessee is now left alone, she will resume all the functions of a state according to the genius and theory of the government.[3]

The President was also favorable to an early restoration of the state. A committee, sent by the Union convention to request that he issue a proclamation declaring Tennessee to be no longer in insurrection, reported on February 13 that,

The President replied that he knew of no impediment in the way of according to our first proposition, except the extent to which it might affect the present trade regulations—that the matter presented might also involve some grave legal considerations and that in order to do justice to our subject, he should have to take some time to consider it, intimating that we might expect as favorable a response as the nature of the case admitted, and with the least avoidable delay.[4]

The state press was also optimistic. On January 17, the Nashville *Union* said,

We shall expect to see Tennessee once more enjoy the blessings of civil government within four or five months, and we have no fears that the next Congress will fail to welcome Senators and Representatives from this state.[5]

On February 22, the *Daily Times,* in an article entitled "The Duty of Today," pointed to the future with bright hope.

A bright destiny is ours if we have the manliness to claim it. If we fail to do our duty today, we deserve to be still more oppressed and degraded. Our action today will be indelibly recorded in the country's history, and what man is willing that we shall hereafter be spoken of as a people who voluntarily chose anarchy, guerrilla marauding, military rule, desolation,

---

[3] *O.R.,* series III, vol. IV, p. 1050.
[4] Nashville *Daily Times,* Feb. 13, 1865. This committee was composed of J. B. Bingham of Shelby, J. W. Bowen of Smith, and John Caldwell of Sevier.
[5] Nashville *Union,* Jan. 17, 1865.

violence and bloodshed, to peace and freedom under the mild
sway of civil law.[6]

At the beginning of his administration the new governor was equally hopeful. In his first message to the
legislature he called attention to threatening reports that
were coming from the North but refused to regard them
seriously,

It is with profound regret that I have observed several Republican journals and some leading politicians, of ability and influence, are opposed to the admission of Senators and Representatives from Tennessee. They take the ground that this state
should be treated as a territory, and continued under military
government, subject to the arbitrary orders of military rule. If
their dangerous and revolutionary doctrine is adhered to by
any considerable portion of Senators and Representatives in
Congress, I shall, for one, dread the consequences. My confidence in the wisdom and patriotism of Senators and Representatives leads me to believe that they will discard, indignantly,
any such proposition. The loyal people of Tennessee have resolved through the ballot-box to rule themselves under the
Federal flag; taking the ground that the state has never been
out of the Union, and boldly denying that the unconstitutional
and treasonable acts of those in rebellion ever carried them
out of the Union.[7]

At the same time he suggested that the legislature should
continue to demonstrate its loyalty by proceeding to the
ratification of the recently adoped Thirteenth Amendment. With regard to this amendment he added,

It is in this way, and in no other, that a uniform rule can be
provided, and an end put thereby, in all time to come, to a possi-
bility of reviving that which has been the fatal cause of all
the mischief in the country. To insist upon excluding slavery
from a state by amending her constitution, before recognizing
her again as within the pale of the Union would look awkward,
and fall below the dignity of political sagacity. Our state has

[6] Nashville *Daily Times*, Feb. 22, 1865. This was the day upon which
the new constitutional amendments were submitted to the people for ratification.
[7] *Senate Journal, 34th Tenn. General Assembly, 1st Session, 1865*, p. 39.

shown her hand, and placed herself square upon the record; and I flatter myself that her representatives here assembled are ready for a measure which shall forever exclude slavery from the United States.[8]

This suggestion was really unnecessary, for the legislature had, on the day before (but presumably after the message was written), unanimously ratified the Thirteenth Amendment.[9] On April 21 the announcement of this action was formally made to President Johnson, who was known to share Lincoln's views as to reconstruction, and he was requested

to make known to the loyal citizens of the State of Tennessee, by proclamation or otherwise, that the State of Tennessee be no longer considered in a state of insurrection, and that the loyal people of that state be granted all the rights and privileges that are granted or allowed to the loyal citizens of any of the sister states, that are not considered in a state of rebellion against the Government of the United States.[10]

On April 29 the President removed the interdict on all domestic and coastwise intercourse in that portion of the late Confederate States east of the Mississippi River and within the lines of national military occupation.[11] Relying upon this act as an indication of the character of Johnson's future policy, and still adhering to the contention that the state had never been out of the Union, the legislature proceeded, on May 4, to elect two United States Senators. David T. Patterson and Joseph S. Fowler were chosen to succeed Andrew Johnson and A. O. P. Nicholson, respectively.[12] On June 9 an act was passed, reapportioning the representation in Congress,[13] and on June 12 the Governor ordered that an election for

[8] Ibid., p. 22.
[9] Acts, 34th Tenn. General Assembly, 1st Session, 1865, p. 39.
[10] Ibid., p. 142.
VI, 333.
[11] James D. Richardson, ed., Messages and Papers of the Presidents,
[12] Senate Journal, 34th Tenn. General Assembly, 1st Session, 1865, pp. 91-96.
[13] Acts, 34th Tenn. General Assembly, 1st Session, 1865, p. 52.

congressmen be held on the following August 2 in each of the eight districts into which the state had been divided.[14]

The legislature adjourned on June 12.[15] On the following day, the President issued a proclamation declaring the insurrection hitherto existing in the State of Tennessee at an end. The authority of the United States, he said, was unquestioned within the limits of the commonwealth, and duly commissioned Federal officers were in undisturbed exercise of their functions. All disabilities attached to the state and its inhabitants were therefore removed, except that nothing contained in the order was to be construed as affecting any of the penalties and forfeitures for treason which had previously been incurred.[16] On August 2 the congressional election was held, and eight congressmen were duly elected. Two of these men had held commissions as judicial officers under the late Confederate Government, but there was no objection to the delegation as a whole on grounds of personal disloyalty to the United States Government.[17]

It is to be observed that, in all their action thus far, both Johnson and the people of Tennessee had adhered to the presidential theory that the states had never left the Union. This attitude continued to be manifested by the people of Tennessee. On September 4 General Gideon J. Pillow, A. O. P. Nicholson, W. C. Whitthorne, and other former Confederates arranged a meeting at Columbia and adopted resolutions expressing a belief that the states had never been out of the Union, and that as soon as its suspended civil and political relations were revived Tennessee would become entitled to all its former benefits and rights as a member of the United States. They also approved of the policy of Andrew Johnson and

---

[14] Nashville *Dispatch*, June 13, 1865.

[15] *Senate Journal, 34th Tenn. General Assembly, 1st Session, 1865*, 230.

[16] Richardson, *op. cit.*, p. 318.

[17] *Cong. Globe*, 39 Cong., 1 Sess., p. 33.

expressed a willingness to abide by the provisions of the Thirteenth Amendment.[18]

About the same time General Rousseau, in command at Nashville, addressed a letter to William B. Campbell, Dorsey B. Thomas, and Edmund Cooper, all members of the recently elected congressional delegation, and inquired specifically as to their attitude toward the national administration. They replied that they were not, and never had been, hostile to the government of the United States; that they had uniformly supported the policy of Andrew Johnson; that they recognized the validity of the Brownlow government; and that they were in accord with the Thirteenth Amendment.[19] This statement was published in the Northern newspapers, and it had its effect when the delegation came to demand seats at the next session of Congress.

Other public meetings followed, all supporting Johnson and the national administration. On September 23 resolutions were passed at Nashville assuring the President of the support of the people of that city and counselling all citizens "to meet all fellow citizens, socially and politically, as brothers of one great nationality."[20] On September 30 there was a great public meeting at Clarksville. Cave Johnson spoke, and resolutions were adopted to the effect that,

President Johnson, in his effort to reunite the people under the constitution of the United States, leaving to the states their sacred and inestimable rights, deserves and should receive the approbation of the whole country regardless of past political differences, and we hold it to be the duty of all Southern men to uphold and encourage his efforts by every manifestation of approval and support.[21]

The legislature met again on October 2, and ten days later the House gave further indication of its support of

[18] Nashville *Daily Union*, Sept. 13, 1865.
[19] Nashville *Dispatch*, Sept. 20, 1865.
[20] Nashville *Daily Union*, Sept. 24, 1865.
[21] Nashville *Dispatch*, Oct. 11, 1865.

the President by the adoption of a resolution endorsing "the Administration of His Excellency, Honorable Andrew Johnson, President of the United States, especially his declaration that 'Intelligent treason must be made odious and traitors punished'."[22]

This then was the situation when the Thirty-ninth Congress assembled on December 4, 1865. Tennessee, along with several other Southern states, had fulfilled all of the requirements specified in the presidential plan of reconstruction, and Johnson had indicated his willingness to restore the state on that ground.[23] The majority of the people in the North seem to have been in sympathy with the President's plan of restoration. Party conventions, Democratic and Union, endorsed it in nearly every state. Few newspapers opposed it, although a certain element of the press advocated that Negro suffrage should be made a fourth condition precedent to readmission.[24]

As the time for the meeting of Congress approached, however, it became evident that there was an element in that body that would not support the President. This element was composed of the Radical members of Congress and was led by Thaddeus Stevens, a politician of no ordinary ability. For several reasons this element opposed the presidential plan of reconstruction. Some desired to assure the ascendency of the Republican party in the South; others were anxious that the legislative branch of the government should resume that superiority which, during the war, had been usurped by the executive; still others felt a sincere or pretended apprehension of danger to the Negroes unless something were done to guarantee their safety; a fourth group hoped to strengthen the Union by the nationalization of civil rights; and lastly there was the desire to "feed fat the ancient

[22] *Acts, 34th Tenn. General Assembly, 2nd Session, 1865-6*, p. 413.
[23] Richardson, *op. cit.*, VI, 310.
[24] J. F. Rhodes, *History of the United States*, V, 533-34.

grudge'' against the South.[25] By whatever motives they were actuated, it was evident that the Radicals were attempting to bring Congress back to the position asserted in the Wade-Davis bill—that the reconstruction of the seceded states was a congressional and not a presidential function.

Congress met at noon on December 4, 1865. The Tennessee members were allowed seats on the floor of the House as a special favor, but their names, along with those of the other members from the Southern states, were excluded from the official roll. This action had been arranged by Stevens through the connivance of his friend, Edward McPherson, the clerk of the House.[26] When the clerk, in calling the roll, reached Indiana, Horace Maynard arose and attempted to speak, but McPherson would allow no interruption.[27] At the close of the roll-call, Maynard again attempted to obtain the floor, but he was called to order by Stevens, on the ground that his name did not appear on the official roll of the House.[28] In accordance with a plan previously agreed upon in the Republican caucus Stevens then secured the appointment of the famous joint committee on reconstruction. This committee consisted of fifteen members, nine from the House and six from the Senate, and to it all papers, resolutions, and bills relating to reconstruction were referred without debate. The creation of the joint committee resulted in successfully removing the matter of reconstruction from the hands of the President and placing it under the control of Congress.

There was a strong feeling among the Republicans, both in and out of Congress, that Tennessee ought to be

[25] *Ibid.*, V, 531 *et seq.* W. A. Dunning, *Reconstruction, Political and Economic*, p. 52.

[26] Rhodes, *op. cit.*, p. 544.

[27] *Cong. Globe*, 39 Cong., 1 Sess., p. 3.

[28] *Ibid.*, p. 3. Gideon Welles thought that this was the result of a previous understanding between Maynard and the Radical leaders. Gideon Welles, *Diary of Gideon Welles*, II, 388.

excepted from the jurisdiction of the joint committee. Henry J. Raymond of New York made a notable effort to have the credentials of the Tennessee delegation referred to the committee on elections, on the ground that each house was "the judge of the elections, returns and quali- fications of its own members."[29] The Radicals became alarmed at this and said that the question involved was not the mere admission of congressmen, but the creation of a state, which required the joint action of the two houses and the consent of the president.[30] On March 2, 1866, the Radical ascendency was secured by the adop- tion of a concurrent resolution declaring that no senator or representative should be admitted from any insurrec- tionary state until Congress should have declared the state entitled to representation.[31] The congressional theory of reconstruction thus succeeded the presidential theory, and the hopes of an early restoration of Ten- nessee were shattered.

Meanwhile a sub-committee was appointed to inquire into the condition of Tennessee and report whether the state was entitled to be represented in either house of Congress. This committee was composed of James W. Grimes of Iowa, on the part of the Senate, and John A. Bingham of Ohio and Henry Grider of Kentucky on the part of the House. Grider was a Democrat, and Grimes and Bingham were not extreme Radicals—a distinct ad- vantage to the state. The sub-committee began taking tes- timony and examining witnesses on January 25, 1866, and concluded its labors on February 13. It took depositions of Fowler and Patterson, the Senators-elect, and of Cooper, Leftwich, Stokes, and Maynard, of the congressional del- egation. All of these men declared that their admission into Congress would strengthen the cause of the loyalists

[29] *Cong. Globe,* 39 Cong., 1 Sess., pp. 31-32.
[30] *Ibid.,* p. 32.
[31] *Ibid.,* p. 1132.

in the state, while their continued exclusion would diminish if not entirely destroy their influence.[32]

Nine other witnesses were called. Of these five were United States army officers stationed in Tennessee, and four were loyal citizens of the state.[33] Each of the nine answered categorically that in his opinion the complete restoration of the state to its place in the Union would strengthen the loyal government in Tennessee, thereby confirming the opinion of the members-elect.[34] It should be observed that the testimony of the army officers was entitled to more credence than that of the congressional delegation. The latter were clearly not in the position of disinterested parties, as the readmission of the state would result in their securing the seats to which they had been elected. On the other hand such action would result in the withdrawal of the Federal forces from the state, with the consequent danger of a reduction of the number of military officers. Thus the army officers were virtually testifying against themselves in stating that they favored the readmission of the state.

The sub-committee was impressed with the testimony and other evidence received, and on February 17 Bingham reported to the joint committee a resolution stating that as Tennessee had adopted a constitution, which on examination had been ''found to be republican in its form of government,'' the state was entitled to representation in Congress and ''to be one of the United States of America, on an equal footing with the other states in all respects whatever.''[35] This resolution was discussed at this meeting and at the next, on February 17, and, al-

[32] *House Reports*, 39 Cong., 1 Sess., No. 30, pp. 98-104.

[33] The army officers were: Major General Edward Hatch, Major General George H. Thomas, Major General Clinton B. Fisk, Lieutenant Colonel John H. Cochrane, and Lieutenant R. H. Barnard. The others were William Spence of Murfreesboro and Oliver P. Temple, John Williams, and Abner G. Jackson, all of Knoxville.

[34] *House Reports*, 39 Cong., 1 Sess., No. 30, pp. 105-28.

[35] B. B. Kendrick, ed., *The Journal of the Joint Committee of Fifteen on Reconstruction*, p. 65.

though it was slightly amended, its principle was not departed from.[36] It did not, however, meet with the approval of the radicals, and it was moved and passed that "the whole subject of Tennessee be referred to a select committee of three members to be appointed by the Chairman." This committee was composed of George H. Williams of Oregon, Roscoe Conkling of New York, and George S. Boutwell of Massachusetts, all radicals.[37]

In addition to their inherent radicalism, the eight radicals who had opposed the Bingham resolution were actuated in this procedure by certain events which had recently occurred in Tennessee. On January 9 a memorial had been sent to the joint committee by the "Union Central and German Union Central Committees of the State of Tennessee and the Union Members of the Tennessee Legislature," expressing fear as to the consequences of the removal of the Federal forces from the state.

Your memorialists will say, however, that they desire to be represented in Congress. The loyal people of Tennessee have not forfeited their civil rights by the misfortune of being surrounded by rebels and if difficulties should occur hereafter, as is to be feared, in that event, they desire to have a voice in the councils of the nation. But if our form of government is such that to admit our representatives to Seats in Congress will compel the withdrawal of the supervising control of the national government over our internal affairs, thereby insuring the ascendency of the rebel majority, your memorialists prefer, and they are sure the loyal people of the state would prefer, to

---

[36] *Ibid.*, p. 66.

[37] *Ibid.*, p. 67. Conkling was an able and prominent statesman, but he was the protege and favorite of Thaddeus Stevens and "generally took his cue in matters concerning the South from that ancient radical."—Kendrick, *op. cit.*, p. 186. Boutwell was a professional politician whose chief interest was to keep his party in power and himself in office. Gideon Welles referred to him as "an ardent narrow-minded partizan, without much judgment, not devoid of talents, with more industry than capacity, ambitious of notoriety, with a mind without comprehension nor well trained; an extreme radical where party is involved."—Welles, *op. cit.*, III, 239. Welles called Williams "a revolutionary, whiskey-drinking radical."—*Ibid.*, II, 412.

live in a territorial condition, and even under a military government.[38]

On January 21 the Knoxville *Whig* predicted that a great financial depression would result, in the coming spring and summer, if the army and the paymasters were withdrawn from Tennessee.[39]   Moreover, it was stated in the Northern newspapers, though he denied it, that the governor had expressed, in a letter to Schuyler Colfax, the Speaker of the House, an opposition to the seating of the Tennessee delegation.[40]

By taking advantage of these conditions which were said to exist in Tennessee, Stevens determined to prevent the readmission of the state except with such restrictions as would embarrass the President.   It was a well known fact that Johnson was exceedingly desirous that his native state should be restored to the Union at the earliest possible date.   If therefore he should sign a resolution admitting Tennessee with conditions additional to those which he had prescribed, he would commit himself to the fundamental principle of the radicals that his conditions were not sufficient; if, on the other hand, he should veto such a measure, the argument that the radicals were alone in their opposition to the admission of the seceded states would lose its force.[41]

With this purpose in view Conkling, from the select committee on Tennessee, reported on February 19 a resolution provided that senators and representatives from that state should be admitted when certain conditions had been complied with.   These conditions included a repudiation of the Confederate debt, the insertion and maintenance of a provision in the constitution disavowing the doctrine of secession, the disfranchisement of all former Confederates for a period of five years, and the ratifi-

---

[38] *House Reports*, 39 Cong., 1 Sess., No. 30, pp. 91-95.

[39] Knoxville *Whig.*, Jan. 21, 1866.

[40] *Ibid.*, Feb. 7, 1866.

[41] Welles, Gideon, *op. cit.*, II, 442.

cation of the foregoing conditions by a majority of the qualified voters of the state.[42]   No action was taken on this resolution, however, as the joint committee adjourned soon after it was presented in order to await the announcement of the President's action upon the freedmen's bureau bill.

The action of Johnson in vetoing this bill was a severe blow to those who hoped for an early readmission of Tennessee.   The cause of the Tennessee delegation had been ably championed by Brooks, the leader of the Democratic minority, and the joint committee was on the point of yielding and seating the members when this veto came.[43]   Stevens now saw an opportunity to set Congress against the policy of the President without bringing in the question of Tennessee at all.   On the next day he introduced a resolution in the House providing that no senators or representatives should be seated until Congress should give its consent.   Henry Grider made an attempt to have Tennessee exempted from this provision and introduced a resolution allowing its delegation to take their seats.[44] The Stevens resolution passed without amendment, however, and the admission of Tennessee was indefinitely postponed.[45]

On March 5, however, the joint committee adopted a resolution providing for the admission of Tennessee with essentially the same conditions as those reported in the Conkling resolution of February 19.[46]   This resolution was reported to the House by Bingham on the same day that it was adopted by the committee.[47]   At that same time minority reports were presented by both Boutwell and Rogers.   These two disagreed with the majority report, but upon very different ground.   Boutwell

[42] *Journal of the Joint Committee,* p. 68.
[43] *Cong. Globe,* 39 Cong., 1 Sess., pp. 3-4.
[44] *Ibid.,* p. 943.
[45] *Ibid.,* p. 1132.
[46] *Journal of the Joint Committee,* pp. 72-81.
[47] *Cong. Globe,* 39 Cong., 1 Sess., p. 1189.

thought that the adoption of Negro suffrage should be made a condition precedent to the readmission of Tennessee,[48] while Rogers denied that the state had ever been out of the Union and recommended the admission of its senators and congressmen without any restrictions whatever.[49] In reporting the majority resolution to the House, Bingham asked that it be recommitted and stated that he would bring it up again within a fortnight.[50] As a matter of fact, it was not called up again for four months.[51]

Meanwhile events in Tennessee were gradually shaping themselves in such a way as to secure the readmission of the state to the Union. On February 13 four of the congressmen-elect, Edmund Cooper, Horace Maynard, John W. Leftwich, and William B. Stokes, presented a memorial to the joint committee. Characterizing the Brownlow government as "republican in form as well as in spirit" they asked that it "be recognized and its perpetuity be guaranteed as the true and proper government of the state of Tennessee, entitled to the same immunities, functions, and prerogatives as the state enjoyed by virtue of an act of Congress approved on the 1st day of June, 1796."[52] On February 21 Elijah Simerly of Carter County, speaking in the legislature on the Conkling resolution of February 19 expressed similar sentiments,

Let us speak out manfully and sustain our patriotic President and demand of Congress the full and prompt recognition of our inalienable rights to participate in the legislation of this great

[48] *House Reports*, 39 Cong., 1 Sess., No. 29.

[49] *Ibid.*

[50] *Cong. Globe*, 39 Cong., 1 Sess., p. 1189.

[51] Kendrick suggests as a hypothesis in explanation of the motives of the Republicans, in allowing action on the resolution to be delayed so long, that the conservatives, led by Fessenden, were disappointed by the President's veto of the civil rights bill, while the radicals, led by Stevens, had secured the fulfillment of their desires in this veto and were ready to allow the Tennessee question to drop.—*Journal of the Joint Committee*, pp. 256-60.

[52] *House Reports*, 39 Cong., 1 Sess., No. 30, pp. 1-2.

and good government which the loyal people of Tennessee have always loved and clung to, in peace and in war, and to preserve whose existence they have suffered and sacrificed far more than many who are now trying to class us with the rebels and traitors and even deny us the rights of freemen.[53]

More important than the action of the Congressmen-elect or that of the legislature, however, was that of the Governor. He was not willing to "sustain our patriotic President," but preferred rather to be numbered among the supporters of the radicals in Congress. In a private letter to Oliver P. Temple on March 8, 1866, he said that Johnson was supporting the "rebels".[54]

They extol Johnson to the skies, claim him as "Head Center" and what is more deplorable to all, he is with them. We shall have a more desperate and bloody war than we have passed through. Johnson will place himself at the head of the rebels and Democrats. He will in less than twelve months, invite the Southern states to send up delegates, and he will undertake to put them in their seats at the point of a bayonet—if indeed he doesn't attempt to turn out the present Congress as Cromwell did the Long Parliament. God only knows what we are coming to.[55]

[53] Nashville *Daily Union,* Feb. 22, 1866.

[54] Brownlow's opposition to Johnson's policy was expressed at times in a facetious as well as a serious manner. An example of the former is found in the following:

COPPERHEAD CATECHISM

Question—Who was the first man?
Answer—Andrew Johnson.
Q.—How many are there of him?
A.—Three.
Q.—Can you name them?
A.—I, me, and my policy.
Q.—What agents are employed in making known his will to man?
A.—Treasury agents.
Q.—Do you believe in the existence of my policy?
A.—I do.
Q.—Upon what grounds do you base your belief?
A.—New Orleans Burial Grounds.
Right. The class may take their seats with the elect.—Knoxville *Whig,* No. 14, 1866.

[55] This letter in the private collection of the late Miss Mary Boyce Temple of Knoxville had reference to a Conservative convention held in Nashville on February 22, where resolutions had been adopted supporting

On March 24, in a speech before the German Union League at Knoxville, he again avowed his hostility to the President and the Democratic party,

The President, backed by the whole South, and by the Democracy of the North can never transfer me to that party. I have taken my stand on the side of Congress, and the party who elected the President, and put down the rebellion, and I propose to fight it out on that line, if I am left in the gang by myself. I am opposed to men taking their seats in Congress and making laws to govern men, who, four years ago, indignantly took up their hats and canes, walked out, and swore that no earthly power could keep them in the Union.[56]

It was thus evident that the policy of the Governor was adhering closely to that of the congressional radicals.

During the late spring and early summer of 1866, however, a number of events occurred in Washington which prompted Brownlow to take positive action toward securing the readmission of the state. On April 30 the joint committee on reconstruction reported a bill to Congress providing that whenever a "rebel" state had ratified the proposed Fourteenth Amendment, and it had become a part of the Constitution, the state should be entitled to representation in Congress.[57] This measure was postponed and failed in the end, but it aroused sufficient interest in Tennessee to cause the Radicals in that state to urge that the legislature, instead of adjourning *sine die,* should merely take a recess so as to be ready to ratify the amendment immediately upon its adoption by Congress.[58] This proposal received support in Congress. On May 10 John A. Bingham, speaking in the House on the proposed amendment, expressed the hope that Tennessee would be the first state to ratify it,

Johnson and denouncing the Radical party and its legislation in Congress. Accounts of the convention are given in Nashville *Daily Union,* Feb. 23, 1866, and Nashville *Union and American,* Feb. 24, 1866.

[56] Knoxville *Whig,* Apr. 4, 1866.

[57] *Cong. Globe,* 39 Cong., 1 Sess., p. 2287.

[58] Nashville *Dispatch,* June 17, 1866.

Let that great example be set by Tennessee and it will be worth a hundred thousand votes to the loyal people in the free North. Let this be done, and it will be hailed as the harbinger of that great day for which all good men pray, when the fallen pillars of the republic shall be restored without violence, or the noise of words, or the sound of the hammer, each in its original place in the sacred temple of our national liberties.[59]

After the Fourteenth Amendment was adopted by Congress, forty members of that body addressed a letter to the Governor, asking him to convene the legislature for the purpose of ratifying the new amendment.[60] At the same time the Cincinnati *Commercial* expressed a belief that "if this is done by Tennessee, it is most probable that her congressional delegation will be admitted ere the adjournment for this session."[61] The Washington *Chronicle* stated on June 15 that "the feeling to admit Tennessee before the close of the present session has become almost irresistible."[62]

Influenced by these announcements and desiring that the state should have the honor of being the first to re-enter the Union, Governor Brownlow issued a proclamation, on June 19, calling the legislature to meet in extra session, on July 4, for the purpose of considering action upon the new amendment.[63] His procedure, however, met with much opposition. The Nashville *Dispatch* was openly skeptical, fearing the implied proposition of Congress as "a bait, which may be withdrawn when we have been caught."[64] The *Union and American* opposed the Governor's plan on the ground that the legislature had not been elected with reference to this question and on the further ground that such a body did not represent the sentiment of the entire population of the state. The amendment itself was also opposed on principle.

[59] *Cong. Globe*, 39 Cong., 1 Sess., p. 2544.
[60] Nashville *Dispatch*, June 17, 1866.
[61] Cincinnati *Commercial*, June 15, 1866.
[62] Washington *Chronicle*, June 15, 1866.
[63] *Proclamation Book*, p. 53.   [64] Nashville *Dispatch*, June 30, 1866.

The whole people of this state are not ready to accept the perfect social and political equality of the blacks with them. They are not prepared to admit the negro to the jury box, to the ballot-box, to indiscriminate mingling in the social circle, at church, in the ball room, in the theater, in the concert hall, in railroad cars, in the parlor, and at the hotels and watering-places. They have not yet satisfied themselves of the superiority of the theory of miscegenation and the improving results of amalgamation; and are not, therefore, ready to open the doors of marriage between the races, either by legal enactment or in the more solemn form of constitutional provision.[65]

On July 2 Joseph R. Dillon of Washington, a former member of the Tennessee legislature, addressed an open letter to A. W. Moss, representative from Williamson County, making the point that the legislature had not been elected with reference to the present question now before it.[66] On July 4 the *Dispatch* published a letter from John W. Leftwich, one of the congressmen-elect, asking that the members of the legislature refuse to ratify the amendment. It was too great an extension of the power of the central government, he said, and only an attempt to make valid the "unconstitutional" civil rights bill. The Constitution, he thought, was held in reverence "because it came from our fathers," and he hoped that Tennessee would not "mar the beautiful and harmonious portions of that sacred instrument, so perfect in its adaptability to our varied wants, as rather to challenge increased veneration, as the gift of inspiration."[67]

Leftwich also adopted a more forceful and practical method of opposing the ratification of the amendment than the language of this florid letter would suggest. On July 24 he wrote to Reuel Hough, revenue collector at Memphis, whose appointment he had been instrumental in securing,

I want you to see our friend, Richards, and if he cannot be induced to oppose the ratification of the constitutional amend-

---

[65] Nashville *Union and American*, June 27, 1866.
[66] Nashville *Dispatch*, July 10, 1866.   [67] *Ibid.*, July 4, 1866.

ment, let him take sick and stay at home, and he and you shall never regret it. The Northern ''people'' do not require of us any such ruinous legislation, but recognize, as you and I do, that in giving the negro freedom and all the civil rights, that we have done quite enough without giving him the right to interfere with our elections, and this is all the amendment means. This is the most important political issue ever presented, and if we ratify it, there is no telling what will be the next requirement. A refusal to ratify it may keep us from our seats for a while, but that is nothing when principles are at stake.[68]

The legislature met on July 4, in pursuance to the Governor's proclamation. Conditions in Nashville were not at all peaceful at this time. According to the statement of General Thomas,

There was considerable excitement. I could observe it from the conversations various persons had with me, and what I read in the newspapers published in the city at that time. The comments of the papers were very severe on both sides, and so were the remarks of those persons who conversed with me. . . . It was my opinion that there was a disposition to break up the legislature, and that opinion was formed from conversations with different persons and from reading the newspapers published at the time.[69]

On the other hand, Judge John S. Brien thought ''that the Brownlow government had no more regard for law than if there had not been any law on the statute book, and that he [Brownlow] acted only in accordance with his own opinions, and that he was not governed by any statutes at all.''[70]

The Senate met, effected its organization, and promptly ratified the amendment. There was an ineffectual attempt to secure the submitting of the question of ratification to the people of the state on the part of Benjamin Frazier,[71] of Knox, but, on the whole, there was little op-

[68] *Proceedings of the High Court of Impeachment, in the Case of the People of the State of Tennessee versus Thomas N. Frazier*, p. 94. Commonly cited as *The Frazier Impeachment Trial*.

[69] *Ibid.*, p. 47.   [70] *Ibid.*, p. 107.
[71] Nashville *Dispatch*, July 12, 1866.

position to the amendment in the Senate. The enemies of the Brownlow regime had determined to carry on their fight against the ratification in the House.

The House met on July 5, with forty-nine members present. As this number did not constitute a quorum, no business could be transacted. The House continued to meet from day to day, but no quorum could be secured. It was a well known fact that an open filibuster was in progress, the purpose of which was to secure the defeat of the ratification of the Fourteenth Amendment. According to William Y. Elliott, a representative from Rutherford County,

I observed that in the meeting of the house of representatives on the first day of its session, probably there was a concert of action, and a concert thenceforth, with a certain class of that body; they would absent themselves under certain conditions, first one and then another. But it was so marked that I think it escaped the notice of no one in that body, that whenever we approached a quorum, that either one or the other member would absent himself so as to reduce the house below a quorum.[72]

After six days of this procedure, the House adopted resolutions directing the speaker to issue warrants of arrest for Martin of Jackson, Butler of Smith, Marable of Benton and Humphreys, Porter of Henry, Dunnaway of Bedford, Foster of Hamilton, and Williams of Carter; that Captain Heydt, the sergeant-at-arms, be authorized to employ such assistance as was necessary to carry this order into effect; and that he bring "said members before the house to answer for their conduct and contempt of this house."[73] As authority for this procedure, the House relied upon "Rule No. 14," adopted in 1865, to the effect that no member could be absent without leave.[74] The Governor then applied to General Thomas for military aid in enforcing the attendance of the absent mem-

[72] *The Frazier Impeachment Trial*, p. 57.
[73] *Ibid.*, p. 5.   [74] *Ibid.*, p. 6.

bers, but upon orders from Washington Thomas replied that military interference was not proper in such a case.[75] The *Press and Times* then charged that the filibuster had been instigated by Johnson himself,

The President stirs the great caldron of "double toil and trouble," in Washington, while he tosses into it all the ingredients of that hell broth which he calls "my policy," and the noise we hear at the State House is only the sputtering of a little superfluous gut fat which leaps into the fire.[76]

It was further said that Edmund Cooper, now Johnson's private secretary, had written a letter to a member of the house advising him to "bolt"; and also that the watchword at the White House was "Defeat the amendment at all cost."[77]

On July 16 Heydt, with the assistance of some colored soldiers, arrested Pleasant Williams of Carter, and A. J. Martin of Jackson, brought them to Nashville, and forcibly detained them in the capitol.[78] Williams and Martin immediately applied to Judge Thomas N. Frazier of the Davidson County criminal court for a writ of habeas corpus. This writ was issued on the 16th, but the legislature denied the jurisdiction of the court and directed Heydt to continue the members under arrest. On the 17th the case came up for trial before Judge Frazier. The town was in a feverish excitement. The case "attracted an audience to the criminal court, which in character, intelligence, and make up, is hardly ever found within the same walls."[79]

The greater part of the legislature was present at the trial. The House was represented by Horace H. Harrison, John Trimble, and H. Corley. John S. Brien, A. S. Colyer, and John C. Gaut appeared for the petitioners. Harrison set up the defence that the petitioners were in

[75] *Ibid.*, p. 47.
[76] Nashville *Daily Press and Times*, July 15, 1866.
[77] *Ibid.*, July 18, 1866.   [78] *Ibid.*, July 18, 1866.
[79] Nashville *Dispatch*, July 18, 1866.

the custody of the House of Representatives. Gaut then asked that an attachment be issued to bring both the petitioners and the respondent into court. To this Harrison demurred on the ground that the Governor had called the legislature in extra session and that its power was equal to that of the court. Brien then denied the legality of the Governor's call, and Gaut denounced the arrest of the members as a violation of the bill of rights.[80] Able and eloquent arguments by Trimble and Brien consumed the second day of the trial,[81] and the decision of the court was rendered on the third. The court held that, as the legislature was bound by the constitution and the bill of rights, the respondent had shown no legal defense. An attachment was therefore issued against Heydt for contempt of court, and also an attachment for the release of the petitioners.[82]

Considerable difficulty was encountered in executing the order of the court. The sheriff failed in his first attempt to effect the release of the petitioners, and Judge Frazier promptly ordered him to make a second attempt. Upon arriving at the capitol the second time he found the outside glass door locked, with a large sized African on the inside fingering an immense horse pistol. The Negro peremptorily refused to open the door, stating that he had orders to that effect. Appeals to the Negro proving in vain, Judge Frazier directed that the sheriff collect a *posse comitatus*. When this was done the guard opened the door and released Williams and Martin. Heydt could not be found.[83]

For his action in "corruptly, willfully, maliciously, and feloniously" attempting to "defeat the presence of a quorum of the house, and to disrupt and break up the same" Judge Frazier was later impeached, convicted, removed from office, and disfranchised by the legisla-

[80] *Ibid.*
[81] *Ibid.*, July 19, 1866.
[82] *Ibid.*, July 20, 1866.
[83] *Ibid.*, July 20, 1866.

ture.[84] The *Union and American,* however, was profuse
in its commendation of his opinion in the habeas corpus
case,

Mailed in the panoply of right, fortified by the simple but
strong logic which marks his decision, sustained alike by a
conscientiousness of duty and the approving voice of an intelligent public opinion, the just judge who has declared the law
and enforced it against the usurpers who are storming the state
by their arrant profligacy, may defy their malice in whatever
form it may come.[85]

The decision, however, did not prevent the ratification
of the Fourteenth Amendment. On July 16 the House,
upon the motion of S. M. Arnell, declared that in order to
constitute a quorum it would require only two thirds of
the remaining members "provided a majority of the
whole number or of a full house remain."[86] On the 19th,
while the sergeant-at-arms was still holding Williams and
Martin in custody, the roll was called and the vote taken,
resulting in forty-three affirmative and eleven negative
votes for the ratification of the amendment. Williams and
Martin "failed and refused" to speak or vote. The
speaker William Heiskell, ruled under this state of facts
that there was no quorum, but an appeal from his ruling
was taken and sustained. Heiskell then refused to sign
the resolution ratifying the amendment, but he was forced
to abdicate the chair in favor of John Norman, the
speaker pro tem, who signed the resolution.[87]

On July 20 the Governor wired John W. Forney, the
clerk of the United States Senate, that "We have fought
the battle and won it. We have ratified the constitutional
amendment in the house—43 to 11 against it, two of Andrew Johnson's tools not voting. Give my respects to

[84] *The Frazier Impeachment Trial,* p. 111. A subsequent legislature
removed the disabilities of Judge Frazier.
[85] Nashville *Union and American,* July 21, 1866.
[86] Nashville *Dispatch,* July 18, 1866.
[87] *Ibid.,* July 26, 1866.

the dead dog of the White House."[88]   Within a few
minutes after this dispatch was received in Washington,
Bingham in the House called up the resolution that had
been recommitted on March 5.   Stevens then moved to
lay the Tennessee resolution on the table while the other
radicals moved an adjournment to accomplish the same
result.   The motion to adjourn was defeated, and after
some dilatory tactics on the part of Stevens, Boutwell,
Morrill, Conkling, and about thirty other radicals Bingham was allowed to substitute another resolution simpler
in form and imposing no conditions upon the state as a
prerequisite for readmission.[89]   On the next day Boutwell attempted to secure an amendment to this resolution
so as to make Negro suffrage a condition of representation, but this failed, and the Bingham substitute passed
the House by a vote of 125 to 72.[90]

On the 21st Trumbull reported the House resolution
to the Senate and asked for its immediate consideration.[91]
It was reported to the judiciary committee, and after
being slightly amended there was passed by the Senate on
the 21st.[92] On the 23rd the House concurred in the amendment, and the resolution was sent on the same day to
the President for his signature.[93]   Johnson signed it, but
he opposed the preamble, which was a reassertion of the
principles of the Wade-Davis bill.[94]   To refuse to sign
the resolution would defeat his long cherished wish to
see the state restored.   As he himself said, he was "paired

[88] Nashville *Daily Press and Times*, July 2, 1866. This was in answer
to a recent speech of Johnson calling Forney "a dead duck." When
Brownlow sent the telegram, the *Press and Times* said "His face shone
like that of Moses (not Andy) when he came down from the mount, for he
had made *pseudo*-Moses "come down", and great was the rejoicing in
the camp of Israel over the sons of Amalek and the uncircumcised Ish-
maelites who were gathered round about."—*Press and Times*, Aug. 10,
1866.

[89] *Cong. Globe*, 39 Cong., 1 Sess., pp. 3948-50.

[90] *Ibid.*, pp. 3975-80.   [92] *Ibid.*, pp. 3987-4008.

[91] *Ibid.*, p. 3987.   [93] *Ibid.*, p. 4056.

[94] *United States Statutes at Large*, XIV, 364.

with himself,'' and in signing the measure he virtually acknowledged the congressional theory of reconstruction.

Shortly after the President signed the resolution the entire delegation from Tennessee were admitted to their seats in Congress, and the formal restoration of the state to all its rights under the constitution became an accomplished fact.[95]

[95] There was a slight delay in the seating of Senator Patterson who had held office as a Confederate judge. His credentials were referred to the judiciary committee, however, and upon its recommendation he was allowed to take the oath of office, omitting the reference to accepting and holding office under the late Confederacy.—*Sen. Misc. Docs.*, 39 Cong., 1 Sess., No. 47, pp. 271-74.

CHAPTER X

THE RETURN OF THE CONSERVATIVES

THE ADMINISTRATION of Governor Brownlow came to an end on February 25, 1869, when he resigned in order to take a seat in the United States Senate to which he had recently been elected.[1]   At the same time events were gradually but surely shaping themselves in such a way as to cause the overthrow of the entire Radical regime. The administration had never possessed the support nor inspired the confidence of the majority of the people of the state.   It had been forced to maintain itself in power by the enactment of somewhat questionable legislation and even, at times, by the resort to military force.   Now upon the departure of their leader it soon became evident that the Radicals could not resist the tide of opposition that had arisen against the Brownlow administration.

A number of factors had contributed to produce this opposition.   One of the most important of these factors was the presence and activity of the carpet baggers in the state.   Tennessee was singularly free from the influence of these individuals so far as the general administration of the commonwealth was concerned, but their interference in the municipal affairs of some of the larger cities was both outrageous and disgraceful.   The city of Nashville suffered especially as a result of their peculations.

That the carpet baggers were able to gain control of

[1] Brownlow announced his candidacy for the Senate in a card to the legislature on October 15, 1867.   He was opposed by Horace Maynard and William B. Stokes, both members of Congress, A. J. Fletcher, the secretary of state, and General Joseph A. Cooper, the commander of the state militia. He was elected on the fourth ballot, on October 23, 1867.—Nashville *Union and Dispatch*, Oct. 17, 23, 24, 1867.   For an account of the election and Brownlow's subsequent service in the Senate see James W. Patton, ''The Senatorial Career of William G. Brownlow,'' *Tennessee Historical Magazine* (series ii) I, 153-64.

the municipalities was due in large measure to the aid of the governor and his legislature. In May, 1866, a serious race riot occurred in Memphis, resulting in a large number of deaths,[2] and to prevent the re-occurrence of such an event the legislature enacted the so-called Metropolitan Police Act. This law was intended primarily for Memphis, but it applied to Nashville and Chattanooga also. It provided that the counties of Shelby, Davidson, and Hamilton should be constituted and known as metropolitan police districts and that "the powers and duties connected with, and incident to, the police government and discipline" of each of these districts should be "vested in and exercised by Commissioners of the Metropolitan Police, and a Board of Metropolitan Police composed of said Commissioners, and by a Metropolitan Police force."

The commissioners, three in number, were to be appointed by the governor, with the advice and consent of the senate, for terms ranging from four to eight years, and they in turn should elect the members of the metropolitan police force, consisting of captains, sergeants, and patrolmen. These latter officials were to hold office during good behavior, but they might, at any time, be suspended or removed for misconduct or disobedience. The expenses of this organization were to be defrayed by a special tax levied and collected by the state upon the real and personal property located within the respective districts.[3]

By virtue of this act the Governor was given complete control over the police administration of the three larger cities, and at the same time a large number of lucrative

[2] See *House Reports*, 39 Cong., 1 Sess., No. 101, for a complete account of the Memphis riots as given in the report of the congressional investigating committee.

[3] *Acts, 34th Tenn. General Assembly, 2nd Session, 1865-6*, pp. 52-62. The act was passed on May 14, 1866. It was amended on July 24, 1866, so as to apply to Nashville and Chattanooga, but with the provision that the latter city should have only one commissioner.—*Acts, Tenn. General Assembly, Extra Session, 1866*, pp. 17-19.

appointments were placed either directly or indirectly within his power. This aided the Radical regime by providing a ready force which might be used to guarantee the supremacy of the administration at the polls and by affording, in the bestowal of the patronage, a convenient means whereby the Governor might discharge his obligations to his political supporters.

The law was most severely criticized. The *Union and American* denounced it as "the most wanton and inexcusable interference with the municipal affairs ever undertaken by a legislative body" and said that it was introduced to subserve "those base private ends which have so far controlled the entire action of the present legislature."[4] The *Dispatch* was sarcastic in its description of the office-seekers who appeared in the city in search of positions in the new municipal government:

Swarms of applicants for subordinate positions under the proposed new municipal régime meet you everywhere. They are nearly all armed with documents, some of them numerously signed, and all setting forth the remarkable virtues, startling patriotism, and superior intelligence of their respective bearers. Whew, what an immense amount of loyalty and rare mental endowments are lying in wait, ready to come to the rescue of our municipal government.[5]

Acting under the provision of the law, the Governor proceeded to appoint three metropolitan police commissioners for the city of Nashville. The regular municipal government then instituted injunction proceedings against the new commissioners with the intention of testing the constitutionality of the act. The city was represented by Caruthers and Cooper, John C. Gaut, Edwin H. Ewing, Neill S. Brown, Nathaniel Baxter, Edward H. East, A. L. DeMoss, and A. S. Colyar, and the case was tried before Chancellor David Campbell. It was alleged by the complainants that the Metropolitan Police Act was

[4] Nashville *Union and American.*
[5] Nashville *Dispatch.*

passed by the legislature in an irregular manner and that
the law itself was despotic rather than republican in
principle.[6] On September 22 a temporary injunction was
granted by Judge Campbell.[7] Later in the year the case
was re-argued, and on January 12, 1867, the injunction
was made perpetual. In this decision Judge Campbell
based his action upon the fact that the law had been
passed without the presence of a constitutional quorum
and also that a municipal corporation "is not subject to
the whim and caprice of the legislature, but may acquire
rights which are sacred under the constitution of the
United States."[8] An appeal to the supreme court was
immediately taken by the defendants.

At this point the carpet baggers appeared on the
scene supported by the Governor. On August 17 a convention was held at the capitol, upon the call of "the
city central committee' of the Radical party, and Major
A. E. Alden, Brownlow's commissioner of registration
and a carpet bagger, was nominated for mayor. At the
same hour another Radical convention met and nominated Abram Myers for the same office.[9] The Conservatives led by Matt Brown, the incumbent mayor, combined
with the *Press and Times* faction of the Radical party
and on August 28 nominated H. S. Scoville.[10] On September 7 Myers was killed by a fall from a hotel window
in Louisville, thus leaving the field to Alden and
Scoville.[11]

An interesting and exciting campaign followed. Alden
made every effort to secure the support of the Negroes.
In a speech at the capitol on September 7, accepting the
nomination, he glorified the Negro and declared that the
time had come when "intelligence" and not "houses and

---

[6] Nashville *Union and American*, Aug. 2, 1866.

[7] Nashville *Daily Press and Times*, Sept. 23, 1866.

[8] Nashville *Union and Dispatch*, Jan. 13, 1867.

[9] *Ibid.*, Aug. 24, 1867.

[10] Nashville *Daily Press and Times*, Aug. 29, 1867.

[11] *Ibid.*, Sept. 8, 1867.

money" must rule the country.[12] On the other hand the *Press and Times* denounced Alden and his "ring" as "a close corporation of twenty-five or thirty men who have not the slightest interest in the welfare of the capital of the state" and who had "never done the least service to the colored people." The same newspaper further charged that Alden and his gang "regarded the negroes with contempt, and look upon them as mere animals whom they can ride at will, and use as tools to advance their own purposes. Without ability or personal popularity, their only hope of getting colored votes is that they are Northern men."[13]

The Conservatives hoped to defeat Alden by advancing and sustaining the contention that the state franchise law was not applicable to municipal elections. The *Union and Dispatch* declared that the state "can no more prescribe the qualifications for municipal voting than it can prescribe the mode of electing the directors of the Nashville, Chattanooga, and St. Louis Railroad.'"[14] The Governor, however, was not disposed to follow this line of reasoning. On September 18 he issued a proclamation stating that the francise act applied to municipal as well as state elections,[15] and at the same time J. B. Sheridan, Alden's successor as commissioner of registration, announced his intention of enforcing the law in the approaching mayor's election.[16]

Mayor Brown then issued a proclamation declaring that the appointment of judges and clerks in municipal elections was the function of the common council and stating it to be the fixed purpose of the corporate authorities of Nashville "to assert the chartered rights of the city and to persevere in the resolution heretofore arrived

[12] Nashville *Union and Dispatch*, Sept. 8, 1867.
[13] Nashville *Daily Press and Times*, Sept. 13, 1867.
[14] Nashville *Union and Dispatch*, Sept. 15, 1867.
[15] *Report of the Secretary of War, 1867*, p. 186.
[16] Nashville *Union and Dispatch*, Sept. 15, 1867.

at to hold the approaching municipal election under the charter."[17] Brownlow thereupon ordered General Joseph A. Cooper to bring his entire force of militia to Nashville to protect the judges and clerks appointed under the franchise act and at the same time applied to General Thomas for Federal aid. Thomas referred the request to General Grant and received the reply that, "Your mission is to preserve the peace and not to take sides in political differences until called out in accordance with law. You are to prevent mobs from aiding either party."[18] In the end the mayor, encountering opposition from the city council, acquiesced and allowed the provisions of the franchise act to be applied.

The election was conducted in a manner that was characteristic of the Brownlow regime. There were troops at all of the polling places. All was quiet, but very few white men voted. Large numbers of Negroes, without visible means of support, many of them non-residents, were brought up in "flocks" to the polls, all of them provided with certificates of registration. Blackburn's mounted militia searched the cellars and attics to see that no Conservative election was being held, and General Cooper had his whole force in the city ready to break up such an election should one be discovered. The result was neither unusual nor unexpected. Alden received 2,423 votes to Scoville's 258.[19] Brown and the Conservatives charged that fraud had been committed and applied to Chancellor Horace H. Harrison for an injunction against Alden's taking office. Alden then appealed to Governor Brownlow, and thirty-five mounted militia under Colonel Blackburn and Lieutenant Alloway were sent to his assistance. They forced Brown to vacate the city hall, and Alden took possession.[20]

[17] *Ibid.*, Sept. 21, 1867.
[18] *Report of the Secretary of War, 1867*, p. 90.
[19] Nashville *Union and Dispatch*, Sept. 29, 1867.
[20] *Ibid.*, Oct. 3, 1867.

Almost immediately upon his assuming the duties of his office, Alden settled the controversy between the city and the metropolitan police. The policemen and commissioners agreed to go on duty immediately[21] and forfeit $120,000 in back pay, and the mayor, in return for this, withdrew the injunction case from the supreme court.[22] On October 17 all of the members of the new force, forty-three in number, appeared and were sworn in by the commissioners,[23] and on the next day the old police force was dismissed. At this time Mayor Alden made a short address to the outgoing officers, warning them to submit to the law and declaring that nothing they might do or say would impede its enforcement.[24]

All attempts to remove Alden and the obnoxious metropolitan police proved unsuccessful. In November several of the discharged policemen brought an action against the state, alleging that they had been unjustly deprived of their employment. The case was tried before a justice of the peace, and a decision was rendered against the plaintiffs on the ground that the office of policeman had been abolished by the legislature.[25] On January 13, 1868, Judge M. M. Brien, acting on the part of certain citizens of the city, submitted a brief to Chancellor Horace H. Harrison, praying for an injunction against Alden and the metropolitan police. Alden, it was charged, was ineligible to the office of mayor because of being a non-resident, in addition to being insolvent and not owning five hundred dollars worth of real estate. It was further charged that he had induced a Negro to deed him a tract of land for eight hundred dollars which had not been paid. Several of the city councilmen were declared to be ineligible because they owned no property and did not have sufficient bondsmen. The Metropolitan

[21] *Ibid.*, Oct. 5, 1867.   [22] *Ibid.*, Oct. 18, 1867.
[23] The commissioners were Henry Stone, F. W. Sparling, and James Davis.
[24] Nashville *Union and Dispatch*, Oct. 19, 1867.
[25] *Ibid.*, Nov. 17, 1867.

Police Act was alleged to be unconstitutional. Alden had signed so many checks as mayor[26] that the petitioners feared that the city would become bankrupt and they asked that an attachment be issued for all city property to be held subject to the order of the court. Harrison refused to grant the injunction or to issue the attachment.[27]

Alden was reelected in 1868, his opponents this time being H. H. Thornburg and M. M. Brien.[28] Relief from the "Ring" was again sought through the courts but to no avail. Chancellor Shackleford, to whom an application for an injunction was made in December, declared that "the complainants are not entitled to the injunction or the receiver prayed for, and the application is therefore refused."[29]

Under this state of affairs conditions were virtually intolerable in Nashville. In 1867 the *Union and Dispatch* declared,

Nashville may now be said to be fully at the mercy of Brownlow's government. All elections are controlled at the point of the bayonet, and not even the police are responsible to the mayor for anything they may do. The police commissioners report only to the governor, and their concern is no more an institution of Nashville than is the legislature which will meet in the capitol on Monday next. The odious militia backed by the entire army of the United States are quartered upon the people, ready at any moment to enforce the wicked mandates of the still more odious tyrant, and as a city Nashville has ceased to exist.[30]

---

[26] The extent of Alden's peculations was enormous. "When returns from the collection of taxes were insufficient to satisfy the greed of the ring, checks, warrants, and due bills were made out in the name of the city, payable to bearer or to fictitious persons and were sold to street shavers of notes for any price they would bring."—Moore and Foster, *Tennessee, The Volunteer State*, I, 541.

[27] Nashville *Union and Dispatch*, Jan. 16, 1868.

[28] Nashville *Daily Press and Times*, Sept. 8, 1868.

[29] *Ibid.*, Dec. 9, 1868.

[30] Nashville *Union and Dispatch*, Oct. 5, 1867.

The *Press and Times* was equally critical and demanded that something be done to save the city from the "clutches of the Nashville Ring,"

The universal profligacy and inefficiency of the city government and the crushing burden of taxation which they impose upon the people, thereby attaining the double end of driving hundreds of mechanics and small tradesmen away and effectively keeping out all accessions of a useful nature to the city from abroad—these considerations are making the subject of municipal reform a theme of general interest.[31]

When Alden was finally removed in 1869 it was estimated that $1,323,668 in checks had been issued, of which $769,000 were emitted without authority of law, and that much of the remainder had been expended for illegal purposes.[32] The expenses of the metropolitan police were also enormous. For the year 1866 they amounted to the sum of $51,290.32 for the district of Nashville alone.[33] There is no evidence to show that the Governor profited financially from these transactions, but the ease with which he was beguiled by such plunderers as Alden weakened his influence and reacted unfavorably upon his popularity.[34] "Brownlow is the pipe upon which others play, and from his sounds we are simply enabled to distinguish the tunes being played," said the *Union and American*.[35] The Knoxville *Press and Herald* declared that "offices have been created without number to reward

[31] Nashville *Daily Press and Times*, Aug. 26, 1868.

[32] Nashville *Union and American*, June 2, 1869. The "Ring" had become so thoroughly entrenched in Nashville that the people were helpless. On June 1, 1869, A. S. Colyar filed a bill before Chancellor Charles Smith at Gallatin on the part of four hundred and sixty-six citizens of Nashville against the mayor, the city council, the city treasurer, and others praying that no more checks be issued and that a receiver be appointed. Chancellor Smith granted the petition and appointed John M. Bass as receiver. In August, 1869, Alden was defeated for reelection by K. J. Morris. The members of the "Alden Ring" then packed their carpet bags and departed leaving the city to pay the debt they had contracted.

[33] *Ledger of the State of Tennessee, 1865-1874*, p. 126. State Archives.

[34] Nashville *Daily Press and Times*, Oct. 2, 1867.

[35] Nashville *Union and American*, Aug. 25, 1866.

partizans and friends, and like locusts they are devouring the substance of the people.''[36]

The presence of "Brownlow's militia" in the state also led to much opposition to the Radical regime. Their unwarranted participation in elections has already been referred to, but there were still other complaints against their acts. In July, 1865, it was reported that the members of this organization had formed the habit of going into the country without permission, taking their arms with them, and committing various petty thefts and depredations.[37] In 1867 there was much criticism of their activity. In Franklin County it was said that "the conduct of the militia has been such as to deter many of our citizens from engaging in their ordinary pursuits."[38] Resolutions were adopted at a mass meeting in Wayne County, opposing "Brownlow's War" as subversive of the state government.[39] When it was proposed by the Governor that the militia should be increased the Knoxville *Daily Free Press* said,

Governor Brownlow cannot raise his eight thousand militia. There are not so many outlaws in the state at his service. . . . The good sense and better feelings of even a portion of his own supporters is already so greatly shocked at the barbarities of his militia that he will not likely dare to increase their number even if it should lie within his power.[40]

In 1868 the Knoxville *Daily Press and Herald* declared that the state had two governors, Brownlow and General Thomas,[41] and the next year it stated that the liberty and lives of the people were at the mercy of Brownlow's militia.[42] The Knoxville *Press and Messenger* stated, in 1869, that,

[36] Knoxville *Press and Herald*, July 12, 1868.
[37] Regimental Order Book, 10th Tennessee Cavalry, July 8, 1865. State Archives.
[38] *Report of the Secretary of War, 1867*, p. 226.
[39] Nashville *Republican Banner*, Apr. 12, 1867.
[40] Knoxville *Daily Free Press*, July 7, 1867.
[41] Knoxville *Daily Free Press and Herald*, Mar. 24, 1868.
[42] *Ibid.*, Jan. 17, 1869.

The attempt by a militia levy to trample upon and crush out
the people looks like the crazy freak of a mad-man. Yet we are
assured that the monstrous work is to be undertaken and General Cooper is pushing forward his plans for the campaign at
Nashville.[43]

At the same time the *Press and Herald* said,

We think the time has come for the pepole of Tennessee to make
common cause. It will result in this at last. It is needless to
repeat the old story, or to say that the temper of Tennessee is
not such as to bear with patience such treatment as is now being
inflicted upon the people of Arkansas, by a band of ruffians, mis-
called militia. No resistance will be offered we suppose to
Brownlow's militia, and it should be the duty of the people
to have no conflict with them. The first arrest by them should
be placed, at once, before the Federal courts, as we have before suggested. In the meantime, if petitions are to be offered
and representations made, it would be more appropriate to
make them at the Federal capital, and ask that the provisions
of the Federal Constitution requiring the United States to
guarantee to each state a republican form of government should
be enforced.[44]

In connection with the militia appeared another source
of opposition to the Brownlow regime. It was claimed
that the policy pursued by the administration was serving to repel immigration from the state. In a letter to
the Memphis *Avalanche,* in April, 1868, an immigration
enthusiast, P. T. Scruggs, stated that immigrants would
not come to a place where they would live under a "Negro
government." "I am assured of thousands of good and
worthy men," he wrote, "who would be glad to come
among us and share our fate as a people, and would do so
but for the difficulties above stated."[45] The Knoxville
Press and Herald said that Tennessee's brilliant hopes
of securing immigration had been shattered by the existing political situation:

[41] Knoxville *Daily Press and Herald,* Mar. 24, 1868.
[44] Knoxville *Daily Press and Herald,* Jan. 29, 1869.
[45] Memphis *Avalanche,* Apr. 20, 1868.

Such false statements as that the ex-rebels were inimical to the immigrants were widely diffused for political effect. Senseless and hurtful assertions by the radical press of Tennessee regarding the mythical existence, in many portions of the state, of armed rebel assassins and wrong statements of a want of security for life and property in the state, all tended to drive away the intending immigrants.[46]

The religious affiliations of the governor also contributed to the opposition to his administration. Becoming a Northern Methodist at the close of the war, he was instrumental in establishing that denomination in East Tennessee.[47] The policy of this church was bitterly criticized in 1867, the Knoxville *Free Press* being especially strong in its condemnation of the Northern Methodist ministers,

They have made the church in fact a church *militant,* and now that carnage has ceased—now that a million lives have been sacrificed to the accursed spirit of fanaticism a Northern and sectional branch of one church arrogates to itself the claim of being the church *triumphant.* Triumphant, not in the spirit of the Prince of Peace, but rather with the greed and rapacity of priestly plunderers.[48]

The same newspaper denounced the activities of the Northern Methodist bishops as "crimes and pious frauds,"

The Methodist Episcopal Church, North, has come to the South. They arrogate to themselves the right to seize upon churches and church property which was paid for by Southern people, and who have worshipped in these churches 'time whereof the memory of man runneth not to the contrary,' and exclude them and appropriate them to themselves.[49]

It was also thought there was some connection between the policy of the administration and the hard times that

[46] Knoxville *Daily Press and Herald,* Mar. 5, 1869.

[47] Interesting information regarding Brownlow's religious activities while Governor is given in W. B. Hesseltine, "Methodism and Reconstruction in East Tennessee," *East Tennessee Historical Society Publications,* III, 42-61.

[48] Knoxville *Daily Free Press,* Nov. 5, 1867.

[49] *Ibid.,* Nov. 6, 1867.

were prevalent in the state during the greater part of the reconstruction period.   This charge is not surprising when one remembers that the state debt was increased $21,647,000 during the four years of the Brownlow regime.   Over fourteen millions of dollars were issued in bonds to railroads under the provisions of the so-called "Omnibus Bill" of 1866.[50]   The scandals attending the passage of this bill were disgraceful.   A subsequent legislative investigating committee reported that,

Many corporate presidents, agents, and representatives came to Nashville to attend the sittings of the legislature. All known influences were used upon the supposed representatives of the people. From the pulpit to the bagnio, recruits were gathered for the assault upon the treasury of the state. Fine brandy by the barrel was on hand to fire thirst and muddle the brain, and first-class suits of clothing to capture the vanity or avarice of the gay or needy. Money, and proceeds of the bonds issued by the state, for specific purpose to these men, was here in abundance, and it was used.[51]

While this extravagance was in progress at the capitol, the people of the state were suffering from a severe economic depression.   In Maury County N. R. Wilkes stated, in February, 1867, that,

Our country is in a terribly embarrassed condition . . . and unless the action of our legislature proves to be more conservative than we now anticipate that it will be, we look forward to a horrible state of affairs. It is almost impossible to make collections as it is now, but if the loyal militia bill, as it is called, is passed, public confidence will be so much shaken that each and everyone will be for taking care of themselves, and the collection of money will be impossible.[52]

In November of the same year Wilkes again wrote of the plight of the people of Maury,

We are without hope in any sense of the word. The fall of cotton and the radical legislation of the country have completely

[50] *Acts, 34th Tenn. General Assembly, 2nd Session, 1865-6*, pp. 33-34.
[51] *Report of the Legislative Investigating Committee*, 1879.
[52] Letter of N. R. Wilkes to Mrs. William H. Polk, Feb. 4, 1867, in Polk Papers, North Carolina Historical Commission.

paralyzed the energies of all. Bankruptcy is the order of the day, and there is emphatically no help for us.[53]

In May, 1868, it was reported that five thousand people had left Memphis within ninety days on account of the great commercial depression and the high rents.[54] In June E. B. Pickett, a Memphis attorney, wrote to a friend in Nashville,

I am doing a very good business *on a credit*. I don't get ten dollars in money, although my usual fees are generally two hundred to five hundred dollars per week. . . . Outside of blatant party leaders, I could find a very respectable support, but I do not expect to mingle in the dirty pool we have here. This town is a political cess-pool, and the leading spirits won't let a decent man dare to raise his head. If you won't follow mildly in their lead, you are at once forced to the other side.[55]

In East Tennessee, David Deaderick wrote in his diary, "Jonesboro, the oldest town in the state, held a most respectable population when I was young. There is great deterioration now."[56]

In one way or another, sometimes vaguely and sometimes directly, the administration was held responsible for this state of affairs. In September, 1868, the Knoxville *Press and Herald* quoted with approval an editorial by James Gordon Bennett in the New York *Herald,* which was a severe denunciation of the Governor,

Brownlow himself is the real source of trouble in Tennessee. If that state was less quiet than the others of the Southern states, it is because Brownlow has made it so. . . . Tennessee is the only state that is in the hands of a born swaggerer and bully— a man who has no conception and no care that the surest way to cultivate disturbance is to be always defying it, to be always oppressively irritating those from whom it may come, and to desire nothing so much as to crowd pride into the last possible corner. . . . It is a pity that the quiet of the country should be threatened by the prominence of such a character in public

[53] *Ibid.*, Nov. 30, 1867.
[54] Nashville *Daily Press and Times*, May 6, 1868.
[55] Letter of E. B. Pickett to Jerry Frazer in State Archives, Nashville.
[56] David Deaderick, Diary, p. 77.

life; that the country should hear the murmur of war, even though faintly simply because an irritable, ill-natured, narrow minded, and pugnacious man happens to be governor of Tennessee.[57]

With all these conditions combining to cause opposition to the Brownlow regime, it was evident, even before the resignation of the Governor, that the career of the Radical party in Tennessee was nearing its end. As early as July, 1867, the Knoxville *Free Press said*

We expect to do all in our power to aid in the legitimate overthrow of his [Brownlow's] state policy. We think that he has undertaken to exercise authority not warranted by the constitution, nor sanctioned by the people. We believe that the present state policy, if much longer pursued, will overwhelm the state in financial ruin and social disorder.[58]

A similar view was expressed in January, 1868, by the Knoxville *Press and Messenger,* in an editorial entitled "The Redemption of Tennessee,"

The redemption of Tennessee means this: it means that the liberties of the people shall be dependent upon the laws and the constitution, and not upon the will of Brownlow. It means that white men shall rule and property holders shall have a voice in levying taxes. . . . It means that intelligence, virtue, patriotism, not ignorance, vice, and rascality, shall be the qualifications for offices of public trust. It means, in one word, simply that Brownlowism shall be abolished and freedom and a republican form of government established.[59]

In November of the same year Senator Joseph S. Fowler wrote to H. S. Foote with regard to conditions in the state. He thought that the disfranchisement of "rebels"

[57] Knoxville *Daily Free Press and Herald,* Sept. 25, 1868. These criticisms of Brownlow were greatly enjoyed by his enemies in the state, especially if they came from a Northern source. In 1867 the Knoxville *Free Press* quoted with pleasure a description of the Governor written by Gail Hamilton (Mary Abigail Dodge): "The recklessness, profanity, and uncleanness of his speech are such that it is difficult to conceive of any combination of circumstances which make it the duty of any man to propose or support him as a leader in any measure affecting the welfare of society."—Knoxville *Daily Free Press,* Aug. 28, 1867.

[58] Knoxville *Daily Free Press,* July 2, 1867.

[59] Knoxville *Daily Press and Messenger,* Jan. 18, 1868.

had been justified, but that the time had now arrived when these disabilities should be removed,

It is incompatible with the cherished principles of the Republican party. It is inconsistent with the idea of a republican government, as now maintained, to exclude so large a part of the citizens, and those representing so much of the taxable property of the state, from the ballot.[60]

It seems that Brownlow did not perceive that the end of Radicalism was drawing near and that he expected that his policy would be continued by his successor. In submitting his resignation as governor, he said,

My regrets on retiring would be far greater were it not that the gentleman who will succeed me for the remainder of my term— the honorable speaker of the Senate, Mr. DeWitt C. Senter—is a loyal man, capable, tried, and trusty, who is sound in his principles and who will steadily adhere to them upon the platform of the Union Republican party in Tennessee.[61]

In this view the governor was mistaken. As the Knoxville *Press and Herald* said, "Brownlow was *sui generis,* and Brownlowism was essentially a thing of his creation and nurture."[62] With him it had its origin and with his departure it died. Senter found that the militia was "a white elephant" upon his hands, and, moreover, he was of the opinion that the time had come for the repeal of the franchise acts. He bolted his party when the Radicals nominated William B. Stokes in May, and upon a platform of "suffrage, economy, annihilation of corporation rings, school-funders, swindlers, and bummers" he was elected as a Conservative to succeed himself in August.[63] Stokes raised the cry of fraud and went to Washington in an attempt to have the election cancelled. In this he was not successful. The state had returned to Conservatism.

[60] Nashville *Daily Press and Times*, Nov. 28, 1868.
[61] *Ibid.*, Feb. 13, 1869.
[62] Knoxville *Daily Press and Herald*, Feb. 17, 1869.
[63] *Ibid.*, Aug. 2, 1869.

BIBLIOGRAPHY

A. PRIMARY SOURCES

I. MANUSCRIPTS

Adjutant-General of Tennessee, Letter Books, 1863-1867, 7 vols. Tennessee State Archives. Copies of military orders, letters sent, and letters received. Contains correspondence with the captains of the various companies of state guards that were formed in 1867.

Bell, John, Papers. Library of Congress. Contains a few letters to Brownlow.

Brownlow, William G., Papers. The Library of Congress possesses a small packet of letters written by Governor Brownlow. The remainder of his extant correspondence is in the Tennessee State Library and covers only the period of his governorship. His personal correspondence appears to have been lost or destroyed.

Cavalry, 10th Regiment, Regimental Order Book. Tennessee State Archives. Contains copies of general orders and special orders issued Feb., 1864—July, 1865.

Deaderick, David, The Diary of David Deaderick; Register of Events and Facts Recorded Annually by David Anderson Deaderick, Son of David and Margaretta Deaderick intended chiefly to give to his posterity a knowledge of the matters herein spoken of which, although at present uninteresting, may by being transmitted from father to son, attain an interest, to which their worth intrinsically does not entitle them. Typewritten copy in the Lawson McGhee Library, Knoxville. Deaderick was a Knoxville merchant, and the diary runs from 1827, when it was begun at Jonesboro, to 1872. Contains intimate descriptions of Knoxville life and society during the Civil War and Reconstruction periods.

Governor's Proclamation Record. Tennessee State Archives. Contains copies of all governor's proclamations from Brownlow to Alfred A. Taylor.

Harris, Isham G., Letter Book. Tennessee State Archives. Practically illegible at present this book contains tissue copies of Harris's letters from May 26, 1861 to Mar. 28, 1862. The letters are chiefly of a military nature, many of them addressed to Jefferson Davis. Papers. Tennessee State Library. Copies of letters sent and letters received by Harris while governor.

BIBLIOGRAPHY 243

Johnson, Andrew, Papers. The greatest collection of Johnson
papers is in the Library of Congress. The Tennessee State
Library has a portion of his correspondence as military governor of the state.

Johnson, John M., Memoirs. Typewritten copy in the Tennessee State Library. The recollections of a Confederate soldier,
written at Bristol in 1901.

Military and Financial Board Proceedings. Tennessee State
Archives. Contains the proceedings of the military and
financial board, consisting of W. G. Harding, Gustavus A.
Henry, and Felix K. Zollicoffer, organized by the legislature
and appointed by the governor in April, 1861.

Nelson, Thomas A. R., Papers. Lawson McGhee Library, Knoxville. A valuable source of information on political conditions in East Tennessee. Consists of letters sent and received, newspaper clippings, and broadsides. Also twelve
scrap books, six of which cover the period from 1860 to 1866.

Polk, William H., Papers. North Carolina Historical Society,
Raleigh, North Carolina. Two large boxes of letters written
and received by Major William H. Polk of Columbia and by
his wife, Lucy Williams Polk, of Warrenton, North Carolina,
covering the period, 1860-1869. Major Polk died in 1862,
whereupon his wife returned to her former home in Warrenton but kept in correspondence with friends in Tennessee.
Her letters relate to private, domestic, and social affairs,
giving an intimate description of life in Maury County.

Ramsey, J. G. M., Autobiography, Written at Exile's Retreat,
North Carolina, 1869-1873. Typewritten copy in the Lawson McGhee Library. Relates chiefly to personal experiences
and the military activities of the author's sons. Several valuable letters are appended.

Rennalds, E. H., Civil War Diary. Typewritten copy in the
Lawson McGhee Library. Runs from January to December,
1863. Contains an interesting account of the election of
Aug. 6, 1863.

Senter, DeWitt Clinton, Papers. Tennessee State Library. The
governor's correspondence of the Senter administration.

Temple, O. P., Papers. Library of the University of Tennessee,
Knoxville. Contains a few letters from Governor Brownlow
and several long letters from John Bell Brownlow. The latter letters were written to Judge Temple when he was preparing his *East Tennessee and the Civil War* and are rem-

iniscent of the Civil War and Reconstruction periods in East
Tennessee.

Tennessee State Guards, General Order Book, 1867. Tennessee
State Archives. Contains copies of orders relative to the
organization and distribution of militia companies in 1867.

Tennessee State Guards, Special Order Book, 1867-1869. Tennessee State Archives. Copies of special orders relative to
the organization and personnel of the state militia.

II. PRINTED SOURCES

1. OFFICIAL DOCUMENTS

a. *Tennessee*

Acts, Tennessee General Assembly, 33rd, 34th, and 35th sessions,
1861-1869.

House Journal, Tennessee General Assembly, 33rd, 34th, and 35th
sessions, 1861-1869.

*Proceedings of the High Court of Impeachment in the Case of
the People of the State of Tennessee versus Thomas N. Frazier*, Nashville, 1867.

*Report of G. W. Blackburn, Comptroller of the Treasurer, to the
first session of the 35th General Assembly*, Nashville, 1867.

*Report of Joseph S. Fowler, Comptroller of the Treasury, to the
General Assembly of Tennessee*, Nashville, 1865.

*Report of the Adjutant-General of the State of Tennessee of the
Military Forces of the State from 1861 to 1866*, Nashville,
1866.

Senate Journal, Tennessee General Assembly, 33rd, 34th, and
35th sessions, 1861-1869.

Tennessee Supreme Court Reports.

b. *United States*

Census Reports, 1850-1870.

Century of Population Growth, A, Washington, 1909.

Congressional Documents, 37th Cong.-40th Cong. This volumi-
nous collection, embracing the *House Executive Documents,
House Miscellaneous Documents, House Reports, Senate
Executive Documents*, and *Senate Reports*, contains, in dis-
connected and undigested form, an enormous amount of information bearing upon the Civil War and Reconstruction
periods in Tennessee. Extensive use was made of the following:

Contested Elections: Leftwich *v.* Smith, *House Misc. Docs.*, No. 143, 41 Cong., 2 Sess.; Sheafe *v.* Tillman, *House Misc. Docs.*, No. 53, 41 Cong., 2 Sess.; Thomas *v.* Arnell, *House Misc. Docs.*, No. 6, 39 Cong., 2 Sess.

East Tennessee Relief Association, *Sen. Ex. Docs.*, No. 40, 38 Cong., 1 Sess.

Memphis Riots, *House Reports*, No. 101, 39 Cong., 1 Sess.

Orders issued by the Freedmen's Bureau Commissioner, 1865-1866, *House Ex. Docs.*, No. 70, 39 Cong., 1 Sess.

Readmission of Tennessee, The, *House Misc. Docs.*, No. 55, 39 Cong., 1 Sess.

Refugees in Tennessee, *Sen. Ex. Docs.*, No. 28, 38 Cong., 2 Sess.

Reports of the Assistant-Commissioners of the Bureau of Refugees, Freedmen, and Abandoned Lands: *Sen. Ex. Docs.*, No. 27, 39 Cong., 1 Sess.; *Sen. Ex. Docs.*, No. 6, 39 Cong., 2 Sess.; *House Ex. Docs.*, No. 329, 40 Cong., 2 Sess.

Reports of the Commissioner of the Bureau of Refugees, Freedmen, and Abandoned Lands: *House Ex. Docs.*, No. 11, 39 Cong., 1 Sess.; *House Ex. Docs.*, No. 1, 39 Cong., 2 Sess.; *House Ex. Docs.*, No. 1, 40 Cong., 1 Sess.; *House Ex. Docs.*, No. 1, 40 Cong., 3 Sess.

Report of the Joint Committee on Reconstruction, *House Reports*, No. 30, 39 Cong., 1 Sess.

Congressional Globe, 37th Cong.—40th Cong., 1861-1869.

Reports of the Secretary of War, 1865-1870. A valuable source of information on the Freedmen's Bureau, which was under the supervision of the war department; also much material relating to the movement of troops and the activities of Federal commanders who were stationed in Tennessee during the Reconstruction period.

Revised Statutes of the United States, The, 2 vols., Washington, 1878.

Richardson, James D., comp., *A Compilation of the Messages and Papers of the Presidents, 1789-1897,* 10 vols., Washington, 1896-1899.

United States Statutes at Large, vols. 14-20.

United States Supreme Court Reports, 1 Black—20 Wallace, 1861-1870.

War of the Rebellion, Official Records of the Union and Confederate Armies, 130 vols., Washington, 1880-1901. This collection is chiefly of a military nature, but it contains scattered sections dealing with civil affairs in the insurrectionary states. Although ponderous and unwieldy it is a source of much valuable information on the Reconstruction period in Tennessee.

c. Confederate

Confederate Statutes at Large, The, 8 vols., Richmond, 1861-1864.
Journals of the Congress of the Confederate States, 8 vols., Washington, 1904.
Richardson, James D., comp., *Messages and Papers of the Confederacy,* 2 vols., Nashville, 1905.

2. COLLECTED DOCUMENTS

Fleming, Walter L., ed., *Documentary History of Reconstruction,* 2 vols., Cleveland, 1906.
Hart, A. B., ed., *American History Told by Contemporaries,* 4 vols., New York, 1897-1909.
McDonald, William, ed., *Documentary Source Book of American History,* New York, 1912.
McPherson, Edward, *The Political History of the United States Of America during the Great Rebellion,* Washington, 1865.
———, *The Political History of the United States of America during the Period of Reconstruction,* Washington, 1871.
Miller, Charles A., *The Official and Political Manual of the State of Tennessee,* Nashville, 1890.
Moore, Frank, comp., *Rebellion Record,* 11 vols., New York, 1861-1868.

3. DIARIES, SPEECHES, AND CONTEMPORARY CORRESPONDENCE

Caskie, Jaquelin A., *Life and Letters of Matthew Fontaine Maury,* Richmond, 1928.
Conkling, A. R., *Life and Letters of Roscoe Conkling,* New York, 1889.
Green, William M., *Life and Papers of A. L. P. Green,* Nashville, 1877.
Hallum, John, *The Diary of an Old Lawyer; or Scenes Behind the Curtains,* Nashville, 1895.
Hancock, R. R., *Hancock's Diary; or a History of the Second Tennessee Confederate Cavalry,* Nashville, 1887.
Lapsey, A. B., ed., *The Writings of Abraham Lincoln,* 8 vols., New York, 1906.

Nicolay, J. G., and Hay, John, eds., *Complete Works of Abraham Lincoln*, 11 vols., New York, 1894.

Portrait and Biography of Parson Brownlow, the Tennessee Patriot, together with his last editorial in the Knoxville Whig; also his recent speeches, rehearsing his experience with secession, and his prison life, Indianapolis, 1862.

Welles, Edgar T., ed., *The Diary of Gideon Welles*, 3 vols., Boston, 1911.

4. AUTOBIOGRAPHIES, MEMOIRS, AND REMINISCENCES

Bell, Hiram P., *Men and Things*, Atlanta, 1907.

Blaine, James G., *Twenty Years of Congress*, Norwich, 1884.

Bokum, Hermann, *Testimony of a Refugee from East Tennessee*, Philadelphia, 1863.

——, *Wanderings North and South, a Refugee's Testimony; Sketches of East Tennessee Life*, Philadelphia, 1864.

Brents, J. A., *The Patriots and Guerrillas of East Tennessee and Kentucky, the Sufferings of the Patriots; also the experience of the author as an officer in the Union Army, including sketches of noted Guerrillas and distinguished Patriots*, New York, 1863.

Brownlow, William G., *A Political Register, Setting Forth the Principles of the Whig and Locofoco Parties in the United States, with the Life and Public Services of Henry Clay, also an Appendix Personal to the Author*, Jonesboro, 1844.

——, *Brownlow, the Patriot and Martyr; showing his faith and works as reported by himself*, Philadelphia, 1862.

——, *Helps to the Study of Presbyterianism or an Unsophisticated Exposition of Calvinism, with Hopkinsian Modifications and Policy with a View to a More Easy Interpretation of the Same, to Which is added a Brief Account of the Life and Travels of the Author, Interspersed with Anecdotes*, Knoxville, 1834.

——, *Sketches of the Rise, Progress and Decline of Secession, with a Narrative of Personal Adventures among the Rebels*, Phila., 1862.

Cheat Mountain; or an Unwritten Chapter of the Late War. By a Member of the Fayetteville Bar, Nashville, 1885.

Cox, S. S., *Three Decades of Federal Legislation*, Providence, 1894.

Ellis, Daniel, *Thrilling Adventures of Daniel Ellis, the great Union guide of East Tennessee, for a period of nearly four years during the great Southern Rebellion; Written by himself, containing a short biography of the author*, New York, 1867.

Grant, Ulysses S., *Personal Memoirs*, 2 vols., New York, 1886.

Greeley, Horace, *The American Conflict*, 2 vols., Hartford, 1864.

Hall, C. W., *Three Score Years and Ten*, Cincinnati, 1884.

Hubbard, John M., *Notes of a Private*, St. Louis, 1911.

Hurlburt, J. S., *History of the Rebellion in Bradley County*, Indianapolis, 1866.

Lester, J. C., and Wilson, D. L., *The Ku Klux Klan, Its Origin, Growth, and Disbandment with appendices containing the prescripts of the Ku Klux Klan, specimen orders and warnings*, Revised Edition, ed., W. L. Fleming, New York, 1906.

Poe, Orlando M., *Personal Recollections of the Occupation of East Tennessee and the Defense of Knoxville*, Detroit, 1889.

Ragan, R. A., *Escape from East Tennessee*, Washington, 1910.

Schurz, Carl, *Reminiscences*, 3 vols., New York, 1907-1909.

Sullins, Daniel, *Recollections of an Old Man; Seventy Years in Dixie*, Bristol, 1910.

Toney, M. B., *The Privations of a Private*, Nashville, 1905.

Turnley, P. T., *Reminiscences*, Chicago, 1892.

Wilson, Henry, *History of the Rise and Fall of the Slave Power in America*, 3 vols., Boston, 1872.

5. MISCELLANEOUS PRINTED SOURCES

Bokum, Hermann, *Tennessee Handbook*, Philadelphia, 1868.

Brownlow, William G., *Americanism Contrasted with Foreignism, Romanism, and Bogus Democracy, in the Light of Reason, History, and Scripture; in which certain demagogues in Tennessee, and elsewhere, are shown up in their true colors*, Nashville, 1856.

————, *The Great Iron Wheel Examined or Its False Spokes Extracted and an Exhibition of Elder Graves Its Builder*, Nashville, 1856.

————, and Pryne, Abram, *Ought American Slavery to be Perpetuated, a Debate Held at Philadelphia, September, 1858*, Philadelphia, 1858.

Davis, Jefferson, *The Rise and Fall of the Confederate Government*, 2 vols., New York, 1881.

DeBow, J. D. B., ed., *The Industrial Resources of the Southern and Western States*, 3 vols., New Orleans, 1852-1853.

Everett, Edward, *Account of the Fund for the Relief of East Tennessee*, Boston, 1864.

Graves, J. R., *The Great Iron Wheel or Republicanism Backwards and Christianity Reversed in a Series of Letters Addressed to J. Soule, Senior Bishop of the M.E. Church, South,* Nashville, 1856.

Halstead, Murat, *Caucuses of 1860,* Columbus, 1860.

Humes, Thomas W., ed., *History of the East Tennessee Relief Association,* Knoxville, 1864-1865.

Kendrick, Benjamin B., ed., *The Journal of the Joint Committee of Fifteen on Reconstruction,* New York, 1914.

Proceedings of the East Tennessee Convention Held at Knoxville, May 30-31, 1861 and at Greeneville, June 17, 1861, Knoxville, 1861.

Ross, Frederick A., *Slavery Ordained of God,* Philadelphia, 1859.

Stephens, Alexander H., *Constitutional View of the Late War Between the States,* 2 vols., Philadelphia, 1868-1870.

Trowbridge, J. T., *The South, a Tour of Its Battlefields and Ruined Cities; a Journey through the Desolated States and Talks with the People,* Hartford, 1866.

Wilson, Henry, *History of the Reconstruction Measures of the Thirty-ninth and Fortieth Congresses, 1865-1868,* Hartford, 1868.

6. CONTEMPORARY PAMPHLETS

Bilbo, W. N., *Brownlow Republicanism vs. Etheridge Conservatism; a speech delivered at the State House,* June 4, 1867. Nashville, 1867.

Colyer, Charles B., *Sketch of Parson Brownlow and his speeches at the Academy of Music and Cooper Institute, May, 1862,* New York, 1862.

Crosby, Alpheus, *The Present Position of the Seceded States and the Rights and Duties of the General Government in Respect to them; an address to the Phi Beta Kappa Society of Dartmouth College, July 19, 1865,* Boston, 1865.

Great Panic, by an Eye Witness, The, Nashville, 1862. An account of the evacuation of Nashville by the Confederates in March, 1862.

Hale, Jonathan, *Champ Ferguson, a Sketch of the War in East Tennessee,* Cincinnati, 1862.

[McLeod, Daniel], *Observations on Bishop Otey's Letter to the Hon. William H. Seward, by a Native of Virginia,* Washington, 1862.

Maynard, Horace, *How, by Whom, and For What was the War Begun, Speech in Nashville, March 20, 1862,* Nashville, 1862.

Resolutions and Addresses Adopted by the Southern Convention Held at Nashville, Tennessee, June 3rd to 12th, Inclusive, in the Year 1850, Nashville, 1850.

Shields, James T., *Speech Delivered at Bean's Station, Tennessee, May 18, 1861*, Knoxville, 1861.

Tilton, Theodore, *Sketch of Parson Brownlow*, New York, 1862.

Yeatman, James E., *Report to the Western Sanitary Commission in Regard to Leasing Abandoned Plantations with Rules and Regulations Governing the Same*, St. Louis, 1864.

III. NEWSPAPERS AND PERIODICALS

Brownlow's *Whig*, 1839-1871. Published under various titles and at several places. Established at Elizabethton, as the *Tennessee Whig* in 1839; removed to Jonesboro in 1840 and appeared under the title of *Jonesboro Whig*, 1840-1850; moved to Knoxville at the latter date and appeared as the *Knoxville Whig* from 1850 until Oct. 24, 1861, when it was suppressed by the Confederate authorities; reestablished in October, 1863, under the title of *Knoxville Whig and Rebel Ventilator* and edited by William G. Brownlow until his inauguration as governor in April, 1865; edited by John Bell Brownlow, 1865 to 1869, and by Thomas H. Pearne from the latter date until its final suspension in 1871. A weekly paper of large circulation, noted for its violent partizanship and rabid Union sentiment. Complete file, formerly owned by John Bell Brownlow and containing many pencilled notes in his handwriting on the margins, now in the Library of Congress.

Jonesboro Review, 1847-1848. Published by William G. Brownlow as a quarterly in 1847 and as a monthly in 1848. Devoted chiefly to religious polemics and personal controversies. Complete file bound in one volume in the Library of Congress.

Knoxville Daily Free Press, 1867-1868. Began publication on June 29, 1867, John M. Fleming, editor; supported Johnson's administration and the candidacy of Emerson Etheridge for governor; combined in January, 1868, with the *Herald*. File in the Lawson McGhee Library.

Knoxville Daily Herald, 1867-1867. A Democratic paper, established Oct. 27, 1867, and combined with the *Free Press* in January, 1868. File in the Lawson McGhee Library.

Knoxville Daily Press and Herald, 1868-1870. A Democratic paper, representing a combination of the *Free Press* and the *Herald*. File in the Lawson McGhee Library.

Knoxville Daily Register. Edited and published by J. A. Sperry as the organ of the Confederate administration in East Tennessee. A few scattering issues, 1861-1863, in the Library of the University of Tennessee.

Knoxville Weekly Press and Messenger, 1868-1870. A combination of the *Daily Free Press and the Weekly Messenger.* File in the Lawson McGhee Library.

Nashville Daily Press, 1865. A Union paper, combined with the *Times* in May, 1865. Carried little state news and contained few editorials. File in the Carnegie Library, Nashville.

Nashville Daily Press and Times, 1865-1869. A Union paper, a combination of the *Press* and the *Times and True Union*, under the editorship of S. C. Mercer. File in the Carnegie Library, Nashville.

Nashville Daily Times and True Union, 1862-1865. A Union paper, established in Nashville by S. C. Mercer, a violent Kentucky Unionist, after the occupation of the city by the Federal forces in April, 1862. The organ of the Johnson military government. Combined with the *Press* in May, 1865. File in the Carnegie Library, Nashville.

Nashville Daily Union, 1865-1866. A conservative Union paper, edited by William Cameron. File in the Carnegie Library, Nashville.

Nashville Daily Union and American, 1865-1866. Edited by F. C. Dunnington, and opposed to the Brownlow administration. Combined with the *Dispatch* in November, 1866. File in the Carnegie Library, Nashville.

Nashville Daily Union and Dispatch, 1866-1868. A combination of the *Union and American* and the *Dispatch,* under the editorship of F. C. Dunnington. Conservative and opposed to the Brownlow administration. File in the Carnegie Library, Nashville.

Nashville Dispatch, 1865-1866. A conservative paper, opposed to the Brownlow administration, and noted for its strong editorials. Combined with the *Union and American* in November, 1866. File in the Carnegie Library, Nashville.

New York Times, 1865-1869. Ably edited by Henry J. Raymond and a supporter of Johnson's policy of reconstruction. Contains considerable news from Tennessee during the period.

New York Tribune, 1865-1869. Edited by Horace Greeley and a strong critic of the Johnson policy. Has a considerable amount of news on Tennessee, especially in connection with the readmission of the state to the Union.

B. *SECONDARY SOURCES*

I. GENERAL WORKS

American Annual Cyclopedia, 1861-1870, New York, 1869-1871.

Channing, Edward, *History of the United States,* 6 vols., New York, 1905-1925.

McMaster, John Bach, *History of the People of the United States,* 8 vols., New York, 1883-1927.

Oberholtzer, E. P., *A History of the United States since the Civil War,* 3 vols., New York, 1925-1928.

Rhodes, James Ford, *History of the United States from the Compromise of 1850,* 9 vols., New York, 1893-1919.

Schouler, James, *History of the United States under the Constitution,* 6 vols., New York, 1880-1899.

Von Holst, Hermann, *Constitutional and Political History of the United States,* 7 vols., Chicago, 1899.

II. BIOGRAPHIES AND COLLECTIONS OF BIOGRAPHICAL SKETCHES

Barclay and Company, pubs., *Miss Maude Brownlow oder Die Helden von Tennessee,* Philadelphia, 1863.

Beadle's Dime Series, pubs., *Parson Brownlow and the Unionists of East Tennessee,* New York, 1862.

Biographical Directory of the American Congress, 1774-1927, Washington, 1928.

Book of Three States; Notable Men of Arkansas, Mississippi, and Tennessee, Memphis, 1914.

Burnett, J. J., *Sketches of Tennessee's Pioneer Baptist Preachers,* Nashville, 1919.

Butler, Pierce, *Judah P. Benjamin,* Philadelphia, 1906.

Caldwell, Joshua W., *Sketches of the Bench and Bar of Tennessee,* Knoxville, 1898.

Davidson, James Wood, *The Living Writers of the South,* New York, 1869.

Drake, James Vaulx, *Life of General Robert Hatton,* Nashville, 1867.

Goodpasture, A. V., and Goodpasture, W. H., *Life of Jackson Dillard Goodpasture,* Nashville, 1897.

Green, William Mercer, *Memoir of Rt. Rev. James Hervey Otey,* New York, 1885.

Hopkins, Alphonso A., *The Life of Clinton Bowen Fiske,* New York, 1910.

Johnson, Allen, and Malone Dumas, eds., *Dictionary of American Biography*, New York, 1929 et seq.

McCall, S. W., *Thaddeus Stevens*, New York, 1899.

Marshall, Park, *Life of William B. Bate*, Nashville, 1908.

Mathes, J. T., *The Old Guard in Gray*, Memphis, 1897.

Nicolay, J. G., and Hay, John, *Abraham Lincoln, a History*, 10 vols., New York, 1890.

Noll, Arthur Howard, *Doctor Quintard, Chaplain C. S. A. and Second Bishop of Tennessee*, Sewanee, 1905.

Savage, John, *The Life and Public Services of Andrew Johnson*, New York, 1866.

Speer, William S., *Sketches of Prominent Tennesseans*, Nashville, 1888.

Stephenson, Nathaniel W., *Lincoln; an Account of his Personal Life, Especially of its Springs of Action as Revealed and Deepened by the Ordeal of War*, Indianapolis, 1922.

Stryker, Lloyd P., *Andrew Johnson, a Study in Courage*, New York, 1929.

Temple, Oliver P., *Notable Men of Tennessee from 1833 to 1875, Their Times and Their Contemporaries*, New York, 1912.

Winston, Robert W., *Andrew Johnson: Plebean and Patriot*, New York, 1929.

Woodburn, J. A., *Life of Thaddeus Stevens*, Indianapolis, 1913.

III. Monographs and Special Works

Barnes, W. H., *History of the Thirty-Ninth Congress*, New York, 1868.

Beale, Howard K., *The Critical Year: a Study of Andrew Johnson and Reconstruction*, New York, 1930.

Beard, J. M., *K. K. K. Sketches, Humorous and Didactic, treating the more important events of the Ku-Klux-Klan movement in the South. With a discussion of the causes which gave rise to it, and the social and political issues emanating from it*, Philadelphia, 1877.

Birkhimer, W. E., *Military Government and Martial Law*, Kansas City, 1914.

Bowers, Claude G., *The Tragic Era; the Revolution after Lincoln*, Boston, 1929.

Brown, William G., *The Lower South in American History*, New York, 1903.

Burgess, John W., *Reconstruction and the Constitution*, New York, 1903.

————, *The Civil War and the Constitution*, 2 vols., New York, 1906.

Caldwell, Joshua W., *Studies in the Constitutional History of Tennessee*, Cincinnati, 1907.

Carter, W. R., *History of the First Regiment of Tennessee Volunteers*, Knoxville, 1902.

Chadsey, C. E., *The Struggle Between President Johnson and Congress*, New York, 1896.

Chandler, J. A. C., et. al., *The South in the Building of the Nation*, 12 vols., Richmond, 1909-1910.

Cisco, J. G., *Historic Sumner County, Tennessee*, Nashville, 1909.

Clayton, W. W., *History of Davidson County, Tennessee*, Philadelphia, 1880.

Cole, A. C., *The Whig Party in the South*, Washington, 1913.

Collins, Charles Wallace, *The Fourteenth Amendment and the States; a study of the operation of the restraint clauses of section one of the Fourteenth Amendment to the Constitution of the United States*, Boston, 1912.

Davis, Susan Lawrence, *Authentic History of the Ku Klux Klan, 1865-1877*, New York, 1924.

DeWitt, David Miller, *The Impeachment and Trial of Andrew Johnson, Seventeenth President of the United States; a History*, New York, 1903.

Drake, E. L., *The Annals of the Army of Tennessee*, 2 vols., Nashville, 1878.

Draper, J. W., *History of the American Civil War*, 3 vols., New York, 1867-1870.

Dunning, William A., *Essays on Civil War and Reconstruction*, New York, 1910.

————, *Reconstruction, Political and Economic*, New York, 1906.

Fertig, James Walter, *The Secession and Reconstruction of Tennessee*, Chicago, 1898.

Flack, Horace E., *The Adoption of the Fourteenth Amendment*, Baltimore, 1908.

Fleming, Walter L., *The Freedmen's Bureau Savings Bank; a Chapter in the Economic History of the Negro Race*, Chapel Hill, 1927.

————, *The Sequel of Appomattox; a Chronicle of the Reunion of the States*, New Haven, 1919.

Garrett, W. R., and Goodpasture, A. V., *History of Tennessee, its people and its institutions*, Nashville, 1900.

[Goodspeed Publishing Company], *History of Tennessee from the Earliest Time to the Present; Together with an Historical and a Biographical Sketch of Giles, Lincoln, Franklin, and Moore Counties; Besides a Valuable Fund of Notes, Reminiscences, Observations, Etc., Etc.*, Nashville, 1886.

Hale, W. T., and Merritt, Dixon, *A History of Tennessee and Tennesseans*, 8 vols., Chicago, 1913.

Hall, Clifton R., *Andrew Johnson, Military Governor of Tennessee*, Princeton, 1916.

Hamilton, J. G. deR., *Reconstruction in North Carolina*, New York, 1914.

Henkel, Socrates, *History of the Evangelical Lutheran Synod of Tennessee*, New Market, Virginia, 1890.

Herbert, Hilary A., *Why the Solid South? or Reconstruction and its Results*, Baltimore, 1890.

Hosmer, James K., *The Appeal to Arms*, New York, 1907.

————, *The Outcome of the Civil War*, New York, 1907.

Humes, Thomas W., *The Loyal Mountaineers of Tennessee*, Knoxville, 1888.

Lindsley, John Berrien, *The Military Annals of Tennessee, Confederate. First Series: Embracing a review of military operations, with regimental histories and memorial rolls, compiled from original and official sources*, Nashville, 1886.

McCarthy, Charles H., *Lincoln's Plan of Reconstruction*, New York, 1901.

McFerrin, John B., *History of Methodism in Tennessee*, 3 vols., Nashville, 1873.

Milton, George Fort, *The Age of Hate*, New York, 1930.

Moore, John Trotwood, and Foster, A. P., *Tennessee, the Volunteer State*, 4 vols., Chicago, 1923.

Neal, John R., *Disunion and Restoration in Tennessee*, New York, 1899.

Noll, Arthur Howard, *History of the Church in the Diocese of Tennessee*, New York, 1900.

Peirce, Paul S., *The Freedmen's Bureau, a Chapter in the History of Reconstruction*, Iowa City, 1904.

Phelan, James, *History of Tennessee, the Making of a State*, New York, 1888.

Porter, James D., *Confederate Military History*, 8 vols., Atlanta, 1899.

Price, R. M., *Holston Methodism from its Origin to the Present Time*, 5 vols., Nashville, 1904-1914.

Rankin, Mrs. Anne, ed., *Christ Church, Nashville*, Nashville, 1929.

Rhodes, James Ford, *History of the Civil War, 1861-1865*, New York, 1917.

Rose, Mrs. S. E. F., *The Ku Klux Klan or Invisible Empire* New Orleans, 1914.

Rule, William; Mellen, George F., and Wooldridge, J., eds., *Standard History of Knoxville, Tennessee, with full outline of the natural advantages, early settlement, territorial government, Indian troubles, and general and particular history of the city down to the present time*, Chicago, 1900.

Scott, Eben Greenough, *Reconstruction during the Civil War in the United States of America*, Boston, 1895.

Seitz, Don C., *The Dreadful Decade, 1869-1879*, New York, 1926.

Shotwell, W. G., *The Civil War in America*, 2 vols., New York, 1923.

Stephenson, Nathaniel W., *Abraham Lincoln and the Union*, New Haven, 1918.

————, *The Day of the Confederacy*, New Haven, 1919.

Tannenbaum, Frank, *Darker Phases of the South*, New York, 1924.

Temple, Oliver P., *East Tennessee and the Civil War*, Cincinnati, 1899.

Wright, M. J., *Tennessee in the War, 1861-1865*, New York, 1908.

IV. ARTICLES, PAMPHLETS, AND FUGITIVE SOURCES

Beaver, R. Pierce, "An Ohio Farmer in Tennessee in 1865," *Tennessee Historical Magazine* (series ii), I (1930), 29-39.

Brown, William G., "Andrew Johnson and 'My Policy'," *Atlantic Monthly*, XCVI (1905), 760-75.

————, "Lincoln's Policy of Mercy," *Atlantic Monthly*, XCVI (1905), 359-76.

————, "The Thirty-ninth Congress," *Atlantic Monthly*, XCVII (1906), 465-88.

Caldwell, Joshua, "John Bell of Tennessee," *American Historical Review*, IV (1898), 652-64.

Cook, Walter Henry, *Secret Political Societies in the South during the Period of Reconstruction, an address before the faculty and friends of Western Reserve University, Cleveland, Ohio*, Cleveland, 1914.

Cooper, Walter Raymond, "Parson Brownlow; a Study of Reconstruction in Tennessee," *Southwestern Presbyterian University Bulletin*, XIX (1931), 3-14.

Dixon, Thomas, "The Story of the Ku Klux Klan," *Metropolitan Magazine*, XXII (1905), 657-69.

Doak, H. M., "The Development of Education in Tennessee," *American Historical Magazine*, VIII (1903), 69-94.

Guild, George B., "Reconstruction Times in Sumner County," *American Historical Magazine*, VIII (1903), 355-70.

Halley, R. A., "A Rebel Newspaper's War Story; being a narrative of the war history of the Memphis *Appeal*," *American Historical Magazine*, VIII (1903), 124-53.

Hamer, Marguerite B., "The Presidential Campaign of 1860 in Tennessee," *East Tennessee Historical Society Publications*, III (1931), 3-22.

Hesseltine, William B., "Methodism and Reconstruction in East Tennessee," *East Tennessee Historical Society Publications*, III (1931), 42-61.

———, "Tennessee's Invitation to Carpet-Baggers", *East Tennessee Historical Society Publications*, IV (1932), 102-15.

Imes, William Lloyd, "The Legal Status of Free Negroes and Slaves in Tennessee," *Journal of Negro History*, IV (1919), 254-72.

"Ku Klux Klan, Prescript of the Order of the * * *," *American Historical Magazine*, V (1900), 3-26.

McDonald, R. L., "The Reconstruction Period in Tennessee," *American Historical Magazine*, I (1896), 307-28.

Patton, James W., "The Progress of Emancipation in Tennessee, 1796-1865," *Journal of Negro History*, XVII (1932), 67-102.

———, "The Senatorial Career of William G. Brownlow," *Tennessee Historical Magazine* (series ii), I (1931), 153-64.

Reeve, Felix A., *East Tennessee in the War of the Rebellion*, Washington, 1902.

Romine, Mr. and Mrs. W. B., *A Story of the Original Ku Klux Klan*, Pulaski, 1924.

Rule, William, *The Loyalists of Tennessee in the Late War*, Cincinnati, 1887.

Ryder, C. J., *The Debt of Our Country to the American Highlanders during the War*, New York, 1907.

Sioussat, St. George L., "Tennessee in National Politics, 1850-1860," *American Historical Association Reports*, I (1914), 248-58.

Thruston, Gates P., "Relic of the Reconstruction Period in Tennessee," *American Historical Magazine*, VI (1901), 243-250.

Walmsley, James Elliott, "The Change of Secession Sentiment in Virginia in 1861," *American Historical Review*, XXXI (1925), 82-101.

Wilson, D. L., "The Ku Klux Klan, its Origin, Growth, and Disbandment," *Century Magazine*, VI (1873), 198-410.

INDEX

ALDEN, A. E., candidate for mayor of Nashville, 229; elected, 231; reëlected, 233; removed from office, 234.

Alden Ring, the, peculations of, 232-3; broken up, 234.

Amnesty act, the, restores lands to owners, 165.

Arnell, S. M., introduces elective franchise bill, 99; speech on elective franchise, 100-1; secures seat in Congress, 112; reports bill to alter elective franchise, 115; reports on Negro testimony bill, 130; attempts made on life, 189; favors ratification of Fourteenth Amendment, 223.

BASS, John M., appointed receiver of Nashville, 234.

Bate, William B., attitude on neutrality of Tennessee, 15; nominated for governor, 39.

Bell, Hiram P., report on secession sentiment in Tennessee, 14.

Bell, John, popularity of, 3; candidate for president, 7; deserts Union cause, 16; attacked by northern writers.

Beman, Amos J., educational missionary, 138.

Benevolent societies, work of, 148-9.

Bennett, James Gordon, denunciation of Brownlow, 239.

"Blood Faction, the," reported to exist, 109.

Bostwick, S. W., report on refugees in Tennessee, 147-8.

Bowen, John W., favors Negro testimony bill, 128-9.

Bradford, H. S., letter to Isham G. Harris, 13.

Bragg, Braxton, sanctions plot to kidnap Andrew Johnson, 33.

Bridge burning in East Tennessee, 60-1.

Bridges, George W., Union candidate for Congress, 29; secures seat in Congress, 29.

Brien, John S., criticism of the Brownlow administration, 219.

Brien, M. M., decides case of House v. Nesbet, 120; asks for injunction against Alden, 232; candidate for mayor of Nashville, 233.

Brown, Matt, mayor of Nashville, 229; proclamation of, 230.

Brown, Neill S., on the duty of Tennessee to arm, 15.

Brown, Randall, criticizes the Brownlow administration, 141.

Brownlow, John Bell, warns Johnson of danger at Kingston, 53; describes his father's financial losses, 69; editor of the Knoxville *Whig*, 78; describes the governor's election, 88-9.

Brownlow, William Gannaway, opposes secession, 6; attitude on the election of Lincoln, 7-8; criticizes action of South Carolina Methodists, 9; attacks proposed ordinance of secession, 18; defends the Union, 20; exposes inconsistency of G. A. Henry, 23; candidate for governor, 26; withdraws from governor's race, 27; antagonism to Andrew Johnson, 30; elected governor, 50; contempt for aristocracy, 52; editor of the Knoxville *Whig*, 54; writes prayer for local preachers, 54-5; letter to Jordan Clark, 55-6; expresses hatred of the Confederacy, 56-7; attitude toward Generals Forrest and Hardee, 57; newspaper suppressed, 61; committed to prison, 61; ill-treated in jail, 68; letter to Judah P. Benjamin, 68; reëstablishes newspaper, 69; early life, 75; education, 75; enters Methodist ministry, 75; crit-

LEA, John M., demands completion of reconstruction, 193.
Leftwich, John W., elected to Congress, 110; opposes ratification of the Fourteenth Amendment, 218.
Lellyet, John, protests to Lincoln, 47.
Lewis, J. R., succeeds General Fisk, 158.
Lewis, William B., attacks elective franchise bill, 115; on the advantage of the Negro testimony bill, 130.
Lincoln, Abraham, effect of election of in Tennessee, 7; calls for troops, 14; sends commissioners to Tennessee, 37; Emancipation Proclamation, 37; instructions to Johnson, 42; amnesty proclamation, 43; impressed with importance of occupying East Tennessee, 59.
Lincoln, Rev. L., murder of, 186.
Live stock, importance in Tennessee, 4.
Lynnville, Negroes beaten at, 185.

McMULLEN, J. C., freedmen's bureau official at Clarksville, 163.
Martial law, declared in West Tennessee, 29; in East Tennessee, 66; proclaimed by the governor, 199.
Martin, A. J., arrested, 221.
Maynard, Horace, elected to Congress, 28; takes seat, 28; attorney general of Tennessee, 34; asks military aid for East Tennessee, 58; speech at Nashville markethouse, 107; election to Congress, 110; speech at Greeneville, 177.
Memphis riots, the, 159, 227; Mercer, S. C., begins and administration newspaper, 35.
Methodist Church, Northern, criticism of, 237; establishment in East Tennessee, 237.
Metropolitan Police act, enacted, 227; provisions, 227; criticism of, 228; injunction against, 228.
Middle Tennessee, the Civil War in, 30; invaded by Morgan and Forrest, 36; economic conditions, 159.
Military League, the, negotiated by Tennessee and the Confederate States, 19.
Militia, the, conditions in, 198-9; criticism of, 235. See also Tennessee State Guards.
Milligan, Samuel, delegate to Washington Peace Conference, 14; administers oath of office to Brownlow, 85; member of the supreme court, 121.
Minnis, J. A., describes conditions in West Tennessee, 19.
Missionaries, northern, encourage defiant attitude of the Negroes, 162.
Morris, K. J., elected mayor of Nashville, 234.
Mount Pleasant, colored school broken up, 163.
Murphy, H. P., opposes Negro testimony bill, 129.
Myers, Abram, candidate for mayor of Nashville, 229.

NASHVILLE, Ku Klux parade at, 186; conditions in, 219; mayoral campaign, 229-31.
Nashville Provident Association, gives relief to Negroes, 156.
Negroes, agitators among, 127; colonization advocated, 129; return to Tennessee, 131; legislation favoring, 131; invited to participate in Conservative convention, 135; convention at Nashville, 136; grand "pow-wow" at Nashville, 138; request arms and ammunition, 139; intimidated by Conservatives, 139; support the Radical ticket, 140; criticize the administration, 141; contraband camps, 145; schools established for, 146; refugees, 147; refugee camps established, 147; abuse of, 148; idleness and discontent, 154; allowed to testify in courts, 156; discriminated against, 157; relation to contract labor system, 157-8; separate schools for, 161; dis-

schools broken up, 164; prosperity
of, 169; at the polls, 231.
Negro soldiers, arrest Emerson Etheridge, 105; at the polls, 176-7.
Negro suffrage, demanded, 94; suggested by Brownlow, 126; contemplated, 128; arguments for,
132; opposition to, 134; enacted,
134.
Negro testimony bill, the, introduced, 128; passed, 130.
Nelson, Thomas A. R., address to
East Tennessee Convention, 23;
submits paper to Greeneville Convention, 24; arrested by Confederates, 28; reassembles Greeneville Convention, 45; attitude to
Emancipation Proclamation, 66;
witnesses fight between Brownlow and Haynes, 78.
Newton, J. W., educational missionary, 163; life threatened, 164.
Nicholson, A. O. P., laments radical
activity, 127.
Norman, John, speaker pro tem of
the senate, 223.

OGDEN, John, opposes segregation
of Negroes, 161-2.
Omnibus bill, the, scandals attending the passage of, 238.
Otey, James H., sermon on the
Union, 5; changes sentiment on
secession, 16.

PARKER, Theodore, challenged to
debate by Brownlow, 81.
Patterson, David T., elected to the
Senate, 204; takes seat, 225.
Pickett, E. B., on economic condi-
tions in Memphis, 239.
Polk, William H., candidate for
governor, 27.
Pryne, Abram, debate with Brown-
low, 81.

QUINTARD, C. T., sermon on
obedience to rulers, 5.

RADICAL party, formation, 106.
Ramsey, J. G. M., on northern tyranny, 3; letter to Governor Harris, 65-6.
Ramsey, John Crozier, Brownlow's
hatred of, 69.
Reedy, Charles, argument on constitutionality of the elective franchise act, 122.
Religious conditions, in West Tennessee, 163; in East Tennessee,
237.
Ridley v. Sherbrook, case of, 120-2.
Robertson, Felix, opposition to secession, 4.
Rodgers, Samuel R., speaker of the
senate, 90.
Rogers, James A., demands restrictions for Negroes, 153.
Ross, Frederick A., controversy with
Brownlow, 80.

SALE v. Ware, case of, 113.
Scoville, H. S., candidate for mayor
of Nashville, 229.
Scruggs, P. T., an immigration enthusiast, 236.
Secession, opposition to, 3-6; forces
against broken down, 7.
Secession, Ordinance of, passed by
the legislature, 18; ratified, 21.
Secession convention, proposition to
call voted down, 12.
Secession propaganda, absence of in
Tennessee, 3; development of, 9-
10; cessation of, 13; success of,
18.
Senter, DeWitt C., opposes Negro
testimony bill, 128; extends promises to the Conservatives, 200;
elected governor, 241.
Sevier, E. G., on the Union, 8.
Sevier, William R., criticism of
secession, 8.
Shackleford, J. P., speech of, 107;
writes opinion in Ridley v. Sherbrook, 121; denies injunction
against Alden, 223.
Sheafe v. Tillman, contested election
of, 106.